COMPLETE YEAR 4

Weekly Learning Activities

Thinking Kids™
Carson-Dellosa Publishing LLC
Greensboro, North Carolina

Thinking Kids™
Carson-Dellosa Publishing LLC
P.O. Box 35665
Greensboro, NC 27425 USA

Printed in the USA • All rights reserved.   ISBN 978-1-4838-0194-0
02-209147784

Table of Contents

Table of Contents

Table of Contents

Introduction to *Complete Year: Grade 4*

The *Complete Year* series has been designed by educators to provide an entire school year's worth of practice pages, teaching suggestions, and multi-sensory activities to support your child's learning at home. Handy organizers are included to help students and parents stay on track and to let you see at a glance the important skills for each quarter and each week of the academic year.

A variety of resources are included to help you provide high-quality learning experiences during this important year of your child's development.

Suggested Calendar (Page 7)
Use this recommended timetable to plan learning activities for your child during all 36 weeks of the school year.

A Guide to School Skills and Subject Areas for Fourth Grade: Reading and Language Arts, Math, Science, and Social Studies (Page 8)
Refer to this useful guide for information about what your child will be learning this school year, what to expect from your fourth grader, and how to help your child develop skills in each subject area.

Quarter Introductions (Pages 14, 108, 202, 296)
Four brief introductions outline the skills covered in practice pages for each nine-week grading period of the school year. In addition, they include a variety of ideas for multi-sensory learning activities in each subject area. These active, hands-on projects are fun for parents and children to do together and emphasize real-world applications for school skills.

Weekly Skill Summaries (Example: Page 17)
Thirty-six handy charts precede the practice pages for each week and give a snapshot of the skills covered. In addition, they provide ideas for fun, multi-sensory learning activities for each subject area.

Practice Pages (Example: Page 18)
Nine practice pages are provided each week for a total of over 300 skill-building activities to help your child succeed this year.

Quarter Check-Ups (Pages 107, 201, 295, 389)
Four informal assessment pages allow students to do a quick self-check of the important skills emphasized during the previous nine weeks. Parents can use these pages to see at a glance the skills their children have mastered.

Suggested *Complete Year* Calendar*

First Quarter: Weeks 1-9
(First nine-week grading period of the school year, usually August–October)

Second Quarter: Weeks 10-18
(Second nine-week grading period of the school year, usually October–December)

Third Quarter: Weeks 19-27
(Third nine-week grading period of the school year, usually January–March)

Fourth Quarter: Weeks 28-36
(Fourth nine-week grading period of the school year, usually April–June)

During Each Nine-Week Quarter:

- Read the **Quarter Introduction** to get an overview of the skills and subject areas emphasized. Choose several multi-sensory learning activities you plan to do with your child this quarter.

- Each week, glance at the **Weekly Skill Summary** to see targeted skills. Make a quick plan for the practice pages and multi-sensory learning activities your child will complete.

- Choose **Practice Pages** that emphasize skills your child needs to work on. Each page should take 10 minutes or less to complete.

- Ask your child to check the boxes on the **Quarter Check-Up** to show what skills he or she has mastered. Praise your child's progress and take note of what he or she still needs to work on.

* This calendar provides a schedule for using *Complete Year* during a typical nine-month academic calendar. If your child attends a year-round school or a school with a different schedule, you can easily adapt this calendar by counting the weeks your child attends school and dividing by four.

A Guide to School Skills for Fourth Grade

This guide provides background information about the skills and subject areas that are important for success in fourth grade. Tips are provided for helping your child develop in each curricular area.

Complete Year supports skills included in the Grade 4 Common Core State Standards for English Language Arts and Mathematics, which have been adopted by most U.S. states. A complete guide to these standards may be found at www.corestandards.org.

In addition, activities in *Complete Year* support the study of science and social studies topics appropriate for fourth grade.

 Reading and Language Arts

Reading

Teach reading through books that fit your child's abilities and interests. Use a variety of books from a bookstore or library. You will find book suggestions throughout *Complete Year*, and an extended list on page 394. The suggested books are age-appropriate and of the highest quality, but you are also encouraged to choose other literature that may better suit your child's interests and abilities. Reading a wide variety of literature, including fantasy, adventure, biography, and poetry, is highly recommended. There is so much great literature for children available today. Find the latest titles and instill the joy of reading in your child.

- Independent Reading and Reading Aloud
  Set aside 15 to 30 minutes each day for your child to read silently. Let him or her choose which book to read. Silent reading time should be a time to read for pleasure. Do not evaluate your child at this time. On the other hand, do not avoid talking about the book. Also, read books aloud to your child that are at a higher level than his or her independent reading level. This will spark interest in various topics and motivate him or her to improve. Read-aloud time is very special and can continue even after your child is reading independently. Some parents continue reading aloud well into the middle school years.

- Reading Comprehension
  Read to and with your child every day. Build a love of reading through positive experiences with books. A child who loves reading will be a more successful reader. The goal of reading is to acquire meaning from text. After reading a book, ask your child a variety of questions to test comprehension, such as "Explain what the character meant by …" or "Make a timeline of events in the story." Ask questions related to context clues to test your child's comprehension of information that is not overtly given and must be inferred.

Language Skills

Language skills are often taught in the context of reading. Your child may be asked to apply knowledge gained from reading to the study of words, sentences, and texts. When reading aloud to your child, take the opportunity to point to individual words, sentences, and punctuation marks on the page and talk about them. This will give your child a deeper understanding of how language works.

- Vocabulary Development
  Build your child's vocabulary skills by introducing new words. Provide your child with a stack of index cards and a file box for maintaining a word bank throughout the year. If your child comes across an unfamiliar word, discuss it with your child, and see if he or she can use context clues to determine the word's meaning. Then, have your child record unfamiliar words on the index cards (one word per card) and file them alphabetically. Revisit the cards throughout the year to refresh your child's knowledge of the new words. Your child will also work with idioms, similes and metaphors, and common affixes.

- Grammar and Usage
  This year, your child will work with parts of speech (nouns, pronouns, verbs, adjectives, adverbs, etc.), verb tenses, writing complete sentences, and punctuation. Help your child develop these skills by closely examining sentences from a favorite book, pointing out capital letters, punctuation marks, subject-verb agreement, and other features. Avoid emphasizing too many skills at once. If your child's writing shows several types of language errors, choose just one or two to emphasize during rewriting.

Writing

At the fourth-grade level, your child should be able to produce clear and coherent writing in which the development and organization are appropriate to task, purpose, and audience. Devote time each week to writing, whether it is creative writing or writing in other areas of the curriculum. The process of writing generally includes the steps listed below. These steps are not necessarily part of a linear sequence, but rather a cycle.

- Prewriting
  Prewriting activities help prepare your child for a writing activity. They engage the child and get him or her thinking. Typical prewriting activities include brainstorming, reading literature, discussing a topic, going on a field trip, observing art, listening to music, and webbing a topic.

- Writing
  Writing, or composing, is the rough draft stage of the writing process. Encourage your child to get all his or her ideas on a topic down on paper. At this stage, the emphasis is on fluency rather than accuracy—do not worry about mistakes. Always have your child date the drafts and save them in a writing folder.

- Revising and Proofreading
  You and your child should revise the piece to make sure it makes sense, then proofread the revised piece for proper spelling, capitalization, and grammar.

- Publishing
  Encourage your child to copy the corrected proof in an appropriate format. He or she may add illustrations. The piece is now ready to be shared with others.

Speaking and Listening

Good speaking and listening skills are essential to school success. By paying careful attention to what is being said, your child will not only learn more but will develop the skill of being a good conversationalist as well. Make sure to provide ample opportunities for your child to listen to songs, poetry, and stories.

$2_8\,^4_6$ Math

Mathematical literacy is the ability to think mathematically in a variety of real-life situations and to interpret and use mathematical references. Math is much more than mastering a set of basic computation skills. Basic skills are to math as spelling is to writing: They are the tools with which we explore, test, and explain. A good teacher will provide a child with an understanding of basic math skills, as well as the applications of these skills. Such applications include designing and interpreting graphs, discovering patterns, measuring, comparing, and problem solving.

- Place Value
  Learning place value will help your child conceptualize large numbers and will lead to greater understanding of addition, subtraction, multiplication, and division. Each digit of a number is given a place value. This distinguishes **4** from **40**. Use models to teach the concept of ones, tens, and hundreds, then lead your child to generalize the pattern for larger numbers.

- Multiplication and Division
  Fourth graders will learn to multiply by multiples of 10, 100, and 1,000. They should recognize and demonstrate multiplication patterns, and will use multiplication to solve real-life problems. Using division, fourth graders will solve real-world problems having up to two-digit divisors and three-digit dividends, with and without remainders.

- Fractions and Decimals
  This year, your child will continue working with fractions and decimals, and comparing the two. Your child will add and subtract fractions, compare fractions as greater than and less than, and find equivalent fractions. He or she will also work with decimals through the hundredths.

- Measurement

  During fourth grade, your child will measure length to the nearest half-inch or centimeter, weight to the nearest ounce or gram, capacity, angles, and more. He or she will learn about feet, yards, miles, millimeters, meters, kilometers; ounces, pounds, tons, grams, kilograms; cups and milliliters. He or she will measure length, area, volume, and perimeter, and will also work with temperatures on the Celsius and Fahrenheit scales.

- Geometry

  In this school year, your child will work with many aspects of geometry, including polygons, three-dimensional shapes, lines, line segments, rays, angles (right, acute, and obtuse), and more. He or she will also be expected to recognize and draw a line of symmetry for a two-dimensional figure as a line across the figure such that the figure can be folded along the line into matching parts.

 **Science**

Fourth graders are learning about life, physical, and earth sciences, as well as what scientists do and how to perform science experiments. Science experiments will involve a series of steps that allow your child to ask a question, make a hypothesis, and determine the answer. For example, a science lesson may begin with a question that sparks the curiosity of your child. Follow up the question with an exploration involving experimentation, observation, play, debate, and other methods of inquiry. Encourage your child to use descriptive language, measure when appropriate, and keep a log of observations. Then, propose explanations and solutions for the initial question. The explanation may prove or disprove the earlier hypothesis. This is a time of writing, talking, and evaluating. After this step, your child may need to return to the second step of the cycle to explore the topic further. Applying the knowledge to your child's world makes the event more meaningful. This may also spark new questions that begin the cycle again.

Do not worry if you don't have answers to all your child's questions. This learning cycle promotes exploration and encourages your child to construct his or her own knowledge based on experience. The more experience you provide, the clearer and more accurate your child's understanding will be.

Encourage your child to satisfy his or her curiosity about the world by reading nonfiction books from the library, exploring science Web sites for kids, and conducting supervised, hands-on experiments. In addition, feature a different scientist each week. Encourage your child to do independent research about that scientist and list some facts about his or her accomplishments. Supply resource books about the scientist and his or her field of expertise.

 **Social Studies**

At the fourth-grade level, the social studies curriculum should expand a child's knowledge of explorers and exploration, Native Americans, the states, and the Middle Ages. Encourage your child's interest in these topics and expand on the concepts as they pertain to your experience. Also, encourage your child to read about current events in newspapers, watch local and national news, and listen to NPR (National Public Radio). Discuss news events with your child daily. Listen to his or her interpretation of current events, and help your child gather the necessary information to make careful judgments.

First Quarter Introduction

Fourth grade is a time of transition for your child, as he or she prepares to enter middle school or junior high school. This year should challenge your child, as well as ready him or her with knowledge and skills needed in the school years ahead. During the first weeks of school, utilize the opportunity to acquaint your child with the new material and what is expected of him or her in the upcoming year.

First Quarter Skills

Practice pages in this book for Weeks 1–9 will help your child improve the following skills.

Reading and Language Arts
- Identify long and short vowel sounds **a**, **e**, **i**, **o**, and **u**
- Recognize vowel sounds for words containing vowel pairs
- Identify common and proper nouns, including subject and object pronouns, and plural nouns
- Form plural nouns from words that end in **y** or **f**
- Understand present-, past-, and future-tense verbs
- Identify and use irregular verbs correctly
- Work with helping verbs, action verbs, and linking verbs
- Use correct subject/verb and pronoun/verb agreement
- Understand adjectives, including comparative adjectives

Math
- Understand place value up to the millions place
- Work with expanded notation
- Round up to the nearest ten thousand
- Practice one-, two-, three-, and four-digit addition problems
- Practice one-, two-, three-, and four-digit subtraction problems
- Skip-count by twos, threes, fours, and tens
- Multiply one-, two-, three-, and four-digit numbers

Multi-Sensory Learning Activities

Try these fun activities for enhancing your child's learning and development during the first quarter of the school year. Be sure to choose activities that include speaking, listening, touching, and active movement.

Reading and Language Arts

Read *The Boxcar Children* by Gertrude Chandler Warner with your child. After you are both finished reading, discuss the book. Then, give your child several sentences from the book and have him or her rewrite them using pronouns wherever possible.

Give your child a choice of 12 action verbs. Have him or her choose eight and write a sentence using each, underlining the verb.

Have your child write a list of at least 20 nouns. Then, ask him or her to write an appropriate adjective in front of each noun.

 **Math**

Create a place-value board. Choose four different colors of construction paper, and designate one color for each place value. Cut out 10 small squares of each color. Then, divide a large sheet of construction paper into four columns and label as shown. Test your child by naming a four-digit number and asking him or her to place the appropriate amount of squares in each column to represent the number. For example, if you say "4,398," your child should

Thousands	Hundreds	Tens	Ones

place four green squares in the thousands column, three red squares in the hundreds column, nine purple squares in the tens column, and eight blue squares in the ones column.

Provide opportunities for your child to estimate numbers by rounding. When you are in a crowded room, ask, "How many people do you think are here?" Or, put a large number of items in a jar for your child to estimate. Count the objects to see how close your child guessed.

Go outside and use chalk to write a number line (0–60) on the sidewalk. Teach your child how to use the number line as an aid in multiplication. Give your child a problem, such as 4 x ____ = 20. Starting at 0, have your child jump by fours to 20. Because it took five jumps, your child can determine that 4 x 5 = 20. Repeat with other problems.

Challenge your child with this variation on the number line activity.

First Quarter Introduction, cont.

Have your child jump to a given number in a specific number of jumps: "Jump to 63 in 9 jumps." Then, ask what each interval was and have your child state the multiplication problem. Repeat with other numbers.

 **Social Studies**

Write the following categories on a large piece of paper: **desert**, **mountain**, **river**, **archipelago**, **island**, and **sea**. The following proper nouns name particular landforms. Have your child list each name under the appropriate category. Use reference materials if he or she needs help.

Mediterranean	Alps	North Bering	Madagascar	Hawaii
Galapagos	Kalahari	Congo	Beaufort	Japan
Jamaica	Yangtze	Arkansas	Gobi	Atlas
Australia	Baffin	Canary	Ural	Atacama
Philippines	New Guinea	Appalachian	Andes	Caribbean

 **Science**

Go to the library with your child and gather books related to the solar system. Then, divide a large sheet of paper into four columns. Label the columns: **What I Know, What I Want to Know, How I Will Get the Information,** and **What I Learned**. Have your child list facts and thoughts under the first three columns. Read several books together before filling out the fourth column.

 Seasonal Fun

Conduct a spooky science experiment with your child. First, find a large drinking glass or glass jar. Then, pour several liquids into the glass in the following order: molasses, corn syrup, water (with a few drops of food coloring), and vegetable oil. Then, ask your child to drop in several small spooky objects, such as a toy bug or a fake eyeball. Which layer do the items float on? Then, ask your child to make his or her predictions for more items and see if he or she is correct.

Week 1 Skills

Subject	Skill	Multi-Sensory Learning Activities
Reading and Language Arts	Identify long and short vowel sounds **a**, **e**, **i**, and **o**.	• Complete Practice Pages 18–22. • Make flash cards, one for each long and short vowel sound. Lay out the cards. Then, name a word and ask your child to show you the card that matches the word's vowel sound. • Read several poems with your child. Ask him or her to highlight the words with long vowel sounds, and encourage him or her to write a new poem using those words.
Math	Understand place value up to the millions place.	• Complete Practice Pages 23–25. • Count a handful of small objects by ones. When you reach 10, put the 10 objects in a paper cup. Count that as 1 ten. It is important for your child to see 10 as a unit. Continue counting the remaining objects, naming the number of tens and ones (for example, **12** should be read as "1 ten, 2 ones").
	Work with expanded notation.	• Complete Practice Page 26. • Challenge your child to write a very large number (with six or more digits) on a large sheet of paper. Then, can he or she write the number in expanded notation? See page 26.

A Is for Apple

ache
admit
animal
April
bacon
bathroom
camera
flap
grateful
happiness
manage
navy
plane
radish
waste

Write the words that contain a **short a** that sounds like the **a** in **apple**.

_____   _____

_____   _____

_____   _____

_____   _____

List all the words that contain a **long a** that sounds like the **a** in **cake**.

_____   _____

_____   _____

_____   _____

_____

Use the words to complete the word search. The words are written vertically, horizontally, and diagonally.

```
T F I U H F C B K Q G H E N P N
M X G O A X J K I W G T I U R M
O C S B P J I P R E J T D P V R
C Q A I P M W L P H M F C F J Z
E E Y Y I N U A H W T L L N A V
B C V Y N F Y D C E W V L B X L
W A S T E L B O A T A D X S M H
N M C T S S A B L K A V J J U X
I E A O S R T O A U B P U J E M
G R T K N I H E P G O T E G U R
G A E A M U R R R M S A A C H E
D F K D U Y O B I D L N U U O A
A W A B V M O X L R A D I S H N
G L N C U Z M X E M N Y F Z A H
H U V I Z K U K J U I S E L T E
K S Y K Q R H T Q W M N T V W L
M D T B H T C R F L A P T I F K
L C L N A V Q H R L L D Z Y A J
S B N T D J K M P C U I I E H A
```

As Are Back

afraid
aide
bay
break
chain
delay
failure
great
maize
payment
prey
refrain
remain
stain
waist

Write the words in which the letters **ai** have a **long a** sound.

_____ _____ _____

_____ _____ _____

_____ _____ _____

Write the words in which the letters **ea** have a **long a** sound.

_____ _____

Write the words in which the letters **ay** have a **long a** sound.

_____ _____ _____

Which word is left? _____

Which two letters make the **long a** sound? _____

Homophones are words that sound like another word but are spelled differently and have different meanings.

The words contain six homophones.
List each below with its missing sound-alike.
The first pair is given.

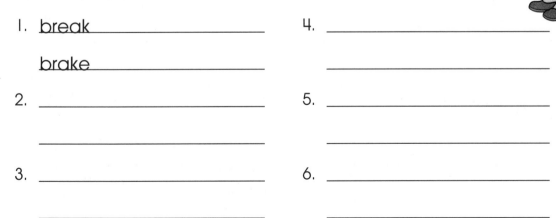

1. break _____
   brake _____

2. _____
   _____

3. _____
   _____

4. _____
   _____

5. _____
   _____

6. _____
   _____

Easy Does It

bedtime
being
beverage
cedar
decoy
elegant
female
jelly
lemon
medicine
meteor
rectangle
recycle
secret
skeleton

Use words containing the **short e** sound to fill in the blanks.

1. A _____ is sour.

2. The new living room carpet was stained by grape

   _____ and a spilled _____.

3. For your sore throat, you can take _____

   before _____.

4. The body's bony frame is called a _____.

5. A queen would probably be _____.

6. A _____ has four sides.

Use words containing a **long e** sound to fill in the blanks.

1. In the night sky, a _____ could be seen near the Big Dipper.

2. It is no _____ that the _____ star of the movie is quite ill.

3. Our neighbor is _____ thoughtful of the environment because

   he tries to _____ things like newspaper, aluminum cans and plastic milk jugs.

4. For his birthday, Dad received a _____ to use when he goes duck hunting.

5. The storm damaged a large _____ tree in our yard.

Still Easy

Put a check to the left of the words in which the letters **ea** make the **long e** sound.

Put a star to the right of the words in which the letters **ee** make the **long e** sound.

Which word uses the letters **eo** for the **long e** sound? _____

agree	easel	preach
between	greenery	season
breathe	greetings	wheat
disease	meek	wheel
eagle	people	yeast

Fill in the blanks.

1. During the holiday _____, our family sends lots of

   _____.

2. The Reverend Smith will _____ to _____ a shorter time because of extra musical selections.

3. In earlier times, _____ was ground into flour with a large stone

   _____.

4. The soaring _____ is a proud creature, not _____ or timid.

5. In the park surrounded by _____ stood the artist painting at his

   _____.

6. The swimming coach taught the swimmers to _____ evenly

   _____ strokes.

7. Two topics or terms studied in life science are _____ and

   _____.

Long I and O

Long $\bar{\text{i}}$ can be spelled **i** as in **wild**, **igh** as in **night**, **i-e** as in **wipe**, or **y** as in **try**. Long $\bar{\text{o}}$ can be spelled **o** as in **most**, **oa** as in **toast**, **ow** as in **throw**, or **o-e** as in **hope**.

stripe	fry
groan	sight
glow	stove
toast	toads
grind	flight

Complete the exercises with words from the box.

1. Write each word from the box with its vowel sound.

   $\bar{\text{i}}$ _____

   $\bar{\text{o}}$ _____

2. Complete these sentences using a word with the given vowel sound. Use each word from the box only once.

   We will ($\bar{\text{i}}$) _____ potatoes on the ($\bar{\text{o}}$) _____.

   I thought I heard a low ($\bar{\text{o}}$) _____, but when I looked, there was

   nothing in ($\bar{\text{i}}$) _____.

   The airplane for our ($\bar{\text{i}}$) _____ had a ($\bar{\text{i}}$) _____
   painted on its side.

   I saw a strange ($\bar{\text{o}}$) _____ coming from the toaster while

   making ($\bar{\text{o}}$) _____.

   Do ($\bar{\text{o}}$) _____ live in the water like frogs?

   We need to ($\bar{\text{i}}$) _____ up the nuts before we put them in the
   cookie dough.

Place Value

1 , 2 3 4 , 5 6 7

millions
hundred thousands
ten thousands
thousands
hundreds
tens
ones

1. The number 8,672,019 has:

   _____ thousands   _____ ten   _____ hundred thousands

   _____ millions   _____ ones   _____ ten thousands

   _____ hundreds

2. What number has
   6 ones   3 millions   9 tens
   7 hundreds   4 ten thousands   8 thousands
   5 hundred thousands

   The number is _____.

3. The number 6,792,510 has:

   _____ ten thousands _____ millions   _____ hundreds

   _____ ones   _____ thousands   _____ ten

   _____ hundred thousands

4. What number has
   5 millions   3 tens   6 thousands
   1 hundred   8 ten thousands   4 ones
   0 hundred thousands

   The number is _____.

Place Value

Place value is the value of a digit, or numeral, shown by where it is in the number. For example, in 1,234, 1 has the place value of thousands, 2 is hundreds, 3 is tens, and 4 is ones.

Write the numbers in the correct boxes to find how far the car has traveled.

one thousand

six hundreds

eight ones

nine ten thousands

four tens

two millions

five hundred thousands

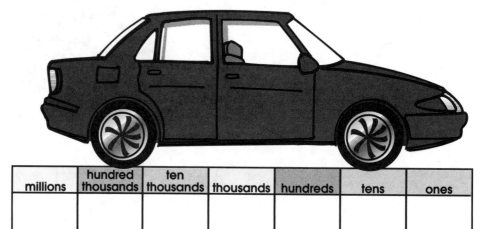

millions	hundred thousands	ten thousands	thousands	hundreds	tens	ones

How many miles has the car traveled? _____

In the number . . .

2,386 _____ is in the ones place.

4,957 _____ is in the hundreds place.

102,432 _____ is in the ten thousands place.

489,753 _____ is in the thousands place.

1,743,998 _____ is in the millions place.

9,301,671 _____ is in the hundred thousands place.

7,521,834 _____ is in the tens place.

Place Value: Standard Form

For this activity, you will need a number spinner or number cube.

Roll the cube or spin the spinner the same number of times as there are spaces in each place value box. The first number rolled or spun goes in the ones place, the second number in the tens place, and so on.

Example:

thousands	hundreds	tens	ones
4	5	6	7

Standard Form

4,567

	hundreds	tens	ones

	thousands	hundreds	tens	ones

ten thousands	thousands	hundreds	tens	ones

hundred thousands	ten thousands	thousands	hundreds	tens	ones

millions	hundred thousands	ten thousands	thousands	hundreds	tens	ones

Write the number words for the numerals above.

_____

_____

_____

_____

_____

Place Value: Expanded Notation and Standard Form

Use the number cube or spinner to create numbers for the place value boxes below. Then write the number in expanded notation and standard form.

Example:

thousands	hundreds	tens	ones
8	6	2	4

Standard Form _____ 8,624

Expanded Notation _____ 8,000 + 600 + 20 + 4

thousands	hundreds	tens	ones

Standard Form _____

Expanded Notation _____

ten thousands	thousands	hundreds	tens	ones

Standard Form _____

Expanded Notation _____

hundred thousands	ten thousands	thousands	hundreds	tens	ones

Standard Form _____

Expanded Notation _____

Write the value of the 4 in each number below.

742,521 _____

456 _____

1,234,567 _____

65,504 _____

937,641 _____

Week 2 Skills

Subject	Skill	Multi-Sensory Learning Activities
Reading and Language Arts	Identify long and short vowel sounds **i**, **o**, and **u**.	• Complete Practice Pages 28–30. • Make a list of about 40 different words containing long and short vowel sounds. Create a "Bingo" card for your child, writing a word from the list in each square. Then, make cards for the caller, writing clues on each one, such as "**long a** sound and begins with **b**," etc. Have the caller pull one card at a time out of a bag and call out the clue. Once your child marks five words in a row correctly, he or she should call out "Bingo!"
	Recognize vowel sounds for words containing vowel pairs.	• Complete Practice Pages 31 and 32. • Name several words containing vowel pairs, such as **break**, **leave**, **weigh**, and **view**. Ask your child to show you the flash card (see page 17) of the vowel sound he or she hears.
Math	Review place value.	• Complete Practice Page 33. • Show your child how to add columns up to the millions place on the place-value chart (see page 15). Teach comma placement and how to read a seven-digit number aloud.
	Practice rounding to the nearest ten thousand.	• Complete Practice Pages 34–36. • Test your child on real-life situations involving rounding. For example, say "If I have $147.36 in the bank, about how much money do I have?"

Long I and O

Read the words. After each word, write the correct long vowel sound. Underline the letter or letters that spell the sound. The first one has been done for you.

Word	Vowel		Word	Vowel
1. br<u>igh</u>t	i	9. white	
2. globe		10. roast	
3. plywood		11. light	
4. mankind		12. shallow	
5. coaching		13. myself	
6. prize		14. throne	
7. grind		15. cold	
8. withhold		16. snow	

Below are words written as they are pronounced. Write the words that sound like:

1. thrōn _____   5. brīt _____

2. skōld _____   6. grīnd _____

3. prīz _____   7. plīwood _____

4. rōst _____   8. mīself _____

Often-Used Os

auto	doctor	object
bobbin	elbow	poetry
bony	frozen	solemn
closet	hotel	solve
cobra	knot	total

Put a check to the left of the words in the list that have a **short o** sound as in **hot**. Put a star to the right of the words in the list that have a **long o** sound as in **open**.

Write a word to answer each question.

1. What's another word for "sum"? ___ ___ ___ ☐ ___

2. Which word names a snake? ☐ ___ ___ ___ ___

3. Which word describes ice cream? ___ ___ ___ ___ ☐ ___

4. Where might you stay on a vacation? ☐ ___ ___ ___ ___

5. Where is thread kept? ___ ___ ___ ☐ ___ ___

6. What can be tied in a rope? ☐ ___ ___ ___

7. What happens when you find a solution? ___ ___ ☐ ___ ___ ___

8. What word means serious? ___ ___ ___ ☐ ___ ___

9. What's between the wrist and the shoulder? ___ ___ ___ ☐ ___

10. Which word describes rhyming verse? ☐ ___ ___ ___ ___ ___

11. Where do clothes hang? ___ ___ ___ ☐ ___ ___

12. Who helps those who are sick? ___ ___ ___ ☐ ___ ___

13. Which word means "car"? ___ ☐ ___ ___

14. Which word describes a skeleton? ___ ___ ___ ☐

Match the boxed letter from each line to the numbered lines below to answer the riddle. *Where can you always find a lost object?*

___ ___ ___ ___ ___ ___ ___ ___ ___
5   8   12   4   3   7   1   11 12

___ ___ ___ ___ ___ ___ ___ ___
10   7   1   2   3   14   9   13

___ ___ ___ ___!
7   9   9   6

You Can Spell Us

Circle the words that contain the **short u** sound as in **cup**. Use your calculator to find the point value of each word that contains the **long u** sound as in **use**.

Assign a number to each letter in the alphabet.

(A = 1, B = 2, C = 3, and so forth)

a ____	n ____
b ____	o ____
c ____	p ____
d ____	q ____
e ____	r ____
f ____	s ____
g ____	t ____
h ____	u ____
i ____	v ____
j ____	w ____
k ____	x ____
l ____	y ____
m ____	z ____

amuse
bubble
budding
budge
computer
customer
duty
humor
hungry
husky
Jupiter
number
sundown
summer
usual

Example: music = 13 + 21 + 19 + 9 + 3 = 65

_____ = _____

_____ = _____

_____ = _____

_____ = _____

_____ = _____

_____ = _____

Which word has the greatest point value? _____

Which has the least? _____

Now, find the point value of your own words. _____

_____ _____ _____

I Before E or Not?

Write the **ei** words in alphabetical order.

1. _____   6. _____

2. _____   7. _____

3. _____   8. _____

4. _____   9. _____

5. _____   10. _____

How many **ei** words have a **long a** sound? _____

How many **ei** words have a **long e** sound? _____

Which of the **ei** words is left? _____

What sound does it have? _____

Write the **ie** words in alphabetical order.

beige
believe
conceited
eight
field
fiend
freight
friend
height
leisure
neighbor
receive
sleigh
thief
weigh

1. _____

2. _____

3. _____

4. _____

5. _____

What sound do you hear in four of the **ie** words? _____

What sound do you hear in the remaining **ie** word? _____

Write the word. _____

Fill in the blanks with four different letters in this helpful spelling rule.

The letter _____ comes before _____ except after _____, or if it sounds like _____.

You Are Beautiful

argue
beautiful
beauty
cue
feud
few
hue
mew
newt
pew
queue
review
view
you
yule

Write the words that contain the letters **ew** or **iew** (as the **yoo** sound) in alphabetical order.

1. _____   4. _____

2. _____   5. _____

3. _____   6. _____

Use the words to fill in the blanks. Not all words are used; one is used twice.

1. TV announcers read from ☐ ___ ___ cards.

2. It's good manners to say "Thank ___ ☐ ___" when someone gives you something.

3. A cat says ☐ ___ ___.

4. A church seat is called a ☐ ___ ___.

5. Christmas is sometimes called ___ ___ ☐ ___.

6. Roses are ___ ___ ___ ___ ___ ___ ☐ ___ ___ ___ flowers.

7. A hungry kitten says ☐ ___ ___.

8. Look at the ___ ___ ☐ ___ out the window.

9. A salamander is related to a ☐ ___ ___ ___.

10. ___ ___ ___ ___ ☐ ___ is only skin-deep.

Read the letters in the box to answer the question: What have you received if

someone says, "You are beautiful"? _____

What four words have not been used?   _____

_____

_____

_____

The First State

What state is known as the first state? Follow the directions below to find out.

1. If 31,842 rounded to the nearest thousand is 31,000, put an A above number 2.

2. If 62 rounded to the nearest ten is 60, put an E above number 2 .

3. If 4,234 rounded to the nearest hundred is 4,200, put an R above number 7.

4. If 677 rounded to the nearest hundred is 700, put an L above number 3.

5. If 344 rounded to the nearest ten is 350, put an E above number 5.

**Peach Blossom
State Flower**

**Blue Hen Chicken
State Bird**

6. If 5,599 rounded to the nearest thousand is 6,000, put an A above number 4.

7. If 1,549 rounded to the nearest hundred is 1,500, put an A above number 6.

8. If 885 rounded to the nearest hundred is 800, put a W above number 2.

9. If 521 rounded to the nearest ten is 520, put an E above number 8.

10. If 74 rounded to the nearest ten is 80, put an R above number 6.

11. If 3,291 rounded to the nearest thousand is 3,000, put an L above number 3.

12. If 248 rounded to the nearest hundred is 300, put an R above number 4.

13. If 615 rounded to the nearest ten is 620, put a D above number 1.

14. If 188 rounded to the nearest ten is 200, put a W above number 1.

15. If 6,817 rounded to the nearest thousand is 7,000, put a W above number 5.

**Fort Christina—site of the first
state's first permanent settlement.
Built by the Swedes and Finns.**

$$\overline{}\ \overline{}\ \overline{}\ \overline{}\ \overline{}\ \overline{}\ \overline{}\ \overline{}$$
   1   2   3   4   5   6   7   8

Rounding: Tens

Rounding a number means expressing it to the nearest ten, hundred, thousand, and so on. Knowing how to round numbers makes estimating sums, differences, and products easier. When rounding to the nearest ten, the key number is in the ones place. If the ones digit is 5 or larger, round up to the next highest ten. If the ones digit is 4 or less, round down to the nearest ten.

Examples:

- Round 81 to the nearest ten.

- 1 is the key digit.

- If it is less than 5, round down.

- Answer: <u>80</u>

- Round 246 to the nearest ten.

- 6 is the key digit.

- If it is more than 5, round up.

- Answer: <u>250</u>

Round these numbers to the nearest ten.

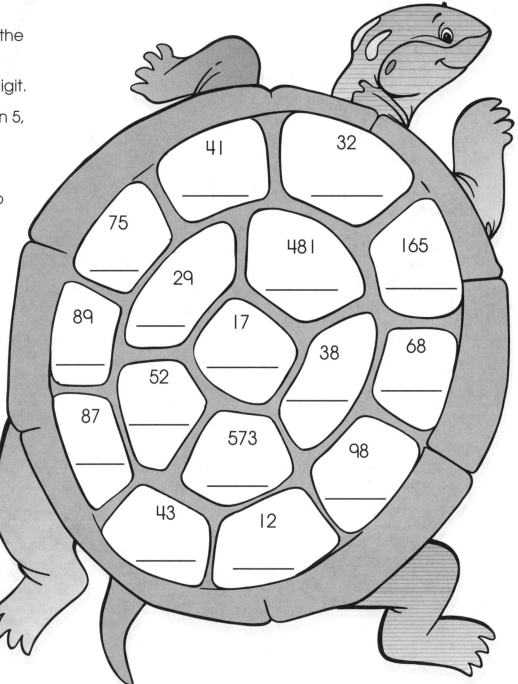

Rounding: Hundreds and Thousands

When rounding to the nearest hundred, the key number is in the tens place. If the tens digit is 5 or larger, round up to nearest hundred. If the tens digit is 4 or less, round down to the nearest hundred.

Examples:

Round 871 to the nearest hundred.
7 is the key digit.
If it is more than 5, round up.
Answer: <u>900</u>

Round 421 to the nearest hundred.
2 is the key digit.
If it is less than 4, round down.
Answer: <u>400</u>

Round these numbers to the nearest hundred.

255 _____   368 _____   443 _____   578 _____

562 _____   698 _____   99 _____   775 _____

812 _____   592 _____   124 _____   10,235 _____

When rounding to the nearest thousand, the key number is in the hundreds place. If the hundreds digit is 5 or larger, round up to the nearest thousand. If the hundreds digit is 4 or less, round down to the nearest thousand.

Examples:

Round 7,932 to the nearest thousand.
9 is the key digit.
If it is more than 5, round up.
Answer: <u>8,000</u>

Round 1,368 to the nearest thousand.
3 is the key digit.
If it is less than 4, round down.
Answer: <u>1,000</u>

Round these numbers to the nearest thousand.

8,631 _____   6,229 _____   8,461 _____

999 _____   4,963 _____   99,923 _____

9,654 _____   798 _____

1,248 _____

Rounding

Round these numbers to the nearest ten.

18 _____   33 _____   82 _____   56 _____

24 _____   49 _____   91 _____   67 _____

Round these numbers to the nearest hundred.

243 _____   689 _____   263 _____   162 _____

389 _____   720 _____   351 _____   490 _____

463 _____   846 _____   928 _____   733 _____

Round these numbers to the nearest thousand.

2,638 _____   3,940 _____   8,653 _____

6,238 _____   1,429 _____   5,061 _____

7,289 _____   2,742 _____   9,460 _____

3,109 _____   4,697 _____   8,302 _____

Round these numbers to the nearest ten thousand.

11,368 _____   57,843 _____

75,302 _____   38,421 _____

14,569 _____   67,932 _____

93,694 _____   49,926 _____

26,784 _____   81,648 _____

29,399 _____   87,065 _____

Week 3 Skills

Subject	Skill	Multi-Sensory Learning Activities
Reading and Language Arts	Identify common nouns and proper nouns, or nouns that name a specific person, place, or thing.	• Complete Practice Pages 38–42. • Read your child several sentences. Ask him or her to identify each noun and proper noun from each sentence. Ask your child to write those words, making sure he or she is using appropriate capitalization for proper nouns.
Math	Practice one- and two-digit addition problems.	• Complete Practice Pages 43–46. • Give your child a copy of the Hundred Chart found on page 390. Then, give your child a sample problem, such as 31 + 27 = ___. Starting at the number **31**, have him or her trace down two rows (adding 2 tens) and over seven columns (adding 7 ones). Your child's finger should land on the correct answer: **58**. Repeat with other problems.
Bonus: Social Studies		• Discuss the broad meaning of the word **exploration**. Give your child the following story starter: "If I were an explorer, I would _____, because…" Be sure your child includes details of the voyage as well as some illustrations.

Nouns

A **noun** names a person, place or thing.

Examples: **Persons** — boy, girl, Mom, Dad
Places — park, pool, house, office
Things — bike, swing, desk, book

Read the following sentences. Underline the nouns. The first one has been done for you.

1. The girl went to school.

2. Grandma and Grandpa will visit us soon.

3. The bike is in the garage.

4. Dad went to his office.

5. Mom is at her desk in the den.

6. John's house is near the park.

7. Her brothers are at school.

8. We took the books to the library.

Read the following words. Underline the nouns. Then categorize the nouns on another sheet of paper into groups of people, places, and things.

tree	Mrs. Smith	Dad	cards	Grandma	skip	sell
house	car	truck	Mom	office	grass	sign
boy	run	Sam	stove	greet	grade	school
girl	camp	jump	weave	free	driver	room
salesperson	sad	teach	treat	stripe	paint	Jane
clay	man	leave	happy	play	desk	tape
watch	lives	painter	brother	rain	window	hop

Nouns

Write nouns that name persons.

1. Could you please give this report to my _____?

2. The _____ works many long
   hours to plant crops.

3. I had to help my little _____ when
   he wrecked his bike yesterday.

Write nouns that name places.

4. I always keep my library books on top of the _____ so I
   can find them.

5. We enjoyed watching the kites flying high in the _____.

6. Dad built a nice fire in the to keep us warm.

Write nouns that name things.

7. The little _____ purred softly as I held it.

8. Wouldn't you think a _____ would get tired of carrying
   its house around all day?

9. The _____ scurried into its hole with the piece of cheese.

10. I can tell by the writing that this _____ is mine.

11. Look at the _____ I made in art.

12. His _____ blew away because
    of the strong wind.

Common and Proper Nouns

Common nouns name general people, places, and things.

Examples: boy, girl, cat, dog, park, city, building

Proper nouns name specific persons, places, and things.

Examples: John, Mary, Fluffy, Rover, Central Park, Chicago, Empire State Building

Proper nouns begin with capital letters.

Read the following nouns. On the blanks, indicate whether the nouns are common or proper. The first two have been done for you.

1. New York City	proper	9. Dr. DiCarlo	_____
2. house	common	10. man	_____
3. car	_____	11. Rock River	_____
4. Ohio	_____	12. building	_____
5. river	_____	13. lawyer	_____
6. Rocky Mountains	_____	14. Grand Canyon	_____
7. Mrs. Jones	_____	15. city	_____
8. nurse	_____	16. state	_____

On another sheet of paper, write proper nouns for the above common nouns.

Read the following sentences. Underline the common nouns. Circle the proper nouns.

1. Mary's birthday is Friday, October 7.

2. She likes having her birthday in a fall month.

3. Her friends will meet her at the Video Arcade for a party.

4. Ms. McCarthy and Mr. Landry will help with the birthday party games.

5. Mary's friends will play video games all afternoon.

6. Amy and John will bring refreshments and games to the party.

Common and Proper Nouns

A **common noun** names any person, place, or thing.

A **proper noun** names a specific person, place, or thing.

A proper noun always begins with a capital letter.

Example: boy, state (common nouns)
Peter, Georgia (proper nouns)

Underline the nouns in the sentences.

1. Bobby was wondering what the weather would be on Friday.

2. The boys and girls from Lang School were planning a picnic.

3. Bobby asked his teacher, Mr. Lewis, how the class could find out.

4. The teacher suggested that the children call a local newspaper, *The Bugle*.

5. Ms. Canyon, the editor, read the forecast to Eddie.

6. Rain was predicted for the day of their picnic.

7. Their town, Grand Forks, also had a radio station.

8. When Rick called the number, he was disappointed.

9. The weatherman, George Lee, said that rain was possible.

10. The children were delighted when the sun came out on Friday.

Now, write each noun you have underlined in the correct category below. Do not use any words more than once.

Proper Nouns

1. _____
2. _____
3. _____
4. _____
5. _____
6. _____
7. _____
8. _____
9. _____
10. _____

Common Nouns

1. _____
2. _____
3. _____
4. _____
5. _____
6. _____
7. _____
8. _____
9. _____
10. _____

11. _____
12. _____
13. _____
14. _____
15. _____
16. _____
17. _____

Proper Nouns

Proper nouns always begin with a capital letter.

Examples: Monday

Texas

Karen

Mr. Logan

Hamburger Avenue

Rover

Cross out the lowercase letters at the beginning of the proper nouns. Write capital letters above them. The first one has been done for you.

1. My teddy bear's name is Cocoa.

2. ms. bernhard does an excellent job at crestview elementary school.

3. emily, elizabeth, and megan live on main street.

4. I am sure our teacher said the book report is due on monday.

5. I believe you can find lake street if you turn left at the next light.

6. Will your family be able join our family for dinner at burger barn?

7. The weather forecasters think the storm will hit the coast of louisiana friday afternoon.

8. My family went to washington, d.c. this summer.

9. Remember, we don't have school on tuesday because of the teachers' meeting.

10. Who do you think will win the game, the cougars or the arrows?

Add 'Em Up!

Addition is "putting together" or adding two or more numbers to find the sum.

Add the following problems as quickly and as accurately as you can.

```
  3        6        5        2
+ 2      + 4      + 4      + 9
```

```
  6        4        9        7        8        8
+ 2      + 1      + 6      + 6      + 7      + 9
```

```
  9        1        4        7        5        5
+ 4      + 8      + 7      + 9      + 6      + 3
```

```
           6        8        7        4
         + 6      + 8      + 7      + 4
```

```
           2        5        3        5
         + 8      + 2      + 6      + 8
```

How quickly did you complete this page? _____

Going in Circles

Where the circles meet, write the sum of the numbers from the circles on the right and left and above and below. The first row shows you what to do.

Magic Squares

Some of the number squares below are "magic" and some are not. Squares that add up to the same number horizontally, vertically, and diagonally are "magic." Add the numbers horizontally and vertically in each square to discover which ones are "magic."

Example:

4	9	2
3	5	7
8	1	6

15
15
15

15 15 15 15

Magic? __yes__

1.

7	2	1
3	4	8
5	9	6

Magic? _____

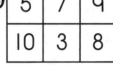

2.

6	11	4
5	7	9
10	3	8

Magic? _____

3.

3	8	1
2	4	6
7	0	5

Magic? _____

4.

2	7	0
1	3	5
6	9	4

Magic? _____

5.

5	10	3
4	6	8
9	2	7

Magic? _____

6.

7	12	5
6	8	10
11	4	9

Magic? _____

7.

1	2	3
4	5	6
7	8	9

Magic? _____

8.

6	7	4
1	5	9
8	3	2

Magic? _____

Challenge: Can you discover a pattern for number placement in the magic squares? Try to make a magic square of your own.

Leafy Addition

Add, then color according to the code.

Code:

green — 79	**orange — 35**	**red — 78**
yellow — 87	**purple — 56**	**brown — 94**

57
+ 21

34
+ 22

23
+ 12

35
+ 52

15
+ 41

62
+ 32

20
+ 74

34
+ 44

47
+ 40

56
+ 23

27
+ 8

63
+ 16

COMPLETE YEAR GRADE 4

Week 4 Skills

Subject	Skill	Multi-Sensory Learning Activities
Reading and Language Arts	Review pronouns; work with subject and object pronouns and plural nouns.	• Complete Practice Pages 48–52. • Write **I**, **you**, **he**, **she**, **it**, **we**, and **they** on a piece of paper. Have your child sort the pronouns into two groups—singular and plural (**you** can be either). Next, write several sentences whose subjects are pronouns. Guide your child to change the verb in each sentence so that it agrees with the singular or plural pronoun.
Math	Practice two-, three-, and four-digit addition problems.	• Complete Practice Pages 53–55. • Roll three dice and arrange them to form a three-digit number. Write the number on lined paper. Roll the three dice again and arrange them to form another number. Write both numbers on a sheet of paper and add them together.
	Practice subtraction problems within 20.	• Complete Practice Page 56. • Create flash cards for subtraction problems within 20. Practice with your child to build speed and memory. How fast can your child correctly answer all the cards?

Pronouns

A **pronoun** is a word that takes the place of a noun in a sentence.

Examples: I, my, mine, me

we, our, ours, us

you, your, yours

he, his, him

she, her, hers

it, its

they, their, theirs, them

Underline the pronouns in each sentence.

1. Bring them to us as soon as you are finished.

2. She has been my best friend for many years.

3. They should be here soon.

4. We enjoyed our trip to the Mustard Museum.

5. Would you be able to help us with the project on Saturday?

6. Our homeroom teacher will not be here tomorrow.

7. My uncle said that he will be leaving soon for Australia.

8. Hurry! Could you please open the door for him?

9. She dropped her gloves when she got off the bus.

10. I can't figure out who the mystery writer is today.

I, We; Me, Us

I and **we** are **subject pronouns**.
Me and **us** are **object pronouns**.

Examples: Mark and **I** are on our way to the park.
(subject pronoun)

We just love to launch rockets!
(subject pronoun)

Will Sara come with **me**?
(object pronoun)

Please feel welcome to join **us**.
(object pronoun)

Choose the correct pronoun for each sentence from those in parentheses. Write it in the blank.

1. _____ plan to launch rockets at the park on Saturday.
   (we, us)

2. Monica bought _____ a two-stage rocket.
   (I, me)

3. Bill and _____ both brought fresh batteries for the rocket launcher.
   (I, me)

4. Curt plans to build _____ a rocket.
   (we, us)

5. Gwen wants _____ to attend the rocket safety course.
   (I, me)

6. _____ always like to paint the fins a bright color.
   (I, me)

7. Tom wants Michele and _____ to chase after his rocket when it lands.
   (I, me)

8. Heather wants _____ to go to the launching site.
   (we, us)

9. Carolyn and _____ just bought a model rocket with a payload section.
   (I, me)

10. Jim will be showing _____ his model rocket.
    (we, us)

Plurals

Nouns come in two forms: singular and plural. When a noun is **singular**, it means there is only one person, place, or thing.

Examples: car, swing, box, truck, slide, bus

When a noun is **plural**, it means there is more than one person, place, or thing.

Examples: two cars, four trucks, three swings, five slides, six boxes, three buses

Usually an **s** is added to most nouns to make them plural. However, if the noun ends in **s**, **x**, **ch** or **sh**, then **es** is added to make it plural.

Write the singular or plural form of each word.

Singular	Plural	Singular	Plural
1. car	_____	9. _____	tricks
2. bush	_____	10. mess	_____
3. wish	_____	11. box	_____
4. _____	foxes	12. dish	_____
5. _____	rules	13. _____	boats
6. stitch	_____	14. path	_____
7. _____	switches	15. _____	arms
8. barn	_____	16. _____	sticks

Rewrite the following sentences and change the bold nouns from singular to plural or from plural to singular. The first one has been done for you.

1. She took a **book** to school.

   She took books to school.

2. Tommy made **wishes** at his birthday party.

   _____

3. The **fox** ran away from the hunters.

   _____

4. The **houses** were painted white.

   _____

Plurals

When a word ends with a consonant before **y**, to make it plural, drop the **y** and add **ies**.

Examples: party   parties
                 cherry   cherries
                 daisy   daisies

However, if the word ends with a vowel before **y**, just add **s**.

Examples: boy   boys
                 toy   toys
                 monkey   monkeys

Write the singular or plural form of each word.

Singular	Plural	Singular	Plural
1. fly	_____	7. _____	decoys
2. _____	boys	8. candy	_____
3. _____	joys	9. toy	_____
4. spy	_____	10. _____	cries
5. _____	keys	11. monkey	_____
6. _____	dries	12. daisy	_____

Write six sentences of your own using any of the plurals above.

_____

_____

_____

_____

_____

Plurals

Some words in the English language do not follow any of the plural rules discussed earlier. These words may not change at all from singular to plural, or they may completely change spellings.

No Change	Examples:	Complete Change	Examples:
Singular	**Plural**	**Singular**	**Plural**
deer	deer	goose	geese
pants	pants	ox	oxen
scissors	scissors	man	men
moose	moose	child	children
sheep	sheep	leaf	leaves

Write the singular or plural form of each word. Use a dictionary to help if necessary.

Singular	Plural	Singular	Plural
1. moose	_____	6. leaf	_____
2. woman	_____	7. _____	sheep
3. _____	deer	8. scissors	_____
4. _____	children	9. tooth	_____
5. _____	hooves	10. wharf	_____

Write four sentences of your own using two singular and two plural words from above.

_____

_____

_____

_____

COMPLETE YEAR GRADE 4

Adding Larger Numbers

When adding two-, three- and four-digit numbers, add the ones first, then tens, hundreds, thousands, and so on.

Examples:

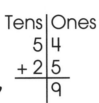

```
Tens | Ones
  5  |  4
+ 2  |  5
─────┼─────
     |  9
```

```
Tens | Ones
  5  |  4
+ 2  |  5
─────┼─────
  7  |  9
```

Add the following numbers.

81	67	34	730
+ 23	+ 22	+ 82	+ 265

76	1,803	523	267
+ 73	+ 1,104	+ 476	+ 12

```
  4,254        111
+  545       + 82
```

```
   164        727
 + 425       + 51
```

Batter Up!

Complete each addition box.

+ →		
492	224	
118	303	

+ →		
3,147	2,394	
1,423	1,387	

+ →		
721	519	
908	286	

+ →		
1,435	2,916	
3,192	2,921	

+ →		
7,540	2,918	
1,387	2,913	

+ →		
5,642	1,829	
2,819	6,425	

+ →		
4,256	1,487	
1,842	2,143	

Addition: Regrouping

Regrouping uses 10 ones to form 1 ten, 10 tens to form 1 hundred, 1 ten and 5 ones to form 15, and so on.

Add using regrouping. Color in all the boxes with a 5 in the answer to help the dog find its way home.

	63 + 22	5,268 4,910 + 1,683	248 + 463	291 + 543	2,934 + 112
1,736 + 5,367	2,946 + 7,384	3,245 1,239 + 981	738 + 692	896 + 728	594 + 738
2,603 + 5,004	4,507 + 289	1,483 + 6,753	1,258 + 6,301	27 469 + 6,002	4,637 + 7,531
782 + 65	485 + 276	3,421 + 8,064			
48 93 + 26	90 263 + 864	362 453 + 800			

Subtraction

Subtraction is "taking away" or subtracting one number from another.

Complete the following problems as quickly and as accurately as you can.

18 − 9	13 − 6	12 − 5	17 − 8	16 − 8
12 − 5	10 − 4	5 − 3	14 − 6	15 − 9
9 − 5	8 − 3	6 − 2	5 − 4	10 − 7
11 − 4	12 − 8	16 − 9	11 − 8	10 − 10

How quickly did you complete this page? _____

Week 5 Skills

Subject	Skill	Multi-Sensory Learning Activities
Reading and Language Arts	Review plural nouns; practice forming plural nouns from words that end in **y** or **f**.	• Complete Practice Pages 58–61. • Give your child a list of nouns, including words that end in **y** or **f**. Ask your child to write the plural form of each word, then use it in a sentence. Then, ask your child to give you another list of nouns that end in **y** or **f**.
Math	Practice two-, three-, and four-digit subtraction problems.	• Complete Practice Pages 62–64. • Go for a walk around your neighborhood. Encourage your child to look around him or her for numbers on houses, street signs, or mailboxes and make a list. Once you return home, ask your child to group the numbers in groups of two. Then, subtract the smaller number in each pair from the larger number.
	Review addition and subtraction.	• Complete Practice Pages 65 and 66. • Give your child a calendar. Ask your child to use addition or subtraction to answer questions, such as, "How many days have passed in this month or year? How many days are still to come in this month or year? How many days until your birthday?"

Plural Nouns

Review these rules for making singular words plural.

For most words, simply add **s**.
Examples: one book — two books   one house — four houses

For words ending with **s**, **ss**, **sh**, **ch** and **x**, add **es**.
Examples: one class — two classes   one church — three churches
one box — four boxes   one crash — five crashes

For words ending with a consonant before **y**, drop the **y** and add **ies**.
Examples: one daisy — three daisies   one cherry — two cherries

For words ending with a vowel before **y**, just add **s**.
Examples: one key — eight keys   one monkey — four monkeys

Write the singular or plural form of each word.

Singular	Plural	Singular	Plural
1. mattress	_____	10. _____	candies
2. _____	bushes	11. try	_____
3. sandwich	_____	12. _____	turkeys
4. fry	_____	13. copy	_____
5. _____	crosses	14. _____	factories
6. marsh	_____	15. _____	foxes
7. _____	supplies	16. ax	_____
8. donkey	_____	17. berry	_____
9. _____	stoves	18. day	_____

Forming Plural Nouns

Most **singular nouns** can be made into **plural nouns** by following one of these rules.

Rules	Examples
1. Add **s** to most nouns.	elephant, elephant**s**
2. If the noun ends in **s**, **sh**, **ch** or **x**, add **es**.	box, box**es**
3. If the noun ends in **y** with a consonant before it, change the **y** to **i** and add **es**.	fly, fl**ies**
4. If the noun ends in **y** with a vowel before it, add **s**.	monkey, monkey**s**
5. To some nouns ending in **f**, add **s**.	chief, chief**s**
6. To some nouns ending in **f** or **fe**, change the **f** to **v** and add **es**.	knife, kni**ves** thief, thie**ves**
7. Some nouns stay the same for singular and plural.	sheep, **sheep**
8. Some nouns have an irregular plural.	goose, **geese**

Change each singular noun to plural. Write the number of the rule you used. Use a dictionary when needed.

Singular	Plural	Rule #	Singular	Plural	Rule #
1. chimney			11. woman		
2. class			12. bus		
3. wolf			13. judge		
4. deer			14. shelf		
5. story			15. chair		
6. elf			16. beach		
7. tooth			17. tax		
8. brush			18. lady		
9. attorney			19. roof		
10. mouse			20. penny		

Tricky Y

batteries
cowboys
delays
donkeys
gravies
ivies
ladies
Mondays
pennies
ponies
stories
trays
Tuesdays
valleys
Wednesdays

Write the singular (S) form of each word. Then, write its plural (P) form below it. The first one is done for you.

1. (S) battery
   (P) batteries

2. (S) _____
   (P) _____

3. (S) _____
   (P) _____

4. (S) _____
   (P) _____

5. (S) _____
   (P) _____

6. (S) _____
   (P) _____

7. (S) _____
   (P) _____

8. (S) _____
   (P) _____

9. (S) _____
   (P) _____

10. (S) _____
    (P) _____

11. (S) _____
    (P) _____

12. (S) _____
    (P) _____

13. (S) _____
    (P) _____

14. (S) _____
    (P) _____

15. (S) _____
    (P) _____

What part of speech is each of these words? _____

Which word can also be used as a verb? _____

How do you know when to change the **y** to an **i** before adding **es**? _____

_____

Plurals With F

| beliefs |
| calves |
| chiefs |
| cliffs |
| cuffs |
| elves |
| halves |
| knives |
| leaves |
| lives |
| loaves |
| roofs |
| scarves |
| shelves |
| wives |

Cross out the word that does not belong in each group. Write the spelling word that fits the category. Write its singular form on the second line.

1. colts, kittens, hogs _____ _____

2. pine cones, tulips, twigs _____ _____

3. canyons, mountains, gorges _____ _____

4. lawyers, aunts, husbands _____ _____

5. totals, fourths, thirds _____ _____

6. collars, shoes, sleeves _____ _____

7. neckties, beads, belts _____ _____

8. pixies, giants, fairies _____ _____

9. followers, leaders, directors _____ _____

10. hatchets, swords, pencils _____ _____

Five words have not been used. Write both the singular (S) and plural (P) forms.

1. (S) _____   4. (S) _____

   (P) _____   (P) _____

2. (S) _____   5. (S) _____

   (P) _____   (P) _____

3. (S) _____

   (P) _____

Subtracting Larger Numbers

When you subtract larger numbers, subtract the ones first, then the tens, hundreds, thousands, and so on.

Example:

Tens	Ones
9	4
− 2	1
	3

Tens	Ones
9	4
− 2	1
7	3

Solve these subtraction problems.

29
− 26

99
− 58

359
− 55

735
− 734

849
− 726

7,678
− 4,321

865
− 731

55
− 25

9,876
− 1,234

Subtraction: Regrouping

Subtract using regrouping.

Examples:

$$\begin{array}{r} 23 \\ -18 \\ \hline \end{array} \qquad \begin{array}{r} \overset{1}{\cancel{2}}3 \\ -18 \\ \hline 5 \end{array} \qquad \begin{array}{r} 243 \\ -\ 96 \\ \hline \end{array} \qquad \begin{array}{r} \overset{1\ 13}{2\cancel{4}\cancel{3}} \\ -\ 96 \\ \hline 147 \end{array}$$

$$\begin{array}{r} 81 \\ -53 \\ \hline \end{array} \qquad \begin{array}{r} 76 \\ -49 \\ \hline \end{array} \qquad \begin{array}{r} 94 \\ -38 \\ \hline \end{array} \qquad \begin{array}{r} 156 \\ -\ 77 \\ \hline \end{array} \qquad \begin{array}{r} 341 \\ -\ 83 \\ \hline \end{array} \qquad \begin{array}{r} 726 \\ -\ 29 \\ \hline \end{array}$$

$$\begin{array}{r} 568 \\ -173 \\ \hline \end{array} \qquad \begin{array}{r} 806 \\ -738 \\ \hline \end{array} \qquad \begin{array}{r} 743 \\ -550 \\ \hline \end{array} \qquad \begin{array}{r} 903 \\ -336 \\ \hline \end{array} \qquad \begin{array}{r} 647 \\ -289 \\ \hline \end{array} \qquad \begin{array}{r} 254 \\ -\ 69 \\ \hline \end{array}$$

$$\begin{array}{r} 730 \\ -518 \\ \hline \end{array} \qquad \begin{array}{r} 961 \\ -846 \\ \hline \end{array} \qquad \begin{array}{r} 573 \\ -\ 76 \\ \hline \end{array} \qquad \begin{array}{r} 604 \\ -\ 55 \\ \hline \end{array} \qquad \begin{array}{r} 265 \\ -\ 19 \\ \hline \end{array} \qquad \begin{array}{r} 372 \\ -\ 59 \\ \hline \end{array}$$

$$\begin{array}{r} 111 \\ -\ 82 \\ \hline \end{array} \qquad \begin{array}{r} 358 \\ -\ 99 \\ \hline \end{array} \qquad \begin{array}{r} 147 \\ -\ 49 \\ \hline \end{array}$$

$$\begin{array}{r} 180 \\ -106 \\ \hline \end{array} \qquad \begin{array}{r} 325 \\ -\ 68 \\ \hline \end{array} \qquad \begin{array}{r} 873 \\ -\ 35 \\ \hline \end{array}$$

Jungle Math

Subtract to complete the crossword puzzle.

Across

2. 517
   − 228

3. 428
   − 249

4. 562
   − 274

5. 924
   − 348

6. 923
   − 346

7. 535
   − 248

8. 857
   − 389

9. 561
   − 247

11. 845
    − 599

13. 325
    − 186

14. 356
    − 168

Down

1. 421
   − 342

2. 627
   − 348

3. 362
   − 194

4. 582
   − 346

5. 824
   − 247

6. 921
   − 346

7. 926
   − 718

8. 721
   − 240

10. 768
    − 292

12. 826
    − 337

13. 247
    − 129

Addition and Subtraction

Add or subtract, using regrouping when needed.

```
  32        183        456
  68        246        398        643
+ 43      +  89      + 597      - 377
```

```
 1,563     3,586      8,711      9,361
-  941   + 4,218    - 4,937    - 7,452
```

```
            293
 5,734      431        743        849
+ 6,298   +  93      - 529        250
                               +  82
```

```
 1,227
 2,431     9,117
+ 5,792  - 3,828
```

68 + 93 + 146 = _____   73 + 246 + 1,579 = _____

43 + 745 – 29 = _____   128 + 403 + 2,571 = _____

156 + 627 + 541 = _____   97 + 51 + 37 + 79 = _____

Tom walks 389 steps from his house to the video store. It is 149 steps to Elm Street. It is 52 steps from Maple Street to the video store. How many steps is it from Elm Street to Maple Street?

_____

Addition and Subtraction

Add or subtract, using regrouping when needed.

```
    38        1,269                        629
    43        2,453       5,792            491        4,697
  + 21      + 8,219     - 4,814          + 308      - 2,988
```

```
                  68         197
  5,280           27         436        7,321          456
- 3,147         + 42       + 213      - 2,789        + 974
```

```
                 492
  3,932          863        9,873        4,978        6,235
+ 4,681        +  57      + 5,483      + 2,131      + 2,986
```

Sue stocked her pond with 263 bass and 187 trout. 97 fish swam away in a flood. How many fish are left?

_____

Week 6 Skills

Subject	Skill	Multi-Sensory Learning Activities
Reading and Language Arts	Understand present-, past-, and future-tense verbs.	• Complete Practice Pages 68–72. • Have your child practice writing sentences in past and future tenses. Discuss the subject/verb agreement (in the past and future tenses, the verb is the same for singular and plural). For example, "Two trees waved in the breeze. One tree waved in the breeze."
Math	Skip-count by twos, threes, fours, and tens.	• Complete Practice Pages 73 and 74. • Have your child count to 100, skip-counting by twos, threes, fours, and tens. Work with your child regularly until he or she has memorized these facts. Then, explain to your child that skip-counting is early practice for multiplication.
	Practice multiplication facts through 9.	• Complete Practice Pages 75 and 76. • Roll two dice. Ask your child to multiply the two numbers together. Test your child to build speed and accuracy. • Encourage your child to notice the grid-like window patterns on large buildings. Ask if he or she can use multiplication to count the number of windows.

Verbs

Verbs are the action words in a sentence. There are three kinds of verbs: action verbs, linking verbs, and helping verbs.

An **action verb** tells the action of a sentence.

Examples: run, hop, skip, sleep, jump, talk, snore
Michael **ran** to the store. **Ran** is the action verb.

A **linking verb** joins the subject and predicate of a sentence.

Examples: am, is, are, was, were
Michael **was** at the store. **Was** is the linking verb.

A **helping verb** is used with an action verb to "help" the action of the sentence.

Examples: am, is, are, was, were
Matthew **was** helping Michael. **Was** helps the action verb **helping**.

Read the following sentences. Underline the verbs. Above each, write **A** for action verb, **L** for linking verb, and **H** for helping verb. The first one has been done for you.

          A

1. Amy <u>jumps</u> rope.

2. Paul was jumping rope, too.

3. They were working on their homework.

4. The math problem requires a lot of thinking.

5. Addition problems are fun to do.

6. The baby sleeps in the afternoon.

7. Grandma is napping also.

8. Sam is going to bed.

9. John paints a lovely picture of the sea.

10. The colors in the picture are soft and pale.

Changing Tenses

accepted
admiring
captured
choking
dining
dozed
fanning
guarded
hoping
invited
pledged
practicing
proving
rearranged
squeezing

For each word, write the present tense of the verb. Watch out for missing or extra letters.

1. _____
2. _____
3. _____
4. _____
5. _____
6. _____
7. _____
8. _____

9. _____
10. _____
11. _____
12. _____
13. _____
14. _____
15. _____

Complete the word search. The 30 words are written vertically, horizontally, and diagonally.

```
R B E S Z C Q U H X O O G X C D K Y D G N
G H I Q H I V T K E E N O M R S E V O G U
U C A U O C X N C V I K I M T Z I L N T B
A C C E P T E D P N S D U N O C Z I A G H
R H C E I R R N N Q E C Z D V U C H O K E
D O E Z N B A A C G U A R D I I G K P D P
E K P E G B F C D U G P O Q T N T W L U L
D I T P N M C E T M S T P C I Q I E E E S
R N D T A O L A L I I U A Z Z Y F N D G Y
T G T L I P J L P H C R E A R R A N G E O
K X A J W H V Y H T P E I A D M I R E J A
N N I Q S Q T S S A U A R N Y C E P O H O
L U M D Z H W Z P Q P R C C G N O G N N O
U Q V G A Z U P S R W R E W I H P S U B I
E V Y C A Y J X R E A A O D J D X F U T G
V B G S N F P U X O L N D V E G G I X Q O
I V W E Z M A T P V V G Q Z I J C N M Y C
F W D F L W I N V I T E O M J N B W C R C
E P M F Y P H M P O X D U Q R A G V M X G
```

Verb Tense

Not only do verbs tell the action of a sentence, but they also tell when the action takes place. This is called the **verb tense**. There are three verb tenses: past, present, and future tense.

Present-tense verbs tell what is happening now.

Example: Jane **spells** words with long vowel sounds.

Past-tense verbs tell about action that has already happened. Past-tense verbs are usually formed by adding **ed** to the verb.

Example: stay — stayed
John **stayed** home yesterday.

Past-tense verbs can also be made by adding helping verbs **was** or **were** before the verb and adding **ing** to the verb.

Example: talk — was talking
Sally **was talking** to her mom.

Future-tense verbs tell what will happen in the future. Future-tense verbs are made by putting the word **will** before the verb.

Example: paint — will paint
Susie and Sherry **will paint** the house.

Read the following verbs. Write whether the verb tense is past, present, or future.

Verb	Tense	Verb	Tense
1. watches	present	8. writes	_____
2. wanted	_____	9. vaulted	_____
3. will eat	_____	10. were sleeping	_____
4. was squawking	_____	11. will sing	_____
5. yawns	_____	12. is speaking	_____
6. crawled	_____	13. will cook	_____
7. will hunt	_____	14. likes	_____

Present, Past, and Future Tense

Read the following sentences. Write **PRES** if the sentence is in present tense. Write **PAST** if the sentence is in past tense. Write **FUT** if the sentence is in future tense. The first one has been done for you.

FUT   1. I will be thrilled to accept the award.

_____ 2. Will you go with me to the dentist?

_____ 3. I thought he looked familiar!

_____ 4. They ate every single slice of pizza.

_____ 5. I run myself ragged sometimes.

_____ 6. Do you think this project is worthwhile?

_____ 7. No one has been able to repair the broken plate.

_____ 8. Thoughtful gifts are always appreciated.

_____ 9. I liked the way he sang!

_____ 10. With a voice like that, he will go a long way.

_____ 11. It's my fondest hope that they visit soon.

_____ 12. I wanted that coat very much.

_____ 13. She'll be happy to take your place.

_____ 14. Everyone thinks the test is easy.

_____ 15. Collecting stamps is her favorite hobby.

Using ing Verbs

Remember, use **is** and **are** when describing something happening right now. Use **was** and **were** when describing something that already happened.

Use the verb in bold to complete each sentence. Add **ing** to the verb and use **is**, **are**, **was** or **were**.

Examples: When it started to rain, we ___were raking___ the leaves.

rake

When the soldiers marched up that hill, Captain

Stevens ___was commanding___ them.

command

1. Now, the police _____ them of stealing the money.

accuse

2. Look! The eggs _____.

hatch

3. A minute ago, the sky _____.

glow

4. My dad says he _____ us to ice cream!

treat

5. She _____ the whole time we were at the mall.

sneeze

6. While we were playing outside at recess, he _____ our tests.

grade

7. I hear something. Who _____?

groan

8. As I watched, the workers _____ the wood into little chips.

grind

Skip-Counting

Skip-counting is a quick way to count by skipping numbers. For example, when you skip-count by 2s, you count 2, 4, 6, 8, and so on. You can skip-count by many different numbers such as 2s, 4s, 5s, 10s, and 100s.

The illustration below shows skip-counting by 2s to 14.

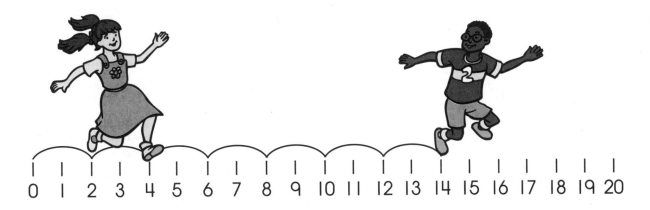

Use the number line to help you skip-count by 2s from 0 to 20.

0, _____, _____, _____, 8, _____, _____, 14, _____, _____, _____

Skip-count by 3s by filling in the rocks across the pond.

Multiples

A **multiple** is the product of a specific number and any other number. For example, the multiples of 2 are 2 (2 x 1), 4 (2 x 2), 6, 8, 10, 12, and so on.

Write the missing multiples.

Example: Count by 5s.
5, 10, 15, 20, 25, 30, 35. These are multiples of 5.

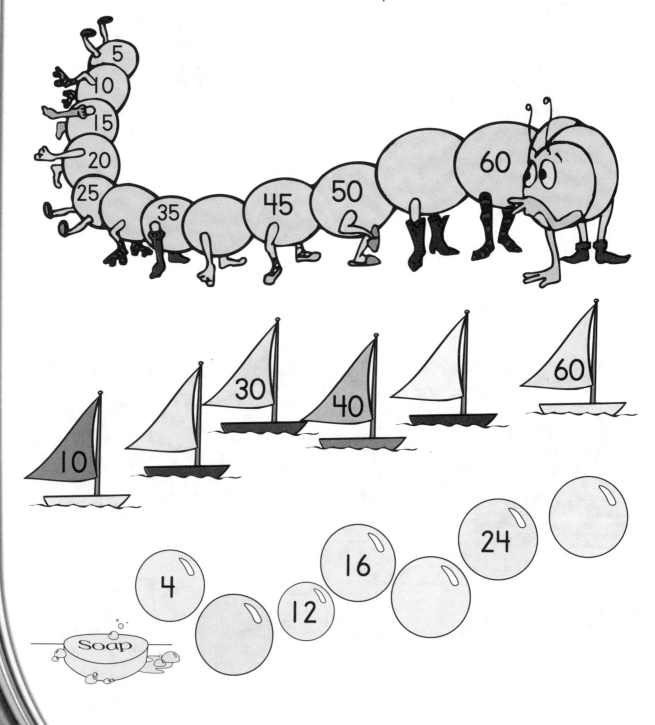

Multiplication

Multiplication is a short way to find the sum of adding the same number a certain amount of times, such as 7 x 4 = 28 instead of 7 + 7 + 7 + 7 = 28.

Multiply as quickly and as accurately as you can.

4	7	0	7	9	1	6
x 7	x 6	x 8	x 2	x 5	x 5	x 4

8	7	4	9	8	6	9
x 3	x 1	x 2	x 6	x 5	x 7	x 8

3	7	3	5	9	7	9
x 5	x 8	x 9	x 6	x 9	x 5	x 4

3	2	8	7
x 6	x 8	x 6	x 7

0	3	5	
x 7	x 3	x 9	

How quickly did you complete this page? _____

Multiplication

Multiply.

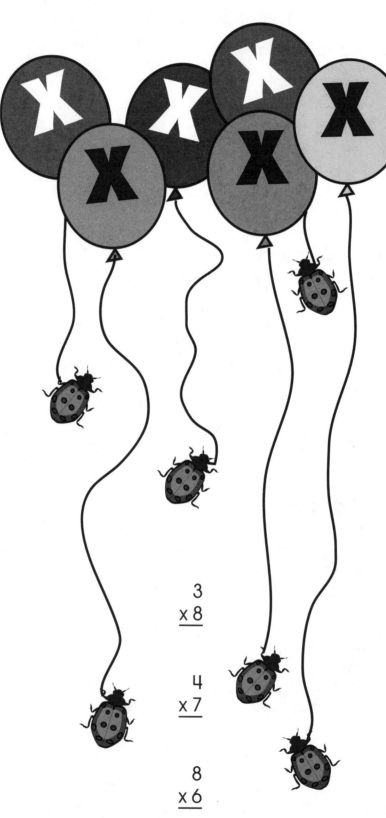

5 x 5	9 x 5		8 x 3
5 x 3	6 x 7		6 x 3
2 x 9	2 x 5	6 x 4	9 x 7
7 x 8	5 x 7	7 x 7	6 x 9
9 x 7	9 x 9	7 x 6	5 x 4
6 x 6	8 x 5	8 x 4	8 x 7
8 x 9	8 x 8	3 x 8	4 x 4	4 x 9
	6 x 5	4 x 7	3 x 9	6 x 8
	9 x 8	8 x 6	7 x 9	7 x 3

Week 7 Skills

Subject	Skill	Multi-Sensory Learning Activities
Reading and Language Arts	Review present-, past-, and future-tense verbs.	• Complete Practice Pages 78–82. • Write several present-, past-, and future-tense sentences for your child, but omit the verb. Ask your child to complete the sentences using the correct verb tense.
Math	Multiply one-digit numbers by two-digit numbers.	• Complete Practice Pages 83–86. • Use a collection of small objects, such as marbles, beans, or pennies. Place a different number of objects in each of several bags. (Use numbers that have multiple factors, like **18**, **24**, and **32**.) Have your child count the items in each bag and divide them into as many different equal sets as possible (for example, 18 = 2 sets of 9, 3 sets of 6, 6 sets of 3, 9 sets of 2). Then, have him or her write multiplication facts based on these sets.
Bonus: Science		• Drop a light object in front of a fan. Gravity pulls the object down while the fan pushes the falling object sideways. Try dropping a heavier object into a bowl of water, then dropping in through the air. Ask your child to observe and describe the difference.

Present-Tense Verbs

Write two sentences for each verb below. Tell about something that is happening now and write the verb as both simple present tense and present tense with a helping verb.

Example: run

   Mia runs to the store.   Mia is running to the store.

1. hatch

   _____

   _____

2. check

   _____

   _____

3. spell

   _____

   _____

4. blend

   _____

   _____

5. lick

   _____

   _____

6. cry

   _____

   _____

7. write

   _____

   _____

8. dream

   _____

   _____

Verb Tense

Read the following sentences. Underline the verbs. Above each verb, write whether it is past, present, or future tense.

1. The crowd <u>was booing</u> the referee. *(past)*

2. Sally will compete on the balance beam.

3. Matt marches with the band.

4. Nick is marching, too.

5. The geese swooped down to the pond.

6. Dad will fly home tomorrow.

7. They were looking for a new book.

8. Presently, they are going to the garden.

9. The children will pick the ripe vegetables.

10. Grandmother canned the green beans.

Write six sentences of your own using the correct verb tense.

Past tense:

_____

_____

Present tense:

_____

_____

Future tense:

_____

_____

Past-Tense Verbs

To write about something that already happened, you can add **ed** to the verb.

Example: Yesterday, we **talked**.

You can also use **was** and **were** and add **ing** to the verb.

Example: Yesterday, we were talking.

When a verb ends with **e**, you usually drop the **e** before adding **ing**.

Examples: grade — was grading   weave — were weaving
tape — was taping   sneeze — were sneezing

Write two sentences for each verb below. Tell about something that has already happened and write the verb both ways. (Watch the spelling of the verbs that end with **e**.)

Example: stream

The rain streamed down the window.

The rain was streaming down the window.

1. grade

_____

_____

2. tape

_____

_____

3. weave

_____

_____

4. sneeze

_____

_____

Review

Write **PRES** for present tense, **PAST** for past tense, or **FUT** for future tense.

_____ 1. She will help him study.

_____ 2. She helped him study.

_____ 3. She helps him study.

_____ 4. She promised to help him study.

Write the past tense form of these verbs.

5. cry _____

6. sigh _____

7. hurry _____

8. pop _____

Write the past tense of these irregular verbs with helpers.

9. (go) have _____

10. (sleep) have _____

11. (sing) have _____

12. (see) have _____

Write the correct form of **be**.

13. They _____ my closest neighbors.

14. I _____ very happy for you today.

15. He _____ there on time yesterday.

16. She _____ still the nicest girl I know.

Circle the correct verb.

17. He went/gone to my locker.

18. I went/gone to the beach many times.

19. Have you went/gone to this show before?

20. We went/gone all the way to the top!

Verb Tenses

A **present-tense** verb shows action that is happening now. A **past-tense** verb shows action that happened earlier. A **future-tense** verb shows action that will take place in the future.

Examples: The clockmaker **repairs** the clock.   (present)
The clockmaker **repaired** the clock.   (past)
The clockmaker **will repair** the clock.   (future)

Write these verbs using the tenses shown in parentheses.

	try	**walk**	**work**
(present)	Tom _____	Karen _____	They _____
(past)	Tom _____	Karen _____	They _____
(future)	Tom _____	Karen _____	They _____

Write the correct verb in each blank below.

1. time (future)   4. use (past)   7. dine (present)   10. invent (past)

2. chart (present)   5. tell (present)   8. move (future)

3. trickle (past)   6. reset (future)   9. help (past)

1. John ___will time___ the runners in the race.

2. A calendar _____ the days of each month.

3. Sand _____ through the hourglass.

4. People _____ the hourglass before clocks were invented.

5. A pendulum _____ time by Earth's rotation.

6. John _____ his watch when changing time zones.

7. He _____ at 8:00 every evening during the week.

8. Martha _____ the hands of the clock.

9. In the distant past, the Sun and the Moon _____ man tell time.

10. The Egyptians _____ the solar calendar.

Multiplying 2 to 12

Multiplication is simply a quick way to add!

Example: 3 x 6

1. The first factor tells how many groups there are. There are 3 groups.

2. The second factor tells how many are in each group. There are 6 in each group.

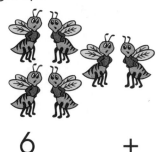   +      +   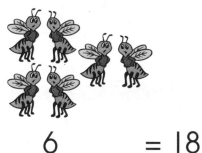   = 18

6   +   6   +   6   = 18

3 groups of 6 equal 18.
3 x 6 = 18

Some helpful hints to remember when multiplying:

- When you multiply by 0, the product is always 0. **Example:** 0 x 7 = 0
- When you multiply by 1, the product is always the factor being multiplied. **Example:** 1 x 12 = 12
- When multiplying by 2, double the factor other than 2. **Example:** 2 x 4 = 8
- The order doesn't matter when multiplying. **Example:** 5 x 3 = 15, 3 x 5 = 15
- When you multiply by 9, the digits in the product add up to 9 (until 9 x 11). **Example:** 7 x 9 = 63, 6 + 3 = 9
- When you multiply by 10, multiply by 1 and add 0 to the product. **Example:** 10 x 3 = 30
- When you multiply by 11, double the factor you are multiplying by (until 10). **Example:** 11 x 8 = 88

Multiply:

2	3	4	2	5	10	7	8
x 9	x 8	x 9	x 11	x 9	x 5	x 6	x 8

11	9	8			
x 12	x 7	x 5	8 x 5 = ____	4 x 8 = ____	10 x 10 = ____
			5 x 5 = ____	6 x 6 = ____	7 x 8 = ____

Multiplication

Follow the steps for multiplying a one-digit number by a two-digit number using regrouping.

Example: **Step 1:** Multiply the ones.
$$\begin{array}{r} \overset{2}{5}4 \\ \times\ 7 \\ \hline 8 \end{array}$$
Regroup.

Step 2: Multiply the tens.
$$\begin{array}{r} \overset{2}{5}4 \\ \times\ 7 \\ \hline 378 \end{array}$$
Add two tens.

Multiply.

27 x 3	63 x 4	52 x 5	91 x 9	45 x 7	75 x 2
64 x 5	76 x 3	93 x 6	87 x 4	66 x 7	38 x 2
47 x 8	64 x 9	51 x 8	99 x 3	13 x 7	32 x 4
25 x 8	15 x 7				

The chickens on the Smith farm produce 48 dozen eggs each day. How many dozen eggs do they produce in 7 days?

_____

Multiplication

Multiply.

Come on, this is easy!

1. 32
    x 3

2. 21
    x 4

3. 43
    x 3

4. 20
    x 3

5. 11
    x 3

6. 34
    x 3

7. 21
    x 3

8. 33
    x 3

9. 24
    x 2

10. 22
    x 4

11. 40
    x 2

12. 32
    x 2

13. 13
    x 3

14. 22
    x 2

15. 20
    x 4

16. 23
    x 2

17. 11
    x 3

18. 41
    x 2

19. 31
    x 3

20. 44
    x 2

21. 23
    x 3

22. 12
    x 4

23. 33
    x 2

24. 30
    x 3

25. 21
    x 2

26. 13
    x 2

27. 42
    x 2

28. 12
    x 3

29. 14
    x 2

30. 22
    x 3

Regrouping

1. Multiply the ones column. Ask: Do I need to regroup?

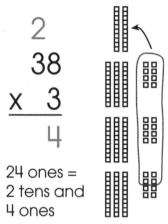

$$\begin{array}{r} 2 \\ 38 \\ \times \ 3 \\ \hline 4 \end{array}$$

24 ones = 2 tens and 4 ones

2. Multiply the tens column. Ask: Do I need to regroup?

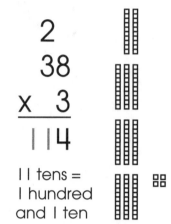

$$\begin{array}{r} 2 \\ 38 \\ \times \ 3 \\ \hline 114 \end{array}$$

11 tens = 1 hundred and 1 ten

$$\begin{array}{r} 38 \\ \times \ 3 \\ \hline \end{array}$$

is the same as

$$\begin{array}{r} 38 \\ 38 \\ + \ 38 \\ \hline \end{array}$$

Multiply.

1. $\begin{array}{r} 29 \\ \times \ 3 \\ \hline \end{array}$

2. $\begin{array}{r} 62 \\ \times \ 4 \\ \hline \end{array}$

3. $\begin{array}{r} 39 \\ \times \ 4 \\ \hline \end{array}$

4. $\begin{array}{r} 86 \\ \times \ 7 \\ \hline \end{array}$

5. $\begin{array}{r} 43 \\ \times \ 6 \\ \hline \end{array}$

6. $\begin{array}{r} 28 \\ \times \ 6 \\ \hline \end{array}$

7. $\begin{array}{r} 48 \\ \times \ 2 \\ \hline \end{array}$

8. $\begin{array}{r} 31 \\ \times \ 9 \\ \hline \end{array}$

9. $\begin{array}{r} 25 \\ \times \ 5 \\ \hline \end{array}$

10. $\begin{array}{r} 55 \\ \times \ 5 \\ \hline \end{array}$

Week 8 Skills

Subject	Skill	Multi-Sensory Learning Activities
Reading and Language Arts	Identify irregular verbs.	• Complete Practice Page 88. • Give your child a list of several irregular verbs, such as **begin**, **draw**, **fall**, and **go**. Ask your child to give you the past tense of the verb and use it in a sentence.
	Work with helping verbs, action verbs, and linking verbs.	• Complete Practice Pages 89 and 90. • Write a complete paragraph on a sheet of paper. Ask your child to circle the helping verbs.
	Use correct subject/verb and pronoun/verb agreement.	• Complete Practice Pages 91 and 92. • Read *The Cricket in Times Square* by George Selden with your child. As you are reading, note several sentences that contain a pronoun and list them for your child, omitting the verb. Ask your child to fill in the blank with a verb that agrees with the given pronoun.
Math	Multiply one-digit numbers by two-, three-, and four-digit numbers.	• Complete Practice Pages 93–95. • Provide your child with a series of multiplication problems and ask him or her to teach you how to solve each one.
	Multiply two-digit numbers by two-digit numbers.	• Complete Practice Page 96. • Have your child read the first number in the equation **436 x 4** as **400 + 30 + 6**. Have him or her multiply each number by 4 and add the products to get the sum. Then, multiply the numbers in the traditional way. Repeat this activity several times.

Irregular Verbs

Verbs that do not add **ed** to form the past tense are called **irregular verbs**. The spelling of these verbs changes.

Examples:

present	past	present	past
begin, begins	**began**	do, does	**did**
break, breaks	**broke**	eat, eats	**ate**

Write the past tense of each irregular verb below.

1. Samuel almost _____ (fall) when he kicked a rock in the path.

2. Diana made sure she _____ (take) a canteen on her hike.

3. David _____ (run) over to a shady tree for a quick break.

4. Jimmy _____ (break) off a long piece of grass to put in his mouth while he was walking.

5. Eva _____ (know) the path along the river very well.

6. The clouds _____ (begin) to sprinkle raindrops on the hikers.

7. Kathy _____ (throw) a small piece of bread to the birds.

8. Everyone _____ (eat) a very nutritious meal after a long adventure.

9. We all _____ (sleep) very well that night.

Many irregular verbs have a different past-tense ending when the helping verbs **have** and **has** are used.

Examples: Steven **has worn** special hiking shoes today.
Marlene and I **have known** about this trail for years.

Circle the correct irregular verb below.

1. Peter has (flew, flown) down to join us for the adventure.

2. Mark has (saw, seen) a lot of animals on the hike today.

3. Andy and Mike have (went, gone) on this trail before.

4. Bill has (took, taken) extra precautions to make sure no cacti prick his legs.

5. Heather has (ate, eaten) all the snacks her mom packed for her.

Helping Verbs

A **verb phrase** is a verb that has more than one word. It is made up of a **main verb** plus one or more **helping verbs**.

Example: verb phrase
Tim **has practiced** hard.

helping verb   main verb

These words are often used as helping verbs with the main verb.
am, **is**, **are**, **was**, **were**, **have**, **has**

Underline the helping verbs and circle the main verbs in the sentences below.

1. The instructor has taught science for several years.

2. The concert pianist was practicing before the performance.

3. Researchers are attempting to find a cure for the disease.

4. The architect has drawn detailed blueprints.

5. The scientist has researched the project carefully.

6. Several patients were waiting in the doctor's office.

7. During his lifetime, the artist has painted many beautiful pictures.

8. A touchdown was scored by the quarterback.

9. The ship's captain is giving orders to the first mate.

10. The clown has performed for many years.

11. The tailor was hemming the man's trousers.

12. The construction workers have finished with the project.

13. The secretary was typing the letters yesterday.

14. Lawyers have passed difficult state examinations.

15. A cab driver has transported many passengers by the end of the day.

Action and Linking Verbs

An **action verb** is a word that shows action.

Examples: We **play** basketball. I **think** about my pet.

Underline the action verb in each sentence below.

1. Have you ever wished for a dog of your very own?
2. Choose the breed of your dog very carefully.
3. Puppies may grow to be very large or very small.
4. Your dog must receive good care, attention and exercise.
5. The right dog will give you years of pleasure and enjoyment.
6. Can you imagine yourself as a dog owner?

A **linking verb** does not show action. Instead, it links the subject with a noun or adjective in the predicate of the sentence. Forms of the verb **be** are common linking verbs.

Example: Puppies **are** cute.

Underline the linking verb in each sentence. Then, fill in the chart.

1. Tom's new puppy is playful and mischievous.
2. His dad's socks are a temptation to that puppy.
3. Mom and Dad were angry when the puppy chewed up a shoe.
4. They were surprised when the puppy got into Mom's flowers.
5. He was so happy rolling around in the dirt.
6. The puppy will be less trouble when he grows up.

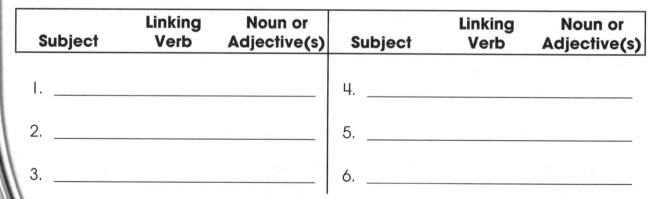

Subject	Linking Verb	Noun or Adjective(s)	Subject	Linking Verb	Noun or Adjective(s)
1. _____			4. _____		
2. _____			5. _____		
3. _____			6. _____		

Subject/Verb Agreement

The **subject** and **verb** in a sentence must *agree*. If the subject is **singular**, add **s** to the verb. If the subject is **plural**, do not add an ending to the verb.

Examples: Lava only **flows** when it is very hot. (singular)
Cinders **shoot** out of an active volcano. (plural)

Complete each sentence below using a form of the verb in parentheses.

1. Some volcanoes _____ quietly. (erupt)

2. The ground _____ around a volcano just before an eruption. (swell)

3. Volcanoes _____ with great fury. (explode)

4. Tremors _____ as magma works its way to the surface. (increase)

5. Magma _____ to the Earth's surface. (escape)

6. A volcano _____ so violently that the mountain can be blown apart. (erupt)

7. Obsidian _____ when flying volcanic debris cools quickly in the air. (form)

8. Volcanoes _____ hot lava high into the air. (spew)

9. The sky _____ from the ash and dust that explode out of a volcano. (darken)

10. Ash _____ the ground for many miles around a volcanic explosion. (cover)

11. Molten lava _____ bright red and yellow as it escapes from underneath the Earth's surface. (glow)

12. Steam _____ when molten lava comes in contact with water. (form)

Pronoun/Verb Agreement

The **subject pronoun** and the **verb** in a sentence must agree. If the subject pronoun is **singular**, add **s** to the verb. If the subject pronoun is **plural**, do not add an ending to the verb.

Examples: He **wears** a helmet every time he rides his bike. (singular)
They **wear** helmets whenever they go roller-blading. (plural)

Circle the verb in parentheses that agrees with the subject pronoun.

1. She (ride, rides) her bike to band practice on Tuesdays.

2. They (zoom, zooms) down the hill to help them get up the steep incline on the other side.

3. He (glide, glides) nicely on his skateboard when he's going around the corners on the skating path.

4. We (travel, travels) as a family every Saturday to the park on our bikes.

5. It (rain, rains) sometimes while we're riding our bikes to school.

6. He (love, loves) to climb the hills on bikes with his mom and dad.

7. She (wear, wears) a helmet and kneepads whenever she goes roller-blading with her friends.

Write the subject pronoun that agrees with the verb.

1. _____ (They, We, He) tries very hard to skate backwards at the skating rink.

2. _____ (I, She, You) tells everyone about all the fun things there are to do at the park.

3. _____ (We, You, He) invites a friend every time he goes to the bicycle acrobatic demonstrations.

4. _____ (She, They, He) look both ways very carefully before crossing the street on their roller-blades.

5. _____ (It, We, He) send invitations to all our friends whenever there is a safety seminar at our school.

COMPLETE YEAR GRADE 4

Fact Factory

Factors are the numbers multiplied together in a multiplication problem. The **product** is the answer.

Write the missing factors or products.

X	5
1	5
5	
4	20
6	
3	
2	10
7	
9	45

X	9
8	72
3	
4	
9	
6	54
7	
2	
1	9

X	7
2	14
5	
	42
8	
7	
4	
	21
0	

X	3
7	
4	
6	
1	
3	
2	
5	
8	

X	1
1	
12	
10	
3	3
5	
7	
6	
4	

X	8
9	
8	
4	
5	
6	
7	
3	
2	

X	2
	24
	2
	22
	4
	20
	6
	18
	8

X	4
2	
4	
6	
8	
	4
	12
	20
	28

X	6
7	
6	
5	
4	
3	
2	
1	
0	

X	10
	20
3	
	40
5	
	60
7	
	80
9	

X	11
4	
7	
9	
10	
3	
5	
6	
8	

X	12
1	
2	24
3	
4	48
5	
6	
7	
8	

Space Math

Blast off into multiplication.

406 x 3	326 x 5	281 x 4	923 x 2	817 x 6
231 x 6	214 x 2	262 x 7	218 x 5	126 x 9
241 x 8	329 x 6	310 x 5	204 x 8	431 x 3
231 x 4	624 x 7			421 x 6
896 x 1				742 x 8
606 x 7				525 x 4
				814 x 9

Amazing Arms

What will happen to a starfish that loses an arm? To find out, solve the following problems and write the corresponding letter above the answer at the bottom of the page.

O. 2,893
x 4

W. 1,763
x 3

W. 7,665
x 5

A. 1,935
x 6

W. 3,097
x 3

E. 2,929
x 4

G. 6,366
x 5

T. 7,821
x 8

L. 6,283
x 7

I. 5,257
x 3

R. 3,019
x 6

N. 2,908
x 7

I. 6,507
x 8

N. 5,527
x 2

L. 6,626
x 3

O. 7,219
x 9

E. 3,406
x 6

| 52,056 | 62,568 | | 5,289 | 15,771 | 43,981 | 19,878 |

| 31,830 | 18,114 | 64,971 | 9,291 | | 11,610 |

| 20,356 | 20,436 | 38,325 | | 11,572 | 11,054 | 11,716 |

Multiplication

Follow the steps for multiplying a two-digit number by a two-digit number using regrouping.

Example:

Step 1: Multiply the ones. Regroup.

```
        2
  63    63
x 68  x 68
       504
```

Step 2: Multiply the tens. Regroup. Add.

```
   1
  63      63
x 68    x 68
3,780    504
       + 3,780
         4,284
```

Multiply.

```
   12        27        65        19        99        35
 x 55      x 15      x 27      x 39      x 13      x 14
```

```
   43        38        53        47        57        48
 x 26      x 17      x 86      x 72      x 62      x 33
```

```
             27        93        64        53
           x 54      x 45      x 16      x 23
```

The Jones farm has 24 cows that each produce 52 quarts of milk a day. How many quarts are produced each day altogether?

_____

Week 9 Skills

Subject	Skill	Multi-Sensory Learning Activities
Reading and Language Arts	Understand adjectives, including comparative adjectives.	• Complete Practice Pages 98–102. • Have your child brainstorm ten nouns (inanimate objects) and ten adjectives (human characteristics). Ask him or her to combine one adjective with one noun and write a sentence, bringing the words to life. Repeat until all the words have been used. Tell your child that these are examples of personification.
Math	Multiply two-digit numbers by two- and three-digit numbers.	• Complete Practice Pages 103–105. • Find up to 20 plastic cups and dozens of small objects, such as coins. Ask your child to give you two numbers between 10 and 20. The first number is the number of cups, and the second number is how many coins you place in each cup. Show your child that the number of total marbles in the cups is the product of the two numbers.
	Multiply three-digit numbers by three-digit numbers.	• Complete Practice Page 106. • On a trip to the grocery store, ask your child to look around for three-digit numbers and make a list of each one he or she sees. At home, pair two numbers together and multiply.

Adjectives

Adjectives tell more about nouns. Adjectives are describing words.

Examples: scary animals   **bright** glow   **wet** frog

Add at least two adjectives to each sentence below. Use your own words or words from the box.

pale	soft	sticky	burning	furry	glistening	peaceful
faint	shivering	slippery	gleaming	gentle	foggy	tangled

Example: The stripe was blue.
The wide stripe was light blue.

1. The frog had eyes.

_____

2. The house was a sight.

_____

3. A boy heard a noise.

_____

4. The girl tripped over a toad.

_____

5. A tiger ran through the room.

_____

6. They saw a glow in the window.

_____

7. A pan was sitting on the stove.

_____

8. The boys were eating French fries.

_____

Adjectives

Adjectives tell a noun's size, color, shape, texture, brightness, darkness, personality, sound, taste, and so on.

Examples: **color** — red, yellow, green, black
size — small, large, huge, tiny
shape — round, square, rectangular, oval
texture — rough, smooth, soft, scaly
brightness — glistening, shimmering, dull, pale
personality — gentle, grumpy, happy, sad

Follow the instructions below.

1. Get an apple, orange or other piece of fruit. Look at it very carefully and write adjectives that describe its size, color, shape, and texture.

_____

_____

2. Take a bite of your fruit. Write adjectives that describe its taste, texture, smell, and so on.

_____

_____

3. Using all the adjectives from above, write a cinquain about your fruit. A **cinquain** is a five-line poem. See the form and sample poem below.

Form: Line 1 — noun

Line 2 — two adjectives

Line 3 — three sounds

Line 4 — four-word phrase

Line 5 — noun

Example: Apple

red, smooth

 cracking, smacking, slurping

drippy, sticky, sour juice

Apple

_____

_____, _____

_____, _____, _____

_____

_____

Descriptive Sentences

Turn a good sentence into a great sentence by using more descriptive words.

Example: The dog chased the boy.
The big brown dog playfully chased the little boy.

Add descriptive words to make each a great sentence.
Write the improved sentence on each line.

1. The man climbed the mountain.

   _____

   _____

2. The group found a buried tomb.

   _____

   _____

3. The girls painted a sign.

   _____

   _____

4. The sunlight came through the window.

   _____

   _____

5. Ice cream dripped down the cone.

   _____

   _____

6. The snake moved down the tree.

   _____

   _____

7. The storm rocked the boat.

   _____

   _____

How Adjectives Compare

There are certain spelling rules to follow when **adjectives** are used to compare people, places, or things.

1. To many adjectives, simply add **er** or **est** to the end.

   fast   fast**er**   fast**est**

2. When an adjective ends with a consonant preceded by a single vowel, double the final consonant and add **er** or **est**.

   fat   fatt**er**   fatt**est**

3. When an adjective ends in an **e**, drop the final **e** and add **er** or **est**.

   brave   brav**er**   brav**est**

4. If an adjective ends in a y preceded by a consonant, change the **y** to **i** and add **er** or **est**.

   heavy   heav**ier**   heav**iest**

Complete the chart below using the spelling rules you have learned. Write the number of the rule you used.

Adjective	Add **er**	Add **est**	Rule
1. weak	weaker	weakest	1
2. kind			
3. easy			
4. clear			
5. close			
6. noisy			
7. large			
8. red			
9. pretty			
10. hungry			
11. big			
12. happy			
13. wet			
14. cute			
15. plain			
16. busy			
17. loud			
18. strong			
19. fresh			
20. hot			

Comparison Words

biggest
brighter
clumsiest
crazier
cruelest
earlier
firmer
flattest
greener
noisiest
prettier
quietest
simpler
tastiest
widest

All the words are adjectives that can be used to compare people, places, or things. An **er** ending is used to compare two things; **est** is used to compare three or more. Fill in the chart below with words and the other missing word that completes the comparison.

List Word	Adding **er**	Adding **est**
1. big	_____	_____
2. _____	_____	brightest
3. clumsy	_____	_____
4. _____	_____	craziest
5. _____	crueler	_____
6. _____	_____	earliest
7. firm	_____	_____
8. _____	flatter	_____
9. green	_____	_____
10. _____	noisier	_____
11. _____	_____	prettiest
12. quiet	_____	_____
13. _____	_____	simplest
14. _____	tastier	_____
15. _____	wider	_____

Elephant Escapades

Multiply.

56 x 43	13 x 24	24 x 56	20 x 93

23 x 54	28 x 43	13 x 82	21 x 64

25 x 34	13 x 64	34 x 21	32 x 55

42 x 23	62 x 31	51 x 43	21 x 64

10 x 84	35 x 24	24 x 30

24 x 53	81 x 46	32 x 27

Multiplication

Follow the steps for multiplying a two-digit number by a three-digit number using regrouping.

Example:

Step 1: Multiply the ones. Regroup.

$$
\begin{array}{r}
287 \\
\times\ 43 \\
\end{array}
\qquad
\begin{array}{r}
{\scriptstyle 2\,2} \\
287 \\
\times\ 43 \\
\hline
861 \\
\end{array}
$$

Step 2: Multiply the tens. Regroup. Add.

$$
\begin{array}{r}
287 \\
\times\ 43 \\
\hline
11{,}480 \\
\end{array}
\qquad
\begin{array}{r}
287 \\
\times\ 43 \\
\hline
861 \\
+\ 11{,}480 \\
\hline
12{,}341 \\
\end{array}
$$

Multiply.

$$
\begin{array}{r} 261 \\ \times\ 36 \end{array}
\qquad
\begin{array}{r} 434 \\ \times\ 48 \end{array}
\qquad
\begin{array}{r} 357 \\ \times\ 75 \end{array}
$$

$$
\begin{array}{r} 231 \\ \times\ 46 \end{array}
\qquad
\begin{array}{r} 754 \\ \times\ 65 \end{array}
\qquad
\begin{array}{r} 614 \\ \times\ 59 \end{array}
$$

$$
\begin{array}{r} 549 \\ \times\ 89 \end{array}
\qquad
\begin{array}{r} 372 \\ \times\ 94 \end{array}
\qquad
\begin{array}{r} 458 \\ \times\ 85 \end{array}
\qquad
\begin{array}{r} 368 \\ \times\ 98 \end{array}
$$

At the Douglas berry farm, workers pick 378 baskets of peaches each day. Each basket holds 65 peaches. How many peaches are picked each day?

_____

Multiplication

Multiply.

25 x 72	70 x 66	844 x 24	124 x 15
45 x 41	76 x 78	74 x 69	261 x 88
48 x 36	263 x 57	37 x 64	52 x 43
321 x 78	544 x 58	797 x 24	998 x 37
249 x 33	24 x 19	48 x 20	817 x 59

Multiplication: Three-Digit Numbers Times Three-Digit Numbers

Multiply. Regroup when needed.

Example:
```
    563
  x 248
  4,504
 22,520
+112,600
139,624
```

Hint: When multiplying by the tens, start writing the number in the tens place. When multiplying by the hundreds, start in the hundreds place.

```
  842        932        759        531
x 167      x 272      x 468      x 556


  383        523        229        738
x 476      x 349      x 189      x 513
```

James grows pumpkins on his farm. He has 362 rows of pumpkins. There are 593 pumpkins in each row. How many pumpkins does James grow?

_____

First Quarter Check-Up

Reading and Language Arts

❑ I can identify long and short vowel sounds **a**, **e**, **i**, **o**, and **u**.

❑ I recognize vowel sounds for words containing vowel pairs.

❑ I can identify common and proper nouns, including subject and object pronouns, and plural nouns.

❑ I can form plural nouns from words that end in **y** or **f**.

❑ I understand present-, past-, and future-tense verbs.

❑ I can identify and use irregular verbs correctly.

❑ I can work with helping verbs, action verbs, and linking verbs.

❑ I use correct subject/verb and pronoun/verb agreement.

❑ I understand adjectives, including comparative adjectives.

Math

❑ I understand place value up to the millions place.

❑ I can work with expanded notation.

❑ I can round up to the nearest ten thousand.

❑ I am fluent in one-, two-, three-, and four-digit addition problems.

❑ I am fluent in one-, two-, three-, and four-digit subtraction problems.

❑ I can skip-count by twos, threes, fours, and tens.

❑ I can multiply one-, two-, three-, and four-digit numbers.

Final Project

Look at a map of your state. Write a paragraph about the information you can gather from the map, such as what state or province is north of your state or what direction the state capital is from your present location. Be sure to use correct capitalization for proper nouns, and highlight the correct subject/verb agreement. Then, choose two cities you'd like to visit. With an adult, look up how many miles each city is from your home. Which city is further away? Subtract the smaller number from the larger number to find out how much farther away it is.

Second Quarter Introduction

During the second quarter of the school year, many children are settled into routines at home and at school. Make sure your family's routines include time for playing, eating and talking together, and reading aloud. Supporting your child's learning and development will build his or her confidence in all areas.

Second Quarter Skills

Practice pages in this book for Weeks 10–18 will help your child improve the following skills.

Reading and Language Arts
- Use adverbs
- Recognize synonyms and antonyms
- Understand homophones
- Recognize up to five-syllable words
- Classify words into similar groupings
- Understand similes, metaphors, and idioms
- Use the correct versions of frequently confused words
- Form contractions
- Understand and write analogies
- Recognize words that are spelled the same but have different meanings
- Recognize double negatives and understand why they should be avoided

Math
- Multiply by powers of 10 and find the missing factor when given one factor and the product
- Divide two-digit dividends by one-digit divisors, divide with remainders, and divide with two-digit divisors
- Use multiplication to check answers of division problems
- Identify missing operations and complete number puzzles
- Create line graphs and work with ordered pairs
- Determine the average of a set of numbers
- Use spinners and coins to determine probability
- Identify fractions as parts of a whole

Multi-Sensory Learning Activities

Try these fun activities for enhancing your child's learning and development during the second quarter of the school year. Be sure to choose activities that include speaking, listening, touching, and active movement.

 Reading and Language Arts

Write the following adverbs on the chalkboard and have your child indicate whether the adverb tells when, where, or how.

easily	today	below	busily	fast	here	carefully
there	thirstily	downhill	slowly	lately	away	perfectly
inside	noisily	yearly	neatly	after	early	annually

Have your child write a news story—including all six elements of who, what, when, where, why, and how—about a recent event that affected your family.

Write 15 words and their antonyms on index cards (one word per card). Shuffle the cards, then have your child match the antonym pairs.

Give your child a list of basic sentences that he or she can transform by adding similes. For example, "I am cold" becomes "I am as cold as an ice cube." Then, give your child several sentence starters to turn into metaphors. For example, "The bustling city…" becomes "The bustling city was a whirlwind of color."

Have your child search online for an image of *The Flower Carrier* by Diego Rivera. Have your child write one simile and one metaphor to describe it.

 **Math**

Tell your child that the average person blinks about 10 times each minute. Ask your child to calculate how many times the average person blinks in five minutes, in 20 minutes, and in one hour.

Use a number line (0–144) to show that division with whole numbers is simply repeated subtraction. Give your child a problem, such as 72 ÷ 9. Starting at 72 on the number line, have your child jump back to zero by increments of 9. Then ask, "How many jumps did it take? How is this like repeated subtraction?"

Second Quarter Introduction, cont.

Play "Math Bingo" with your child. On a piece of paper, write the letters **B**, **I**, **N**, **G**, and **O** in a row. List 15 division problems with two-digit divisors beneath each letter. Give your child a blank Bingo card and let him or her choose five problems from each list on the board to put in the spaces on the card. The problems can be in any order but should stay in the appropriate columns. Read one problem at a time, such as "B—125 ÷ 25." Your child should place a marker over the problem if it is on his or her card. Repeat until your child has five markers in a row. To win, your child must then solve the problems correctly.

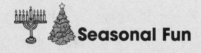 **Science**

Listen to or read weather predictions. Talk about the meaning of words such as **chance**, **likelihood**, **mostly sunny**, and **90%**. Follow local weather forecasts for one week. Compare the predictions with the actual weather. Help your child determine the probability of an accurate weather prediction. Discuss why weather predictions are not always correct and why weather forecasters use probability language.

Seasonal Fun

Make decorative winter trees out of string and glue. First, cut a large circle out of butcher's paper. Fold the circle in half before cutting it in two. Roll one half into a cone shape, using tape to secure. Then, cover a cookie sheet with waxed paper and stand the tree form in the middle of the cookie sheet. In a small bowl, mix two tablespoons of glue with one tablespoon of water. Cut pieces of metallic thread or string about four to eight inches long. Then, start building the tree. Let your child drop pieces of string into the glue, squeezing off any excess. Help him or her put one string on the paper cone at a time, starting at the bottom and working up to the top. Be sure to overlap each string—the more strings that overlap, the stronger the tree will be. When he or she is done adding string, set the tree aside to dry. Once the glue has completely dried, carefully remove the paper cone.

Week 10 Skills

Subject	Skill	Multi-Sensory Learning Activities
Reading and Language Arts	Understand and use adverbs, or words that describe verbs.	• Complete Practice Pages 112–116. • Teach your child how to recognize the elements of a news story: who, what, when, where, why, and how. Read articles from a newspaper and have your child identify the elements in each.
Math	Review multiplication; multiply by powers of 10.	• Complete Practice Pages 117–119. • Make two decks of cards for your child. On one deck, write **10**, **100**, or **1,000** on each card. On the other deck, write any one-, two-, or three-digit number. Ask your child to pull one card from each deck and multiply the numbers together.
	Determine the missing factor or product.	• Complete Practice Page 120. • Find 20 small objects for your child, such as buttons or candies. Then, give your child a multiplication problem with a missing factor, such as **4 x n = 20**. Ask your child to divide the buttons into groups of 4 until all 20 have been placed. Then, count the groups of buttons to determine the missing factor. Repeat with other problems.

Adverbs

Like adjectives, adverbs are describing words. They describe verbs. Adverbs tell how, when or where action takes place.

Examples:

How	When	Where
slowly	yesterday	here
gracefully	today	there
swiftly	tomorrow	everywhere
quickly	soon	

Hint: To identify an adverb, locate the verb, then ask yourself if there are any words that tell how, when, or where action takes place.

Read the following sentences. Underline the adverbs, then write whether they tell how, when, or where. The first one has been done for you.

1. At the end of the day, the children ran <u>quickly</u> home from school.   how

2. They will have a spelling test tomorrow.   _____

3. Slowly, the children filed to their seats.   _____

4. The teacher sat here at her desk.   _____

5. She will pass the tests back later.   _____

6. The students received their grades happily.   _____

Write four sentences of your own using any of the adverbs above.

_____

_____

_____

_____

Adverbs

Adverbs are words that tell when, where, or how.

Adverbs of time tell when.

Example: The train left yesterday.
   Yesterday is an adverb of time. It tells when the train left.

Adverbs of place tell where.

Example: The girl walked away.
   Away is an adverb of place. It tells where the girl walked.

Adverbs of manner tell how.

Example: The boy walked quickly.
   Quickly is an adverb of manner. It tells how the boy walked.

Write the adverb for each sentence in the first blank. In the second blank, write whether it is an adverb of time, place, or manner. The first one has been done for you.

1. The family ate downstairs. ___downstairs___ ___place___

2. The relatives laughed loudly. _____ _____

3. We will finish tomorrow. _____ _____

4. The snowstorm will stop soon. _____ _____

5. She sings beautifully! _____ _____

6. The baby slept soundly. _____ _____

7. The elevator stopped suddenly. _____ _____

8. Does the plane leave today? _____ _____

9. The phone call came yesterday. _____ _____

10. She ran outside. _____ _____

Adverbs of Time

Choose a word or group of words from the box to complete each sentence. Make sure the adverb you choose makes sense with the rest of the sentence.

in 2 weeks	last winter
next week	at the end of the day
soon	right now
2 days ago	tonight

1. We had a surprise birthday party for him _____ .

2. Our science projects are due _____ .

3. My best friend will be moving _____ .

4. Justin and Ronnie need our help _____ !

5. We will find out who the winners are _____ .

6. Can you take me to ball practice _____ ?

7. She said we will be getting a letter _____ .

8. Diane made the quilt _____ .

Adverbs of Place

Choose one word from the box to complete each sentence. Make sure the adverb you choose makes sense with the rest of the sentence.

inside	upstairs	below	everywhere
home	somewhere	outside	there

1. Each child took a new library book _____.

2. We looked _____ for his jacket.

3. We will have recess _____ because it is raining.

4. From the top of the mountain we could see the village far

_____.

5. My sister and I share a bedroom _____.

6. The teacher warned the children, "You must play with the ball

_____."

7. Mother said, "I know that recipe is _____ in this file box!"

8. You can put the chair _____.

Adverbs of Manner

Choose a word from the box to complete each sentence. Make sure the adverb you choose makes sense with the rest of the sentence. One word will be used twice.

> quickly   carefully   loudly   easily   carelessly   slowly

1. The scouts crossed the old bridge _____.

2. We watched the turtle move _____ across the yard.

3. Everyone completed the math test _____.

4. The quarterback scampered _____ down the sideline.

5. The mother _____ cleaned the child's sore knee.

6. The fire was caused by someone _____ tossing a match.

7. The alarm rang _____ while we were eating.

Multiplication Drill

Multiply.

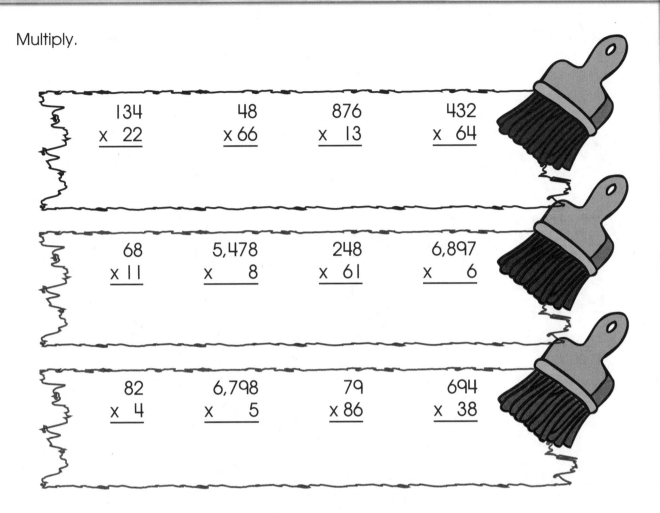

134 x 22	48 x 66	876 x 13	432 x 64

68 x 11	5,478 x 8	248 x 61	6,897 x 6

82 x 4	6,798 x 5	79 x 86	694 x 38

Color the picture by matching each number with its paintbrush.

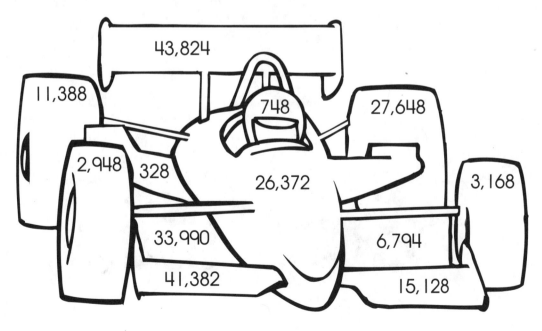

43,824

11,388

748

27,648

2,948   328

26,372

3,168

33,990

6,794

41,382

15,128

Wheels of Wonder

Solve the following problems by multiplying each number by the power of 10 in the center.

Multiplication: Tens, Hundreds, Thousands

When multiplying a number by 10, the answer is the number with a 0. It is like counting by tens.

Examples:

$$\begin{array}{r} 10 \\ \times\ 1 \\ \hline 10 \end{array} \quad \begin{array}{r} 10 \\ \times\ 2 \\ \hline 20 \end{array} \quad \begin{array}{r} 10 \\ \times\ 3 \\ \hline 30 \end{array} \quad \begin{array}{r} 10 \\ \times\ 4 \\ \hline 40 \end{array} \quad \begin{array}{r} 10 \\ \times\ 5 \\ \hline 50 \end{array} \quad \begin{array}{r} 10 \\ \times\ 6 \\ \hline 60 \end{array}$$

When multiplying a number by 100, the answer is the number with two 0's. When multiplying by 1,000, the answer is the number with three 0's.

Examples:

$$\begin{array}{r} 100 \\ \times\ 1 \\ \hline 100 \end{array} \quad \begin{array}{r} 100 \\ \times\ 2 \\ \hline 200 \end{array} \quad \begin{array}{r} 100 \\ \times\ 3 \\ \hline 300 \end{array} \quad \begin{array}{r} 1,000 \\ \times\ 1 \\ \hline 1,000 \end{array} \quad \begin{array}{r} 1,000 \\ \times\ 2 \\ \hline 2,000 \end{array} \quad \begin{array}{r} 1,000 \\ \times\ 3 \\ \hline 3,000 \end{array}$$

$$\begin{array}{r} 4 \\ \times\ 2 \\ \hline 8 \end{array} \quad \begin{array}{r} 400 \\ \times\ 2 \\ \hline 800 \end{array} \quad \begin{array}{r} 8 \\ \times\ 3 \\ \hline 24 \end{array} \quad \begin{array}{r} 800 \\ \times\ 3 \\ \hline 2,400 \end{array} \quad \begin{array}{r} 7 \\ \times\ 5 \\ \hline 35 \end{array} \quad \begin{array}{r} 700 \\ \times\ 5 \\ \hline 3,500 \end{array}$$

Multiply.

Puzzling Numbers

Fill in the tables with the missing factors and products.

factor	factor	product
	4	180
16	8	
	5	275
4		104

factor	factor	product
3		123
	5	10
6		318
47	3	

factor	factor	product
5		125
	7	308
30	3	
	20	840

factor	factor	product
114	2	
6		198
	40	120
2		132

Shade in your answers below to reveal a picture.

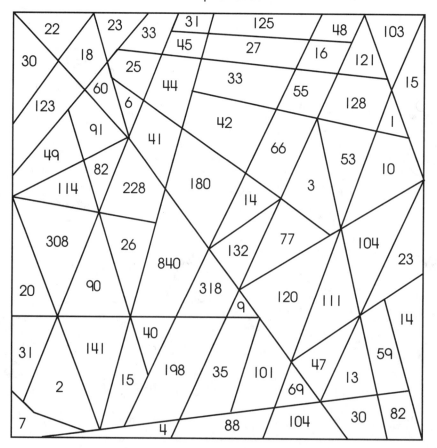

Week 11 Skills

Subject	Skill	Multi-Sensory Learning Activities
Reading and Language Arts	Understand and use synonyms, or words with similar meanings.	• Complete Practice Pages 122, 123, and 126. • Show your child how to use a thesaurus. Have him or her look up a word and find a synonym. Have your child use the original word in a sentence, then replace it with the synonym. Which is more precise?
	Understand and use antonyms, or words that mean the opposite.	• Complete Practice Pages 124–126. • Write several words on a piece of paper, such as **descended**, **impatient**, **mournful**, **resentful**, and **swiftly**. Use each word in a sentence for your child, then have him or her replace the word in each sentence with an antonym.
Math	Divide two-digit dividends by one-digit divisors.	• Complete Practice Pages 127–129. • Give your child a starting number, such as 28. Ask him or her to subtract 7 repeatedly until he or she reaches zero. Then, have your child write the number of times 7 was subtracted as the answer. Repeat with other equations.
	Divide with remainders.	• Complete Practice Page 130. • Tell a story in which something cannot be divided evenly. For example, say, "Darnell has 14 pieces of bubble gum. He wants to share the gum equally with five of his friends. How many pieces each will Darnell and his friends get? How many pieces will be left over?"

Synonyms

A **synonym** is a word that means the same, or nearly the same, as another word.

Example: quick and **fast**

Draw lines to match the words in Column A with their synonyms in Column B.

Column A	Column B
plain	unusual
career	vocation
rare	disappear
vanish	greedy
beautiful	finish
selfish	simple
complete	lovely

Choose a word from Column A or Column B to complete each sentence below.

1. Dad was very excited when he discovered the _____ coin for sale on the display counter.

2. My dog is a real magician; he can _____ into thin air when he sees me getting his bath ready!

3. Many of my classmates joined the discussion about _____ choices we had considered.

4. "You will need to _____ your report on ancient Greece before you sign up for computer time," said Mr. Rastetter.

5. Your _____ painting will be on display in the art show.

Synonyms

For each sentence, choose a word from the box that is a synonym for the bold word. Write the synonym above the word.

> tired   greedy   easy   rough   minute   melted   friend   smart

1. Boy, this road is really **bumpy**!

2. The operator said politely, "One **moment**, please."

3. My parents are usually **exhausted** when they get home from work.

4. "Don't be so **selfish**! Can't you share with us?" asked Rob.

5. That puzzle was actually quite **simple**.

6. "Who's your **buddy**?" Dad asked as we walked onto the porch.

7. When it comes to animals, my Uncle Steve is quite **intelligent**.

8. The frozen treat **thawed** while I stood in line for the bus.

Antonyms

An **antonym** is a word that means the opposite of another word.

Example: difficult and **easy**

Choose words from the box to complete the crossword puzzle.

| friend | vanish | quit | safety | liquids | scatter | help | noisy |

ACROSS:

2. Opposite of **gather**

3. Opposite of **enemy**

4. Opposite of **prevent**

6. Opposite of **begin**

7. Opposite of **silent**

DOWN:

1. Opposite of **appear**

2. Opposite of **danger**

5. Opposite of **solids**

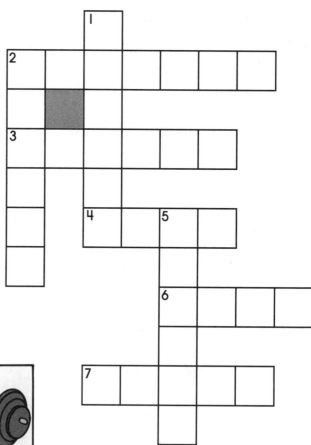

Antonyms

Each bold word below has an antonym in the box. Use these words to write new sentences. The first one is done for you.

friend   vanish   quit   safety   liquids   help   scatter   worse

1. I'll help you **gather** all the papers on the lawn.

   The strong winds will scatter the leaves.

2. The fourth graders were learning about the many **solids** in their classroom.

   _____

   _____

3. "It's time to **begin** our lesson on the continents," said Ms. Haynes.

   _____

   _____

4. "That's strange. The stapler decided to **appear** all of a sudden," said Mr. Jonson.

   _____

   _____

5. The doctor said this new medicine should **prevent** colds.

   _____

   _____

6. "She is our **enemy**, boys, we can't let her in our clubhouse!" cried Paul.

   _____

   _____

7. I'm certain that dark cave is full of **danger**!

   _____

   _____

8. Give me a chance to make the situation **better**.

   _____

   _____

Synonyms and Antonyms

Use the words in the box to write a synonym for each word below. Write it next to the S. Next to the A, write an antonym. The first one is done for you.

appear	gloomy	straight	fancy
under	valuable	late	bumpy
embarrassed	merry	break	plain
icy	unnecessary	old	smooth
proud	bent	repair	above
melted	immediate	new	vanish

1. crooked

   S: ___bent___

   A: ___straight___

2. frozen

   S: _____

   A: _____

3. instant

   S: _____

   A: _____

4. damage

   S: _____

   A: _____

5. important

   S: _____

   A: _____

6. ashamed

   S: _____

   A: _____

7. cheerful

   S: _____

   A: _____

8. elegant

   S: _____

   A: _____

9. rough

   S: _____

   A: _____

10. beneath

    S: _____

    A: _____

11. disappear

    S: _____

    A: _____

12. ancient

    S: _____

    A: _____

Division

Division is a way to find out how many times one number is contained in another number. For example, $28 \div 7 = 4$ means that there are 4 groups of 7 in 28.

Division problems can be written two ways: $36 \div 6 = 6$ or $6\overline{)36}$

These are the parts of a division problem:

dividend ⟶ **36 ÷ 6 = 6** ⟵ **quotient**

divisor

6 ⟵ **quotient**

divisor ⟶ **6)36** ⟵ **dividend**

Divide.

$7\overline{)21}$

$2\overline{)2}$

$5\overline{)25}$

$4\overline{)32}$

$9\overline{)45}$

$2\overline{)4}$

$8\overline{)24}$

$4\overline{)12}$

$6\overline{)24}$

$3\overline{)6}$

$9\overline{)54}$

$7\overline{)14}$

$5\overline{)15}$ $3\overline{)9}$

$6\overline{)12}$

$64 \div 8 =$ ___ $63 \div 7 =$ ___

$81 \div 9 =$ ___

$6\overline{)36}$

$3\overline{)75}$

$72 \div 8 =$ ___

$6\overline{)48}$ $5\overline{)40}$

$27 \div 3 =$ ___ $16 \div 4 =$ ___

$72 \div 9 =$ ___

Division

Divide.

1. $5\overline{)30}$

2. $7\overline{)21}$

3. $4\overline{)28}$

4. $9\overline{)63}$

5. $5\overline{)35}$

6. $1\overline{)9}$

7. $4\overline{)24}$

8. $8\overline{)32}$

9. $6\overline{)36}$

10. $2\overline{)14}$

11. $7\overline{)56}$

12. $4\overline{)36}$

13. $9\overline{)27}$

14. $6\overline{)42}$

15. $8\overline{)8}$

16. $3\overline{)24}$

17. $7\overline{)63}$

18. $9\overline{)54}$

19. $3\overline{)27}$

20. $1\overline{)7}$

21. $8\overline{)24}$

22. $2\overline{)16}$

23. $7\overline{)42}$

24. $6\overline{)54}$

25. $8\overline{)56}$

26. $4\overline{)32}$

27. $9\overline{)72}$

28. $5\overline{)45}$

29. $3\overline{)21}$

30. $8\overline{)64}$

31. $5\overline{)45}$

32. $7\overline{)49}$

33. $9\overline{)54}$

34. $3\overline{)36}$

35. $8\overline{)72}$

36. $7\overline{)28}$

37. $5\overline{)40}$

38. $6\overline{)30}$

Snowball Bash

Help Pete climb down this mound of giant snowballs.

$7\overline{)84}$ $5\overline{)75}$

$3\overline{)45}$ $9\overline{)99}$ $4\overline{)88}$ $5\overline{)80}$

$4\overline{)64}$ $3\overline{)57}$ $3\overline{)78}$ $3\overline{)72}$ $8\overline{)96}$

$2\overline{)86}$ $2\overline{)38}$ $6\overline{)66}$ $5\overline{)65}$ $4\overline{)52}$

$4\overline{)68}$ $6\overline{)78}$ $7\overline{)91}$ $2\overline{)42}$ $6\overline{)72}$

Division With Remainders

Sometimes groups of objects or numbers cannot be divided into equal groups. The **remainder** is the number left over in the quotient of a division problem. The remainder must be smaller than the divisor.

Example:

Divide 18 butterflies into groups of 5.
You have 3 equal groups,
with 3 butterflies left over.

$$18 \div 5 = 3 \text{ R}3$$

or

$$\begin{array}{r} 3 \text{ R}3 \\ 5\overline{)18} \\ -15 \\ \hline 3 \end{array}$$

Divide. Some problems may have remainders.

 $9\overline{)84}$ $7\overline{)65}$ $8\overline{)25}$ $5\overline{)35}$ $5\overline{)34}$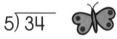

$4\overline{)25}$ $6\overline{)56}$ $4\overline{)7}$ $4\overline{)16}$ $8\overline{)37}$

$7\overline{)27}$ $2\overline{)5}$ $2\overline{)4}$ $8\overline{)73}$ $4\overline{)9}$

$9\overline{)46}$ $5\overline{)17}$ $2\overline{)3}$ $4\overline{)13}$ $5\overline{)25}$

Week 12 Skills

Subject	Skill	Multi-Sensory Learning Activities
Reading and Language Arts	Recognize homophones, or words that sound the same but are spelled differently.	• Complete Practice Pages 132–136. • Give your child a series of word pairs, such as **small** and **little**, **long** and **short**, and **bear** and **bare**. Have your child mark each pair as homophones (H), synonyms (S), or antonyms (A). Then, ask your child to write his or her own word pairs and give them to you to label correctly.
Math	Review division with remainders.	• Complete Practice Pages 137–140. • Give your child a sheet of division problems, with the problems in one column and the answers mixed up in the other column. Ask your child to match the problems with the correct answers. As an added challenge, time your child to see how quickly he or she can correctly match the problems with their answers. • Explain that the average person spends 1,638 hours each year involved in sports and leisure activities. Ask your child to calculate how many hours are spent in sports and leisure activities each month, each week, and each day.

Same Spelling But ...

Homophones are words that have the same spelling but are different in meaning and sometimes pronunciation. Use the spelling words to fill in the blanks. Indicate the part of speech in the parentheses. The same word is used twice in each sentence.

bass
bowl
close
cobbler
does
file
flounder
grave
hawk
list
minute
object
paddle
present
sow

1. The secretary wanted to _____ ( ) her fingernails before she put all the papers in the _____ ( ).

2. Before my dad goes to _____ ( ), he eats a big _____ ( ) of cereal.

3. Our _____ ( ) broke, the boat overturned and we had to _____ ( ) quite a distance.

4. The _____ ( ) singer enjoys fishing for _____ ( ).

5. The ship's captain was reading the _____ ( ) of passengers when he suddenly felt the ship _____ ( ).

6. After the _____ ( ) has repaired shoes all day, he enjoys eating a fruit _____ ( ).

7. The _____ ( ) was hooked tightly, but I couldn't reel it in, so it began to _____ ( ) in the shallow water.

8. As the peddler was getting ready to _____ ( ) his vegetables, a hungry _____ ( ) was perched on a nearby tree branch.

9. The company hired to dig the _____ ( ) realized the cemetery needed _____ ( ) attention.

Circle the correct pronunciation and write the word on the line.

1. The president was so _____ I could shake his hand. klōz   klōs

2. Three _____ were nibbling grass by the road. dōz   dūz

3. After doing our research, we had to _____ a report. prĕz' ent   prĭ zĕnt'

4. The gardener will _____ grass seed for a new lawn. sō   sou

Bizarre Bazaar!

board
bored
coarse
council
counsel
course
creak
creek
knot
lead
led
not
ring
who's
whose
wring

Three pairs of homophones are not next to each other in the spelling list because of alphabetical order. Write those three pairs.

a. _____   a. _____   a. _____

b. _____   b. _____   b. _____

Fill in the blanks with spelling words. Not all words are used.

1. The pipe was made out of __ __ __ ☐.

2. She broke the __ __ ☐ __ __ with a karate chop.

3. In scouting, he learned to tie a __ __ __ ☐.

4. Students will elect class members to the student __ __ ☐ __ __ __ __ __.

5. The umpire shouted, "__ ☐ __ __ __ bat is this?"

6. Grandpa gave me good __ __ __ ☐ __ __ __ whenever I had important decisions to make.

7. With nothing to do, I am ☐ __ __ __ __.

8. It is __ ☐ __ nice to hit anyone.

9. The __ __ __ __ __ ☐ material made my arms itch.

10. The hikers followed a __ __ __ __ ☐ __ to the north.

11. The thief stole a diamond __ __ __ ☐.

12. We sailed paper boats in the __ __ __ __ ☐.

13. The old floor started to ☐ __ __ __ __ when I walked across it.

Match the boxed letter from each sentence to the numbered lines below to answer the riddle: *Why was the man happy to get a job at the bakery?*

____ ____ ____ ____ ____ ____ ____   ____ ____
 7   9   13   2   4   10   9   5   9

____ ____ ____ ____ ____ ____ ____   ____ ____ ____
12   6   9   2   1   9   1   3   5   9

____ ____ ____ ____ ____ .
 1   8   4   11   5

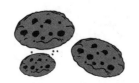

Homophones

Homophones are two words that sound the same, have different meanings, and are usually spelled differently.

Example: write and **right**

Write the correct homophone in each sentence below.

weight — how heavy something is
wait — to be patient

threw — tossed
through — passing between

steal — to take something that doesn't belong to you
steel — a heavy metal

1. The bands marched _____ the streets lined with many cheering people.

2. _____ for me by the flagpole.

3. One of our strict rules at school is: Never _____ from another person.

4. Could you estimate the _____ of this bowling ball?

5. The bleachers have _____ rods on both ends and in the middle.

6. He walked in the door and _____ his jacket down.

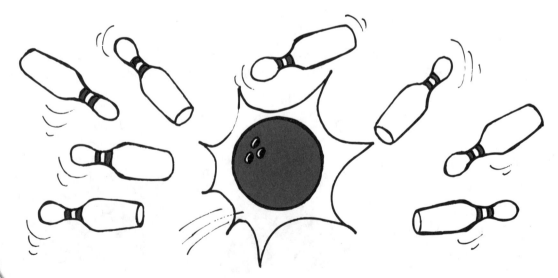

Homophones

Write the correct homophone in each sentence below.

cent — a coin having the value of one penny
scent — odor or aroma

chews — grinds with the teeth
choose — to select

course — the path along which something moves
coarse — rough in texture

heard — received sounds in the ear
herd — a group of animals

1. My uncle Mike always _____
   each bite of his food 20 times!

2. As we walked through her garden, we detected the

   _____ of roses.

3. It was very peaceful sitting on the hillside watching the

   _____ of cattle grazing.

4. Which flavor of ice cream did you _____?

5. The friendly clerk let me buy the jacket even though I was one

   _____ short.

6. You will need _____ sandpaper to make the wood
   smoother.

Words That Sound Alike

Choose the correct word in parentheses to complete each sentence.

1. Jimmy was so _____ that he fell asleep. (board, bored)

2. We'll need a _____ and some nails to repair the fence. (board, bored)

3. Do you want _____ after dinner? (desert, dessert)

4. Did the soldier _____ his post. (desert, dessert)

5. The soldier had a _____ pinned to his uniform. (medal, meddle)

6. I told her not to _____ in other people's lives. (medal, meddle)

7. Don't _____ at your present before Christmas! (peak, peek)

8. They climbed to the _____ of the mountain. (peak, peek)

9. Jack had to repair the emergency _____ on his car. (brake, break)

10. Please be careful not to _____ my bicycle. (brake, break)

11. The race _____ was a very difficult one. (coarse, course)

12. We will need some _____ sandpaper to finish the job. (coarse, course)

Looking to the Stars

Solve the problems. To find the path to the top, color the spaces where the answers match the problem number.

35. $4\overline{)57}$	36. $2\overline{)72}$

32. $3\overline{)96}$	33. $2\overline{)66}$	34. $4\overline{)57}$

27. $3\overline{)63}$	28. $3\overline{)84}$	29. $4\overline{)97}$	30. $6\overline{)74}$	31. $6\overline{)68}$

22. $6\overline{)74}$	23. $2\overline{)46}$	24. $2\overline{)48}$	25. $3\overline{)75}$	26. $6\overline{)96}$

15. $5\overline{)92}$	16. $3\overline{)41}$	17. $3\overline{)57}$	18. $4\overline{)84}$	19. $4\overline{)76}$	20. $7\overline{)86}$	21. $5\overline{)72}$

8. $5\overline{)57}$	9. $3\overline{)65}$	10. $2\overline{)87}$	11. $5\overline{)55}$	12. $7\overline{)84}$	13. $3\overline{)87}$	14. $7\overline{)93}$

1. $3\overline{)96}$	2. $6\overline{)94}$	3. $5\overline{)93}$	4. $9\overline{)36}$	5. $2\overline{)97}$	6. $6\overline{)84}$	7. $3\overline{)68}$

Division: Larger Numbers

Follow the steps for dividing larger numbers.

Example: **Step 1:** Divide the tens first.   **Step 2:** Divide the ones next.

$$
3\overline{)66}
$$

$$
\begin{array}{r} 2 \\ 3\overline{)66} \\ -6 \\ \hline 06 \end{array}
$$

$$
\begin{array}{r} 22 \\ 3\overline{)66} \\ -6 \\ \hline 06 \\ -6 \\ \hline 0 \end{array}
$$

Divide.

$$4\overline{)84} \qquad 2\overline{)90} \qquad 2\overline{)64} \qquad 2\overline{)50} \qquad 3\overline{)45}$$

$$3\overline{)75} \qquad 3\overline{)36} \qquad 4\overline{)92} \qquad 2\overline{)76} \qquad 5\overline{)65}$$

In some larger numbers, the divisor goes into the first two digits of the dividend.

Example:

$$
9\overline{)729}
$$

$$
\begin{array}{r} 81 \\ 9\overline{)729} \\ -72 \\ \hline 09 \end{array}
$$

$$
\begin{array}{r} 81 \\ 9\overline{)729} \\ -72 \\ \hline 09 \\ -9 \\ \hline 0 \end{array}
$$

Divide.

$$7\overline{)630} \qquad 5\overline{)125} \qquad 6\overline{)486} \qquad 5\overline{)100} \qquad 6\overline{)540}$$

Division

Divide.

7) 860   6) 611   8) 279   4) 338   6) 979

3) 792   5) 463   6) 940   4) 647   3) 814

7) 758   5) 356   4) 276   8) 328   9) 306

4) 579   8) 932   3) 102   2) 821   6) 489

The music store has 491 CD's. The store sells 8 CD's a day. How many days will it take to sell all of the CD's?

_____

To Catch a Butterfly

Solve the problems. Draw a line connecting each net with the correct butterfly.

$6) \overline{1279}$

$5) \overline{843}$

168 R3

441 R6

$5) \overline{3742}$

$3) \overline{794}$

796 R7

213 R1

663 R1

$9) \overline{3975}$

264 R2

748 R2

$4) \overline{2653}$

149

422 R2

$2) \overline{1748}$

874

747 R1

691 R5

$7) \overline{5230}$

$6) \overline{894}$

$3) \overline{1268}$

$8) \overline{6375}$

$8) \overline{5533}$

Week 13 Skills

Subject	Skill	Multi-Sensory Learning Activities
Reading and Language Arts	Review homophones.	• Complete Practice Pages 142 and 143. • Work with your child to come up with 26 homophone pairs, each of which begins with a different letter of the alphabet.
	Recognize up to five-syllable words.	• Complete Practice Pages 144 and 145. • A haiku contains 17 syllables: 5 on line one, 7 on line two, and 5 on line three. Encourage your child to write several haikus about the solar system.
	Classifying words into similar groupings.	• Complete Practice Page 146. • Read *The Whipping Boy* by Sid Fleischman with your child. List the actions of the prince throughout the book. Have your child classify his actions as selfish or generous.
Math	Review division; divide with two-digit divisors.	• Complete Practice Pages 147–149. • Buy a large bag of candy and count the pieces. Then, ask your child to count how many students are in his or her class at school. How many pieces would each child get? How many would be left over?
	Use multiplication to check answers of division problems.	• Complete Practice Page 150. • Review the relationship between division and multiplication. Provide your child with a division fact, such as $24 \div 6$. Have him or her draw a representation or build a model of the fact and solve it.

Homophone Hype

```
G S B R I D L E W O J M
E H R Q M N S L H G V A
G N I L A X H E A R W N
D R D W I C R N F A S E
R M A I N E Q I S Z K R
V G L Y W N F S C E N T
N D I N S T L L K H N S
R U U O N P W E I G H T
D E W S P C H D L V E Y
O F A I S L E I L B R L
R L Y O M S Y E R G T A
```

For each word given below, list the homophones in the spaces provided. Find and circle the homophone in the word search. Then, write a sentence using the given word and at least one homophone.

1. Here _____

   Sentence: _____

2. Bridle _____

   Sentence: _____

3. I'll _____ _____

   Sentence: _____

4. Graze (Hint: plural forms of a color) _____ _____

   Sentence: _____

5. Main _____ _____

   Sentence: _____

6. Whey _____ _____

   Sentence: _____

7. Dew _____ _____

   Sentence: _____

8. Scent _____ _____

   Sentence: _____

Is the Bear Bare?

bare
bear
berry
bury
groan
grown
hall
haul
pain
pane
raise
rays
stair
stare
wait
weight

Use each pair of homophones correctly in the sentences.
Indicate the part of speech in the parentheses.

1. When my brother moved into the dormitory, he had

   to _____( ) all his belongings down

   the _____( ).

2. The camper was _____( ) when he

   swam in the lake, but only a _____( )
   saw him.

3. I decided to _____( ) the blinds to let

   in the sun's _____( ).

4. My dad let out a _____( ) when he

   discovered he had _____( ) too large for his pants.

5. I felt a small _____( ) when I cut my hand on the

   _____( ) of glass.

6. It's not polite to _____( ) when someone stumbles on a

   _____( ).

7. When our pet canary died, we decided to _____( ) it near

   the bush with the one red _____( ) on it.

Syllables

A **syllable** is a word—or part of a word—with only one vowel sound. Some words have just one syllable, such as **cat**, **dog**, and **house**. Some words have two syllables, such as **in-sist** and **be-fore**. Some words have three syllables, such as **re-mem-ber**; four syllables, such as **un-der-stand-ing**; or more. Often words are easier to spell if you know how many syllables they have.

Write the number of syllables in each word below.

Word	Syllables	Word	Syllables
1. amphibian	_____	11. want	_____
2. liter	_____	12. communication	_____
3. guild	_____	13. pedestrian	_____
4. chili	_____	14. kilo	_____
5. vegetarian	_____	15. autumn	_____
6. comedian	_____	16. dinosaur	_____
7. warm	_____	17. grammar	_____
8. piano	_____	18. dry	_____
9. barbarian	_____	19. solar	_____
10. chef	_____	20. wild	_____

Next to each number, write words with the same number of syllables.

1 _____ _____ _____

2 _____ _____ _____

3 _____ _____ _____

4 _____ _____ _____

5 _____ _____

Syllables

Write each word from the box next to the number that shows how many syllables it has.

fuss	paragraph	phone	friendship	freedom
defend	flood	alphabet	rough	laughter

One: _____ _____ _____ _____

Two: _____ _____ _____ _____

Three: _____ _____

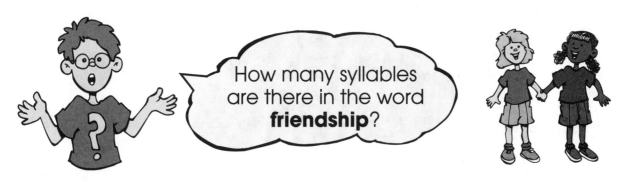

How many syllables are there in the word **friendship**?

Circle the two words in each row that have the same number of syllables as the first word.

Example: fact	(clay)	happy	(phone)	command
rough	freckle	pump	accuse	ghost
jacket	flood	laughter	defend	paragraph
accident	paragraph	carpenter	stomach	castle
comfort	agree	friend	friendship	health
fuss	collect	blend	freedom	hatch
alphabet	thankful	Christmas	enemy	unhappy
glowing	midnight	defending	grading	telephone

Grouping Letters

scheme
scholar
school
schooner
scratch
scream
screw
scrimmage
scrub
straight
strainer
strength
string
stripe
struggle

Cross out the word that does not belong in each group. Write the word that fits the category.

1. filter, mixture, sieve _____

2. polish, claw, rip _____

3. rope, leather, cord _____

4. college, academy, apartment _____

5. soil, wash, clean _____

6. power, weakness, force _____

7. tramp, pupil, learner _____

8. fight, conflict, agreement _____

9. laugh, yell, cry _____

10. plan, vacation, plot _____

11. nail, bolt, hammer _____

12. ship, locomotive, vessel _____

13. band, line, circle _____

Which two words were not used? _____ _____

Write one sentence using both words. _____

_____

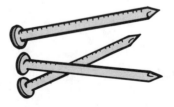

Yum-Yum!

What edible fungus is occasionally found on pizzas or in omelets? To find out, solve the problems. Then, write the corresponding letter above the answer at the bottom of the page.

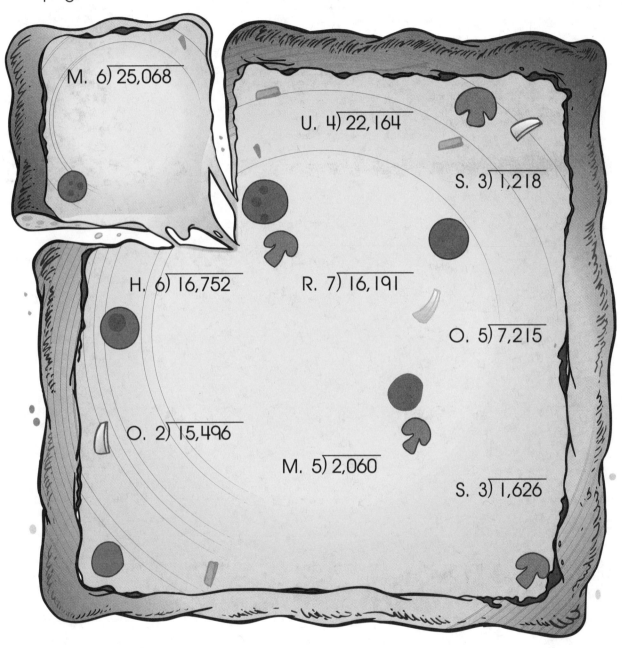

M. 6) 25,068

U. 4) 22,164

S. 3) 1,218

H. 6) 16,752

R. 7) 16,191

O. 5) 7,215

O. 2) 15,496

M. 5) 2,060

S. 3) 1,626

| 412 | 5,541 | 406 | 2,792 | 2,313 | 7,748 | 1,443 | 4,178 | 542 |

Division: Two-Digit Divisors

Divide. Then check each answer on another sheet of paper by multiplying it by the divisor and adding the remainder.

Example:

$$
\begin{array}{r}
2 \\
12\overline{)256} \\
-24 \\
\hline
1
\end{array}
\qquad
\begin{array}{r}
21\text{ R}4 \\
12\overline{)256} \\
-24 \\
\hline
16 \\
-12 \\
\hline
4
\end{array}
$$

Check:

$$
\begin{array}{r}
21 \\
\times 12 \\
\hline
42 \\
210 \\
\hline
252 \\
+\ 4 \\
\hline
256
\end{array}
$$

$27\overline{)880}$ $81\overline{)913}$ $65\overline{)790}$ $42\overline{)674}$ $67\overline{)823}$

$72\overline{)977}$ $54\overline{)743}$ $45\overline{)863}$ $24\overline{)432}$ $18\overline{)372}$

$28\overline{)175}$ $49\overline{)538}$ $77\overline{)936}$ $37\overline{)603}$ $63\overline{)835}$

The Allen farm has 882 chickens. The chickens are kept in 21 coops. How many chickens are there in each coop?

_____

China's Dragon Kite

Solve the problems in this incredible dragon kite!

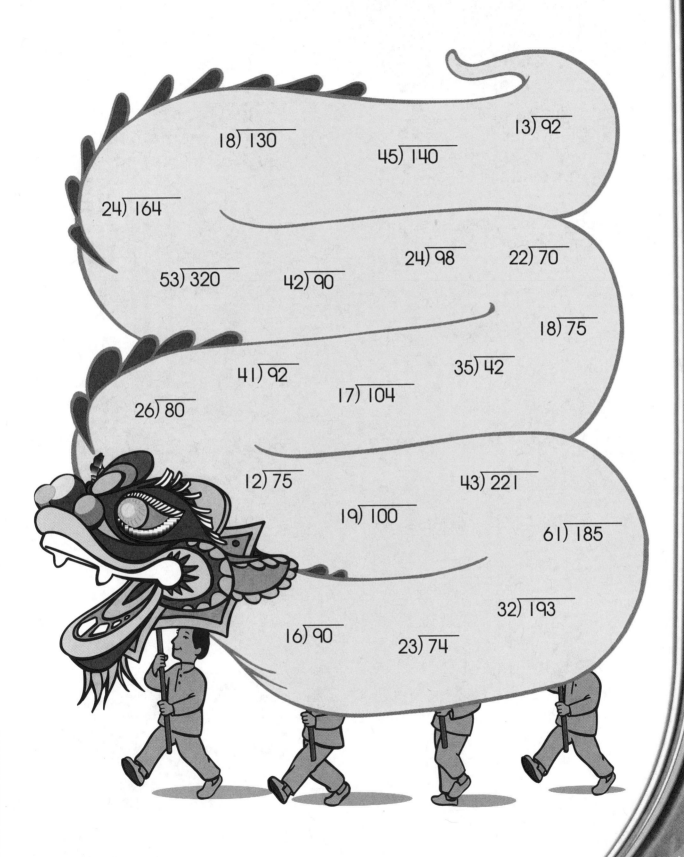

18) 130

45) 140

13) 92

24) 164

53) 320

42) 90

24) 98

22) 70

18) 75

41) 92

17) 104

35) 42

26) 80

12) 75

43) 221

19) 100

61) 185

32) 193

16) 90

23) 74

Division: Checking the Answers

To check a division problem, multiply the quotient by the divisor. Add the remainder. The answer will be the dividend.

Example:

quotient ⟶ **58** R**1**

divisor ⟶ 3) **175**

dividend ⟶ – 15

25

– 24

remainder ⟶ **1**

58 ⟵ quotient

x   3 ⟵ divisor

174

+   1 ⟵ remainder

175 ⟵ dividend

Divide each problem, then draw a line from the division problem to the correct checking problem.

33	53	97	135	113	119
x 7	x 7	x 7	x 7	x 7	x 7
	+ 2	+ 3	+ 1	+ 1	+ 1

7) 682   7) 231   7) 373   7) 792   7) 834   7) 946

The toy factory puts 7 robot dogs in each box. The factory has 256 robot dogs. How many boxes will they need?

_____

Week 14 Skills

Subject	Skill	Multi-Sensory Learning Activities
Reading and Language Arts	Understand similes and metaphors, and recognize the differences between them.	• Complete Practice Pages 152–154. • Have your child write a descriptive article on a topic such as hiking in the woods or baking chocolate chip cookies. Tell him or her to use at least two metaphors and two similes in the article.
	Understand idioms as figures of speech.	• Complete Practice Pages 155 and 156. • Read several examples of idioms. List them on a large piece of paper. Have your child think of others to add to the list. Then, have your child draw a picture of each literal interpretation.
Math	Identify missing operations and complete number puzzles.	• Complete Practice Pages 157–160. • Divide pennies evenly into a given number of sections in an egg carton. Name the two multiplication and two division sentences that the model represents. For example, place 24 pennies in 6 sections of the egg carton so there are 4 in each section. The four sentences are $24 \div 6 = 4$, $24 \div 4 = 6$, $6 \times 4 = 24$, and $4 \times 6 = 24$. Repeat with different equations.

Like...a Simile

In the sentences below, underline the two things or persons being compared. In the blank, write simile or metaphor. Remember, a simile uses **like** or **as**; metaphors do not.

1. Angel was as mean as a wild bull. _____

2. Toni and Mattie were like toast and jam. _____

3. Mr. Ashby expected the students to be as busy as beavers.

   _____

4. The pin was a masterpiece in Mattie's mind. _____

5. The park's peacefulness was a friend to Mattie. _____

6. The words came as slow as molasses into Mattie's mind. _____

7. Mrs. Stamp's apartment was like a museum. _____

8. Mrs. Benson was as happy as a lark when Mattie won

   the contest. _____

9. Mr. Phillip's smile was a glowing beam to Mattie and

   Mrs. Benson. _____

10. Mattie ran as fast as the wind to get her money. _____

11. Angel's mean words cut through Charlene like glass. _____

12. Mr. Bacon was a fairy godmother to Mattie. _____

13. The gingko tree's leaves were shaped like fans. _____

Complete the following sentences using similes.

1. Matt was as artistic as _____.

2. Hannibal's teeth were like _____.

3. Toni's mind worked fast like _____.

4. Mattie was as sad as _____.

5. Mrs. Stamp was like _____.

Similes

A **simile** uses the words **like** or **as** to compare two things.

Examples: The snow glittered **like** diamonds.
                He was **as** slow **as** a turtle.

Circle the two objects being compared in each sentence.

1. The kittens were like gymnasts performing tricks.

2. My old computer is as slow as molasses.

3. When the lights went out in the basement, it was as dark as night.

4. The sun was like a fire, heating up the earth.

5. The young girl was as graceful as a ballerina.

6. The puppy cried like a baby all night.

7. He flies that airplane like a daredevil.

8. The girl was as pretty as a picture.

9. The snow on the mountain tops was like whipped cream.

10. The tiger's eyes were like emeralds.

Complete the simile in each sentence.

11. My cat is as _____ as _____.

12. He was as _____ as _____.

13. Melissa's eyes shone like_____ .

14. The paints were like _____ .

15. The opera singer's voice was as _____ as _____.

16. My friend is as _____ as _____.

Metaphors

A **metaphor** is a direct comparison between two things.
The words **like** or **as** are not used in a metaphor.

Example: The **sun** is a **yellow ball** in the sky.

Underline the metaphor in each sentence.
Write the two objects being compared on the line.

1. As it bounded toward me, the dog was a quivering
    furball of excitement.

    _____

2. The snow we skied on was mashed potatoes.

    _____

3. John is a mountain goat when it comes to rock climbing.

    _____

4. The light is a beacon shining into the dark basement.

    _____

5. The famished child was a wolf, eating for the first time in days.

    _____

6. The man's arm was a tireless lever as he fought to win the wrestling contest.

    _____

7. The flowers were colorful circles against the green of the yard.

    _____

Idioms

An **idiom** is a phrase that says one thing but actually means something quite different.

Example: A **horse of a different color** means something quite unusual.

Write the letter of the correct meaning for each bold phrase. The first one has been done for you.

> a. refusal to see or listen
> b. misbehaving, acting in a wild way
> c. made a thoughtless remark
> d. lost an opportunity
> e. got angry
> f. pay for
> g. unknowing
> h. feeling very sad
> i. get married
> j. excited and happy

_____f_____ 1. My parents will **foot the bill** for my birthday party.

_____ 2. Tony and Lisa will finally **tie the knot** in June.

_____ 3. Sam was **down in the dumps** after he wrecked his bicycle.

_____ 4. Sarah **put her foot in her mouth** when she was talking to our teacher.

_____ 5. I really **missed the boat** when I turned down the chance to work after school.

_____ 6. I got the **brush-off** from Susan when I tried to ask her where she was last night.

_____ 7. Mickey is **in the dark** about our plans to throw a surprise birthday party for him.

_____ 8. The children were **bouncing off the walls** when the baby-sitter tried to put them to bed.

_____ 9. The students were **flying high** on the last day of school.

_____ 10. My sister **lost her cool** when she discovered I had spilled chocolate milk on her new sweater.

Idioms

An **idiom** is a figure of speech that has a meaning different from the literal one.

Example: Dad is **in the doghouse** because he was late for dinner.

Meaning: Dad is in trouble because he was late for dinner.

Write the meanings of the idioms in bold.

1. He was a **bundle of nerves** waiting for his test scores.

   _____

2. It was **raining cats and dogs**.

   _____

3. My friend and I decided to **bury the hatchet** after our argument.

   _____

4. He **gave** me **the cold shoulder** when I spoke to him.

   _____

5. My mom **blew up** when she saw my poor report card.

   _____

6. I was **on pins and needles** before my skating performance.

   _____

7. When the student didn't answer, the teacher asked, "**Did the cat get your tongue**?"

   _____

8. The city **rolled out the red carpet for** the returning Olympic champion.

   _____

9. They hired a clown for the young boy's birthday party to help **break the ice**.

   _____

Identifying Operations

Fill in the correct sign for each problem.

5 ◯ 5 = 10   14 ◯ 59 = 73   21 ◯ 9 = 30   36 ◯ 63 = 99

9 ◯ 9 = 81   56 ◯ 17 = 73   64 ◯ 8 = 8   6 ◯ 9 = 54

56 ◯ 8 = 48   40 ◯ 5 = 8   7 ◯ 8 = 56   33 ◯ 57 = 90

91 ◯ 16 = 75   9 ◯ 3 = 27   76 ◯ 19 = 57   27 ◯ 3 = 9

54 ◯ 6 = 9   29 ◯ 37 = 66   43 ◯ 7 = 50   63 ◯ 9 = 54

28 ◯ 17 = 11   6 ◯ 5 = 30   4 ◯ 9 = 36   8 ◯ 38 = 46

25 ◯ 5 = 5   36 ◯ 5 = 31   48 ◯ 8 = 6   2 ◯ 9 = 18

72 ◯ 9 = 63   56 ◯ 8 = 7   9 ◯ 1 = 9   55 ◯ 37 = 92

64 ◯ 8 = 56   7 ◯ 1 = 7   45 ◯ 5 = 9   81 ◯ 9 = 9

36 ◯ 4 = 9   57 ◯ 9 = 48   36 ◯ 27 = 63   80 ◯ 17 = 63

45 ◯ 5 = 40   7 ◯ 6 = 42   48 ◯ 6 = 42   32 ◯ 4 = 8

82 ◯ 9 = 91   8 ◯ 8 = 64   9 ◯ 8 = 72   71 ◯ 15 = 86

17 ◯ 77 = 94   40 ◯ 6 = 34   47 ◯ 38 = 9   56 ◯ 9 = 47

36 ◯ 6 = 30   15 ◯ 38 = 53   3 ◯ 6 = 18   5 ◯ 9 = 45

72 ◯ 8 = 9   43 ◯ 48 = 91   27 ◯ 18 = 45   6 ◯ 6 = 36

49 ◯ 7 = 7   7 ◯ 7 = 49   8 ◯ 3 = 24   16 ◯ 16 = 32

A Visit to Space Camp

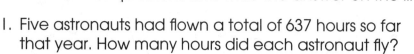

Circle the correct problem and write the answer on the line.

1. Five astronauts had flown a total of 637 hours so far that year. How many hours did each astronaut fly?

    637 + 637   637 ÷ 5   5 x 5   637 x 5 _____

2. Terri's class ate 3 meals in the cafeteria at space camp. The cafeteria served 420 meals in all that day. How many people ate at each meal (breakfast, lunch and dinner) in the cafeteria the day Terri was there?

    420 x 2   3 + 420   420 ÷ 3   3 + 3 _____

3. Eight children can ride the moon gravitation simulator at a time. Ninety-seven children rode the simulator that day. How many groups of 8 rode the simulator?

    8 x 97   97 ÷ 8   8 x 8   97 ÷ 97 _____

4. At the souvenir shop, 9 children bought t-shirts. The total price was $106. They split the cost evenly. How much did each of the children spend on a space camp t-shirt?

    $106 + 9   9 x $106 $106 ÷ 9   9 x 9 _____

5. They drove 193 miles round trip. How many miles is it from the space camp to their hometown?

    193 ÷ 2   2 + 193   2 x 57   193 ÷ 193 _____

6. Terri was in a small group of 8 children who, in one day, spent an accumulated total of 82 hours in the museum. How many hours was that per child?

    8 x 82   82 ÷ 8   8 – 8   8 x 82 _____

7. The children stayed overnight in the dorms with their counselors. There were 124 girls and 8 counselors in the girls' dorm. How many girls was each counselor in charge of?

    124 ÷ 8   8 x 124   8 ÷ 8   124 + 124 _____

Use your calculator.
The Moon is 238,866 miles from Earth. It took 3 days for the rocket to get there. How many miles did the rocket go each day? _____

Number Puzzles

Solve the puzzles.

1

Write your age. _____

Multiply it by 3. _____

Add 18. _____

Multiply by 2. _____

Subtract 36. _____

Divide by 6.(your age) _____

2

Write any number. _____

Double that number. _____

Add 15. _____

Double again. _____

Subtract 30. _____

Divide by 2. _____

Divide by 2 again. _____

3

Write any 2-digit number. _____

Double that number. _____

Add 43. _____

Subtract 18. _____

Add 11. _____

Divide by 2. _____

Subtract 18. _____

4

Write the number of children in your neighborhood. _____

Double that number. _____

Add 15. _____

Double it again. _____

Subtract 30. _____

Divide by 4. _____

Number Puzzles

Use the numbers in each box to make number sentences. Use each number only once.

8	9	7
4	4	6
3	14	36

_____ + _____ = _____

_____ − _____ = _____

_____ × _____ = _____

3	7	5
4	28	9
8	3	12

_____ + _____ = _____

_____ − _____ = _____

_____ × _____ = _____

6	4	13
9	7	27
8	12	3

_____ + _____ = _____

_____ − _____ = _____

_____ × _____ = _____

10	6	13
7	4	5
9	5	42

_____ + _____ = _____

_____ − _____ = _____

_____ × _____ = _____

11	3	15
21	8	6
7	7	5

_____ + _____ = _____

_____ − _____ = _____

_____ × _____ = _____

7	9	12
20	5	16
3	9	4

_____ + _____ = _____

_____ − _____ = _____

_____ × _____ = _____

Week 15 Skills

Subject	Skill	Multi-Sensory Learning Activities
Reading and Language Arts	Understand correct usage of frequently confused words **good** and **well**; **your** and **you're**; **its** and **it's**; and **can** and **may**.	• Complete Practice Pages 162–166. • Dictate several sentences that include the words **your** or **you're**. Have your child to write each sentence using the correct word.
Math	Create graphs.	• Complete Practice Page 167. • Place a thermometer outside. Every morning, check the thermometer and record the data. Using a coordinate grid, ask your child to plot the temperature changes day-to-day.
	Work with ordered pairs.	• Complete Practice Pages 168–170. • Print a coordinate grid labeled A–F on the x-axis (horizontal) and 1–6 on the y-axis (vertical). Place coins in some, but not all, of the grid's squares. Then, have your child toss one regular die and one die labeled A–F (buy wooden cubes at a craft store to make the die, or use stickers to cover the sides of a regular die) to form a coordinate pair (for example, 2B). He or she should pick up the coin, if any, from the appropriate square. At the end of five rounds, ask your child to count the value of his or her coins for the final score.

Good and Well

Use the word **good** to describe a noun. Good is an adjective.

Example: She is a **good** teacher.

Use the word **well** to tell or ask how something is done or to describe someone's health. Well is an adverb. It describes a verb.

Example: She is not feeling **well**.

Write **good** or **well** in the blanks to complete the sentences correctly. The first one has been done for you.

___good___ 1. Our team could use a good/well captain.

_____ 2. The puny kitten doesn't look good/well.

_____ 3. He did his job so good/well that everyone praised him.

_____ 4. Whining isn't a good/well habit.

_____ 5. I might just as good/well do it myself.

_____ 6. She was one of the most well-/good- liked girls at school.

_____ 7. I did the book report as good/well as I could.

_____ 8. The television works very good/well.

_____ 9. You did a good/well job repairing the TV!

_____ 10. Thanks for a job good/well done!

_____ 11. You did a good/well job fixing the computer.

_____ 12. You had better treat your friends good/well.

_____ 13. Can your grandmother hear good/well?

_____ 14. Your brother will be well/good soon.

Your and You're

The word **your** shows possession.

Examples: Is that **your** book?
I visited **your** class.

The word **you're** is a contraction for **you are**. A **contraction** is two words joined together as one. An apostrophe shows where letters have been left out.

Examples: **You're** doing well on that painting.
If **you're** going to pass the test, you should study.

Write **your** or **you're** in the blanks to complete the sentences correctly. The first one has been done for you.

__You're__   1. Your/You're the best friend I have!

_____ 2. Your/You're going to drop that!

_____ 3. Your/You're brother came to see me.

_____ 4. Is that your/you're cat?

_____ 5. If your/you're going, you'd better hurry!

_____ 6. Why are your/you're fingers so red?

_____ 7. It's none of your/you're business!

_____ 8. Your/You're bike's front tire is low.

_____ 9. Your/You're kidding!

_____ 10. Have it your/you're way.

_____ 11. I thought your/you're report was great!

_____ 12. He thinks your/you're wonderful!

_____ 13. What is your/you're first choice?

_____ 14. What's your/you're opinion?

_____ 15. If your/you're going, so am I!

_____ 16. Your/You're welcome.

Good and Well; Your and You're

Choose the correct word for each sentence: **good**, **well**, **your**, or **you're**.

1. Are you sure you can see _____ enough to read with the lighting you have?

2. _____ going to need a paint smock when you go to art class tomorrow afternoon.

3. I can see _____ having some trouble. Can I help with that?

4. The music department needs to buy a speaker system that has

   _____ quality sound.

5. The principal asked, "Where is _____ hall pass?"

6. You must do the job _____ if you expect to keep it.

7. The traffic policeman said, "May I please see

   _____ driver's license?"

8. The story you wrote for English class was done quite _____.

9. That radio station you listen to is a _____ one.

10. Let us know if _____ unable to attend the meeting on Saturday.

Its and It's

The word **its** shows ownership.

Examples: **Its** leaves have all turned red.
Its paw was injured.

The word **it's** is a contraction for **it is**.

Examples: **It's** better to be early than late.
It's not fair!

Write **its** or **it's** to complete the sentences correctly. The first one has been done for you.

_____It's_____ 1   Its/It's never too late for ice cream!

_____ 2. Its/It's eyes are already open.

_____ 3. Its/It's your turn to wash the dishes!

_____ 4. Its/It's cage was left open.

_____ 5. Its/It's engine was beyond repair.

_____ 6. Its/It's teeth were long and pointed.

_____ 7. Did you see its/it's hind legs?

_____ 8. Why do you think its/it's mine?

_____ 9. Do you think its/it's the right color?

_____ 10. Don't pet its/it's fur too hard!

_____ 11. Its/It's from my Uncle Harry.

_____ 12. Can you tell its/it's a surprise?

_____ 13. Is its/it's stall always this clean?

_____ 14. Its/It's not time to eat yet.

_____ 15. She says its/it's working now.

Can and May

The word **can** means am able to or to be able to.

Examples: I **can** do that for you.
                 Can you do that for me?

The word **may** means be allowed to or permitted to. May is used to ask or give permission. **May** can also mean **might** or **perhaps**.

Examples: **May** I be excused?
                 You **may** sit here.

Write **can** or **may** in the blanks to complete the sentences correctly. The first one has been done for you.

_____May_____   1. Can/May I help you?

_____   2. He's smart. He can/may do it himself.

_____   3. When can/may I have my dessert?

_____   4. I can/may tell you exactly what she said.

_____   5. He can/may speak French fluently.

_____   6. You can/may use my pencil.

_____   7. I can/may be allowed to attend the concert.

_____   8. It's bright. I can/may see you!

_____   9. Can/May my friend stay for dinner?

_____   10. You can/may leave when your report is finished.

_____   11. I can/may see your point!

_____   12. She can/may dance well.

_____   13. Can/May you hear the dog barking?

_____   14. Can/May you help me button this sweater?

_____   15. Mother, can/may I go to the movies?

Majestic Mountains

The word **mountain** means different things to different people. Some people who live on vast, level plains, consider a small hill a mountain. While others, who live in the mountains, would not consider a region mountainous unless it was very high and rugged.

Listed below are eight famous mountains of the world along with their heights. Graph each mountain's height. On the bottom of the graph, write the mountain's name and, on the side of the graph, chart the height. When you have finished graphing, use the results to answer the questions below.

Name	Height
Everest	29,022 feet
Lassen Peak	10,453 feet
Kenya	17,058 feet
Pikes Peak	14,110 feet
Fuji	12,388 feet
Mauna Loa	13,680 feet
McKinley	20,320 feet

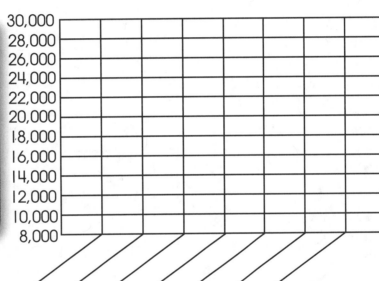

1. Which mountain is the highest? _____

2. What is the average height of the mountains? _____

3. How much higher is McKinley than Pikes Peak? _____

4. What is the height of all the mountains? _____

5. What is the difference between the highest and shortest mountain?

_____

Gliding Graphics

Draw the lines as directed from point to point for each graph.

Draw a line from:
F,7 to D,1
D,1 to I,6
I,6 to N,8
N,8 to M,3
M,3 to F,1
F,1 to G,4
G,4 to E,4
E,4 to B,1
B,1 to A,8
A,8 to D,11
D,11 to F,9
F,9 to F,7
F,7 to I,9
I,9 to I,6
I,6 to F,7

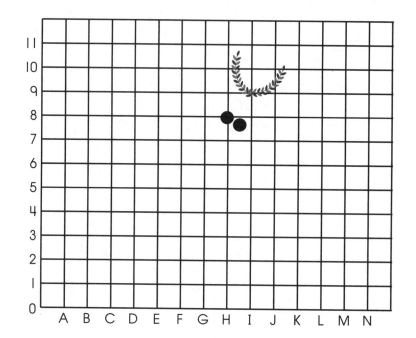

Draw a line from:

J,◆ to N,◣
N,◣ to U,◣
U,◣ to Z,▣
Z,▣ to X,✚
X,✚ to U,◣
U,◣ to S,◉
S,◉ to N,◣
N,◣ to N,◉
N,◉ to J,◆
J,◆ to L,▦
L,▦ to Y,▦
Y,▦ to Z,▣
Z,▣ to L,▣
L,▣ to J,◆

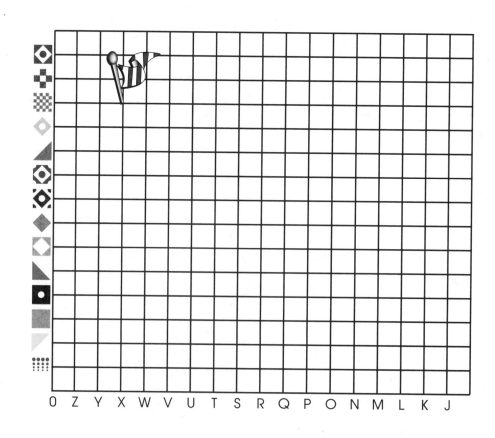

Ordered Pairs

An **ordered pair** is a pair of numbers used to locate a point.

Example: (8, 3)

Step 1: Count across to line 8 on the graph.
Step 2: Count up to line 3 on the graph.
Step 3: Draw a dot to mark the spot.

Map the following spots on the grid using ordered pairs.

(4, 7)   (9, 10)   (2, 1)   (5, 6)   (2, 2)   (1, 5)   (7, 4)   (3, 8)

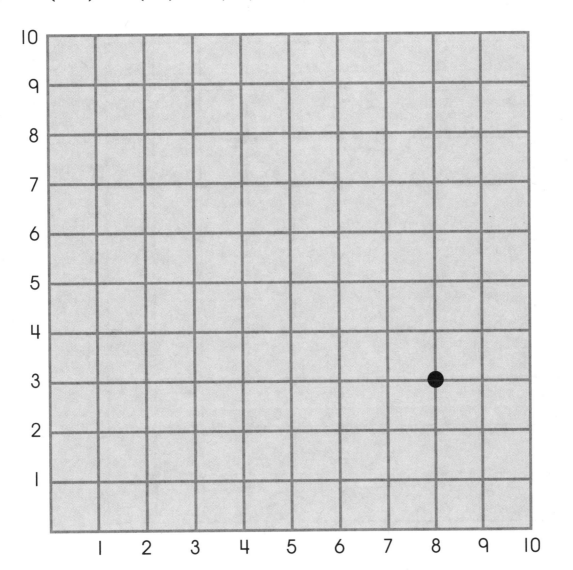

Graphing: Finding Ordered Pairs

Graphs or grids are sometimes used to find the location of objects.

Example: The ice cream cone is located at point (5, 6) on the graph. To find the ice cream's location, follow the line to the bottom of the grid to get the first number — 5. Then go back to the ice cream and follow the grid line to the left for the second number — 6.

Write the ordered pair for the following objects. The first one is done for you.

book __(4, 8)__   bike _____   suitcase _____   house _____

globe _____   cup _____   triangle _____   airplane _____

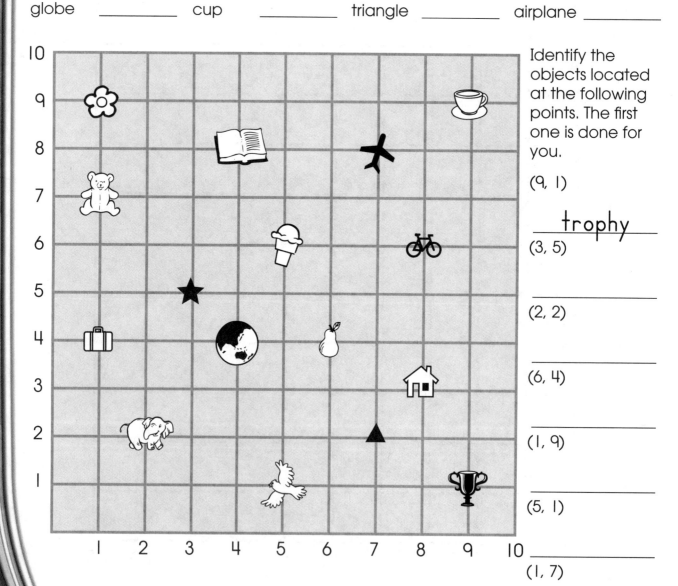

Identify the objects located at the following points. The first one is done for you.

(9, 1)

__trophy__

(3, 5)

_____

(2, 2)

_____

(6, 4)

_____

(1, 9)

_____

(5, 1)

_____

(1, 7)

_____

Week 16 Skills

Subject	Skill	Multi-Sensory Learning Activities
Reading and Language Arts	Understand correct usage of frequently confused words **its** and **it's**; **can** and **may**; **sit** and **set**; **their**, **there**, and **they're**; and **this** and **these**.	• Complete Practice Pages 172–177. • Have your child create a worksheet or crossword puzzle that provides practice for using each of the frequently confused words he or she has learned so far. Encourage your child to share the chart with his or her teacher at school.
Math	Determine the average of a set of numbers.	• Complete Practice Pages 178–180. • Ask your child to choose a set of numbers that he or she would like to know the average for, such as baseball scores, test scores, or temperatures over time. Help him or her compile the numbers to be used in your set and then find the average. • Observe the electric meter just outside your house. Note how the disk spins faster when more electricity is being used. Teach your child how to read the meter in kilowatt hours. Have your child read the meter every day for a week and figure the average daily usage.

Its and It's; Can and May

Choose the correct word for each sentence: **its**, **it's**, **can**, or **may**.

1. "It looks as though your arms are full, Diane. _____ I help
   you with some of those things?" asked Michele.

2. The squirrel _____ climb up the tree quickly with his mouth
   full of acorns.

3. She has had her school jacket so long that it is beginning to lose

   _____ color.

4. How many laps around the track _____ you do?

5. Sometimes you can tell what a story is going to be about by looking at

   _____ title.

6. Our house _____ need to be painted again in two or
   three years.

7. Mother asked, "Jon, _____ you open the door for your
   father?"

8. _____ going to be a while until your birthday, but do you
   know what you want?

9. I can feel it in the air; _____ going
   to snow soon.

10. If I'm careful with it, _____ I borrow
    your CD player?

Sit and Set

The word **sit** means to rest.

Examples: Please **sit** here!
Will you **sit** by me?

The word **set** means to put or place something.

Examples: **Set** your purse there.
Set the dishes on the table.

Write **sit** or **set** to complete the sentences correctly. The first one has been done for you.

_____sit_____ 1. Would you please sit/set down here?

_____ 2. You can sit/set the groceries there.

_____ 3. She sit/set her suitcase in the closet.

_____ 4. He sit/set his watch for half past three.

_____ 5. She's a person who can't sit/set still.

_____ 6. Sit/set the baby on the couch beside me.

_____ 7. Where did you sit/set your new shoes?

_____ 8. They decided to sit/set together during the movie.

_____ 9. Let me sit/set you straight on that!

_____ 10. Instead of swimming, he decided to sit/set in the water.

_____ 11. He sit/set the greasy pan in the sink.

_____ 12. She sit/set the file folder on her desk.

_____ 13. Don't ever sit/set on the refrigerator!

_____ 14. She sit/set the candles on the cake.

They're, Their, There

The word **they're** is a contraction for **they are**.

Examples: **They're** our very best friends!
Ask them if **they're** coming over tomorrow.

The word **their** shows ownership.

Examples: **Their** dog is friendly.
It's **their** bicycle.

The word **there** shows place or direction.

Examples: Look over **there**.
There it is.

Write **they're**, **their**, or **there** to complete the sentences correctly. The first one has been done for you.

There 1. They're/Their/There is the sweater I want!

_____ 2. Do you believe they're/their/there stories?

_____ 3. Be they're/their/there by one o'clock.

_____ 4. Were you they're/their/there last night?

_____ 5. I know they're/their/there going to attend.

_____ 6. Have you met they're/their/there mother?

_____ 7. I can go they're/their/there with you.

_____ 8. Do you like they're/their/there new car?

_____ 9. They're/Their/There friendly to everyone.

_____ 10. Did she say they're/their/there ready to go?

_____ 11. She said she'd walk by they're/their/there house.

_____ 12. Is anyone they're/their/there?

_____ 13. I put it right over they're/their/there!

Sit and Set; They're, Their, There

Choose the correct word for each sentence: **sit**, **set**, **they're**, **there**, or **their**.

1. _____ your pencil on your desk when you finish working.

2. When we choose our seats on the bus will you _____ with me?

3. _____ is my library book! I wondered where I had left it!

4. My little brother and his friend said _____ not going to the ball game with us.

5. Before the test, the teacher wants the students to sharpen _____ pencils.

6. She blew the whistle and shouted, "Everyone _____ down on the floor!"

7. All the books for the fourth graders belong over _____ on the top shelf.

8. The little kittens are beginning to open _____ eyes.

9. I'm going to _____ the dishes on the table.

10. _____ going to be fine by themselves for a few minutes.

This and These

The word **this** is an adjective that refers to things that are near. **This** always describes a singular noun. Singular means one.

Example: I'll buy **this** coat.
(Coat is singular.)

The word **these** is also an adjective that refers to things that are near. **These** always describes a plural noun. A plural refers to more than one thing.

Example: I will buy **these** flowers.
(Flowers is a plural noun.)

Write **this** or **these** to complete the sentences correctly. The first one has been done for you.

_____these_____ 1. I will take this/these cookies with me.

_____ 2. Do you want this/these seeds?

_____ 3. Did you try this/these nuts?

_____ 4. Do it this/these way!

_____ 5. What do you know about this/these situation?

_____ 6. Did you open this/these doors?

_____ 7. Did you open this/these window?

_____ 8. What is the meaning of this/these letters?

_____ 9. Will you carry this/these books for me?

_____ 10. This/These pans are hot!

_____ 11. Do you think this/these light is too bright?

_____ 12. Are this/these boots yours?

_____ 13. Do you like this/these rainy weather?

Review

Complete the sentences by writing the correct words in the blanks.

_____ 1. You have a good/well attitude.

_____ 2. The teacher was not feeling good/well.

_____ 3. She sang extremely good/well.

_____ 4. Everyone said Josh was a good/well boy.

_____ 5. Your/You're going to be sorry for that!

_____ 6. Tell her your/you're serious.

_____ 7. Your/You're report was wonderful!

_____ 8. Your/You're the best person for the job.

_____ 9. Do you think its/it's going to have babies?

_____ 10. Its/It's back paw had a thorn in it.

_____ 11. Its/It's fun to make new friends.

_____ 12. Is its/it's mother always nearby?

_____ 13. How can/may I help you?

_____ 14. You can/may come in now.

_____ 15. Can/May you lift this for me?

_____ 16. She can/may sing soprano.

_____ 17. I'll wait for you to sit/set down first.

_____ 18. We sit/set our dirty boots outside.

_____ 19. It's they're/their/there turn to choose.

_____ 20. They're/Their/There is your answer!

_____ 21. They say they're/their/there coming.

_____ 22. I must have this/these one!

_____ 23. I saw this/these gloves at the store.

_____ 24. He said this/these were his.

Averaging

An **average** is found by adding two or more quantities and dividing by the number of quantities.

Example:

Step 1: Find the sum of the numbers.
24 + 36 + 30 = 90

Step 2: Divide by the number of quantities.
90 ÷ 3 = 30

The average is 30.

Find the average of each group of numbers. Draw a line from each problem to the correct average.

12 + 14 + 29 + 1 =	410
4 + 10 + 25 =	83
33 + 17 + 14 + 20 + 16 =	40
782 + 276 + 172 =	15
81 + 82 + 91 + 78 =	13
21 + 34 + 44 =	33
14 + 24 + 10 + 31 + 5 + 6 =	14
278 + 246 =	20
48 + 32 + 18 + 62 =	262

A baseball player had 3 hits in game one, 2 hits in game two, and 4 hits in game three. How many hits did she average over the three games?

_____

Averaging

Find the averages.

Ted went bowling. He had scores of 112, 124, and 100. What was his average?

_____

Sue ran 3 races. Her times were 9 seconds, 10 seconds, and 8 seconds. What was her average?

_____

The baseball team played 6 games. They had 12 hits, 6 hits, 18 hits, 36 hits, 11 hits, and 7 hits. What is the average number of hits in a game?

_____

In 3 games of football, Chris gained 156, 268, and 176 yards running. How many yards did he average in a game?

_____

Jane scored 18, 15, 26, and 21 points in 4 basketball games. How many points did she average?

_____

Work It Out

The **average** is the result of dividing the **sum** of addends by the **number** of addends. Match the problem with its answer.

1. 80 + 100 + 90 + 95 + 10   _____   A.   53

2. 52 + 56 + 51   _____   B.   190

3. 85 + 80 + 95 + 95 + 100   _____   C.   410

4. 782 + 276 + 172   _____   D.   75

5. 125 + 248 + 214 + 173   _____   E.   91

6. 81 + 82 + 91 + 78   _____   F.   55

7. 40 + 60 + 75 + 45   _____   G.   83

8. 278 + 246   _____   H.   33

9. 75 + 100 + 100 + 70 + 100   _____   I.   3

10. 0 + 0 + 0 + 0 + 15   _____   J.   262

11. 21 + 34 + 44   _____   K.   89

12. 437 + 509 + 864 + 274   _____   L.   94

13. 80 + 80 + 100 + 95 + 95   _____   M.   8

14. 4 + 6 + 7 + 12 + 11   _____   N.   90

15. 75 + 100 + 100 + 100 + 95   _____   O.   521

Week 17 Skills

Subject	Skill	Multi-Sensory Learning Activities
Reading and Language Arts	Review frequently confused words.	• Complete Practice Pages 182 and 183. • Write a paragraph for your child, using some incorrect forms of the frequently confused words he or she has learned. Give the paragraph to your child to see if he or she can spot and correct the mistakes.
	Recognize the two words that form contractions.	• Complete Practice Page 184. • Read *Frindle* by Andrew Clements. Locate a passage that contains several contractions. Have your child identify the contractions and name the two words that make up the contraction.
	Understand and write analogies.	• Complete Practice Pages 185 and 186. • Write analogies on a piece of paper, including antonyms (for example, **backward** is to **forward** as **sit** is to **stand**), synonyms (for example, **touch** is to **poke** as **step** is to **stomp**), and parts to wholes (for example, **toe** is to **foot** as **finger** is to **hand**). Then, ask your child to write his or her own analogies in each category.
Math	Use spinners and coins to determine probability.	• Complete Practice Pages 187–190. • Ask your child to predict what color sock you will pull out of a bag of two red socks and three blue socks. Then, let him or her pull a sock out of the bag. Discuss the result.

Review

Write the correct answers in the blanks using the words in the box.

good	well	your	you're	its
it's	can	may	sit	set
they're	there	their	this	these

1. _____ is an adjective that refers to a particular thing.

2. Use _____ to tell or ask how something is done or to describe someone's health.

3. _____ is a contraction for **it is**.

4. _____ describes a plural noun and refers to particular things.

5. _____ means to rest.

6. _____ means am able to or to be able to.

7. _____ is a contraction for **they are**.

8. _____, _____, and

   _____ show ownership or possession.

9. Use _____ to ask politely to be permitted to do something.

10. _____ is a contraction for **you are**.

11. _____ means to place or put.

12. _____ describes a noun.

13. Use _____ to show direction or placement.

Misused Words

Sometimes people have difficulty using **good**, **well**, **sure**, **surely**, **real**, and **really** correctly. This chart may help you.

Adjectives	Adverbs
Good is an adjective when it describes a noun. That was a **good** dinner.	**Good** is never used as an adverb.

Well is an adjective when it means in good health or having a good appearance.
    She looks **well**.
	Well is an adverb when it is used to tell that something is done capably or effectively.
	    She writes **well**.

Sure is an adjective when it modifies a noun.
    A robin is a **sure** sign of spring.
	Surely is an adverb.
	    He **surely** wants a job.

Real is an adjective that means genuine or true.
    That was a **real** diamond.
	Really is an adverb.
	    Mary **really** played a good game.

Use the chart to help you choose the correct word from those in parentheses. Write it in the blank.

1. You did a very _____ job of writing your book report. (good, well)

2. The detective in the story used his skills _____. (good, well)

3. He _____ solved the case before anyone else did. (sure, surely)

4. I _____ want to read that book now. (real, really)

5. Did it take you long to decide who the _____ criminal was? (real, really)

6. The doctor said the child was _____ and healthy. (well, good)

7. Detective Rains read the clues _____ as he worked on the case. (good, well)

8. You will _____ get a good grade on that report. (surely, sure)

9. You had to _____ work hard to get those good grades. (real, really)

Shortening Words

aren't
couldn't
doesn't
hasn't
he'd
I'd
she's
should've
they'll
wasn't
weren't
what's
who'd
won't
you've

Write each contraction and the two words that form it.

1. _____ _____ _____
2. _____ _____ _____
3. _____ _____ _____
4. _____ _____ _____
5. _____ _____ _____
6. _____ _____ _____
7. _____ _____ _____
8. _____ _____ _____
9. _____ _____ _____
10. _____ _____ _____
11. _____ _____ _____
12. _____ _____ _____
13. _____ _____ _____
14. _____ _____ _____
15. _____ _____ _____

Sometimes a contraction can represent different words. Circle the correct answer in each of the following.

1. In the sentence, "He'd had a cold," the '**d** stands for . . .

   a. would   b. had   c. did

2. In the sentence, "He'd like to go," the '**d** stands for . . .

   a. would   b. had   c. did

3. In the question "Who'd volunteer?" the '**d** stands for . . .

   a. would   b. had   c. did

4. In the question "Who'd you say it was?" the '**d** stands for . . .

   a. would   b. had   c. did

Analogies

An **analogy** indicates how different items go together or are similar in some way.

Examples: **Petal** is to **flower** as **leaf** is to **tree**.
            Book is to **library** as **food** is to **grocery**.

If you study the examples, you will see how the second set of objects is related to the first set. A petal is part of a flower, and a leaf is part of a tree. A book can be found in a library, and food can be found in a grocery store.

Fill in the blanks to complete the analogies. The first one has been done for you.

1. Cup is to saucer as glass is to _____ coaster _____.

2. Paris is to France as London is to _____.

3. Clothes are to hangers as _____ are to boxes.

4. California is to _____ as Ohio is to Lake Erie.

5. _____ is to table as blanket is to bed.

6. Pencil is to paper as _____ is to canvas.

7. Cow is to _____ as child is to house.

8. State is to country as _____ is to state.

9. Governor is to state as _____ is to country.

10. _____ is to ocean as sand is to desert.

11. Engine is to car as hard drive is to _____.

12. Beginning is to _____ as stop is to end.

Write three analogies of your own.

_____

_____

_____

Prize Words

Fill in the blanks. Each word is used only once.

1. **One** is to **once** as **two** is to _____ .

2. **Reverse** is to **forward** as **sit** is to _____ .

3. **Book** is to **library** as **typewriter** is to _____ .

4. **Shiny** is to **dull** as **foolish** is to _____ .

5. **Teacher** is to **education** as **judge** is to _____ .

6. **Illness** is to **doctor** as **crime** is to _____ .

7. **Tag** is to **label** as **cost** is to _____ .

8. **1, 2, 3** is to **count** as **A, B, C** is to _____ .

9. **Imagine** is to **think** as **guess** is to _____ .

10. **Wordy** is to **long-winded** as **brief** is to _____ .

alphabetize	memorize	service
arise	office	surmise
concise	police	surprise
enterprise	price	twice
justice	prize	wise

Use the remaining words from the list to answer each question.

1. What do you usually get when you win a contest? _____

2. What do actors do with their lines? _____

3. What is a risky or important project? _____

4. What is a synonym for "helpfulness"? _____

5. What is a synonym for "astonish"? _____

Spinner Fun

Using what you know about probability, try to predict how many times your spinner would land on the following numbers if you were to spin the spinner 20 times.

Predictions

	Number of Times
Spinning a 1	
Spinning a 2	
Spinning a 3	
Spinning a 4	

Now, actually spin the spinner 20 times and compare your predictions with what you actually spin. Use tally marks to record the number of spins.

Actual Spins

	Number of Times
Spinning a 1	
Spinning a 2	
Spinning a 3	
Spinning a 4	

1. Were your predictions close to the actual? _____

2. What did you notice about your predictions and the actual spinning?

   _____

   _____

3. Why do you think this is? _____

   _____

More Spinner Fun

What is the probability that the arrow will land on . . .

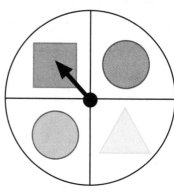

1. a circle?_____

2. a square? _____

3. a triangle?_____

Which shape has the greatest chance (probability) of having the arrow land on it?

_____

Why do you think that? _____

What is the probability that the arrow will land on . . .

1. a shape?_____

2. a number? _____

3. a number or shape? _____

4. a circle?_____

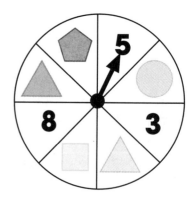

5. a triangle?_____

6. a pentagon? _____

7. a square? _____

8. a three?_____

9. an eight?_____

10. a five?_____

11. a five or eight?_____

Probability

One thinking skill to get your brain in gear is figuring probability. **Probability** is the likelihood or chance that something will happen. Probability is expressed and written as a ratio.

The probability of tossing heads or tails on a coin is one in two (1:2).

The probability of rolling any number on a die is one in six (1:6).

The probability of getting a red on this spinner is two in four (2:4).

The probability of drawing an ace from a deck of cards is four in fifty-two (4:52).

Write the probability ratios to answer these questions.

1. There are 26 letters in the alphabet. What is the probability of drawing any letter from a set of alphabet cards?

   _____

2. Five of the 26 alphabet letters are vowels. What is the probability of drawing a vowel from the alphabet cards?

   _____

3. Matt takes 10 shots at the basketball hoop. Six of his shots are baskets. What is the probability of Matt's next shot being a basket?

   _____

4. A box contains 10 marbles: 2 white, 3 green, 1 red, 2 orange, and 2 blue. What is the probability of pulling a green marble from the box?

   _____

   A red marble?

   _____

5. What is the probability of pulling a marble that is not blue?

   _____

Probability

Write the probability ratios to answer these questions.

1. Using the spinner shown, what is the probability of spinning a 4? _____

2. Using the spinner show, what is the chance of not spinning a 2? _____

3. Using the spinner shown, what is the probability of spinning a 6, 7, or 3? _____

4. What is the probability of getting heads or tails when you toss a coin? _____

Toss a coin 20 times and record the outcome of each toss. Then answer the questions.   _____ Heads   _____ Tails

5. What was the ratio of heads to tails in the 20 tosses? _____

6. Was the outcome of getting heads or tails in the 20 tosses the same as the probability ratio? _____

7. Why or why not? _____

The probability ratio of getting any number on a cube of dice is 1:6.

Toss a die 36 times and record how many times it lands on each number. Then answer the questions.

_____ one   _____ two   _____ three   _____ four   _____ five   _____ six

8. What was the ratio for each number on the die?

_____ one   _____ two   _____ three   _____ four   _____ five   _____ six

9. Did any of the numbers have a ratio close to the actual probability ratio?

_____

10. What do the outcomes of flipping a coin and tossing a die tell you about the probability of an event happening?

_____

COMPLETE YEAR GRADE 4

Week 18 Skills

Subject	Skill	Multi-Sensory Learning Activities
Reading and Language Arts	Recognize words that are spelled the same but have two different meanings.	• Complete Practice Pages 192–195. • List several words that have two different meanings, such as **play**, **fly**, and **duck**. Ask your child to write one sentence for each meaning of the words, then draw a picture to illustrate the sentences.
	Recognize double negatives and understand why they should be avoided.	• Complete Practice Page 196. • List words that are negatives (**not**, **no**, **never**, **none**, **no one**, **nobody**, **nothing**, **nowhere**) and contractions containing a negative such as **can't** (**cannot**), **doesn't** (**does not**), and **won't** (**will not**). Write the following sentences on a piece of paper and discuss the difference: "The store didn't have no paper plates. The store didn't have any paper plates." Then, write several more sentences containing double negatives and ask your child to correct them.
Math	Identify fractions as parts of a whole.	• Complete Practice Pages 197–200. • Model fractions with round candies. Using 12 pieces of candy, have your child divide the candies into two equal groups. What is the fraction symbolized by one group? Both groups? Repeat with thirds, fourths, sixths, and twelfths.

Watch for Grandpa's Watch

Each "watch" in the title of this activity sheet has a different meaning. One means "to look for," and the other means "a timepiece." Write two meanings for the words below.

	Meaning 1	**Meaning 2**
1. spring		
2. run		
3. ruler		
4. duck		
5. suit		
6. cold		
7. fall		
8. tire		
9. rose		
10. face		
11. train		
12. play		
13. foot		
14. pen		
15. box		
16. fly		
17. seal		
18. bowl		
19. ride		
20. line		

Double Trouble

Fill in the blanks with the correct definition number for each bold word.

Example: ____3____ I was covered with **pitch** after climbing the pine tree.

winding	1. having bends or curves
	2. the act of turning something around a central core
wolf	1. to gulp down
	2. a large carnivorous member of the dog family
pitch	1. to sell or persuade
	2. to throw a ball from the mound to the batter
	3. a resin that comes from the sap of pine trees

_____ 1. Do the children's clubs **pitch** cookies?

_____ 2. We are **winding** the top's string tightly.

_____ 3. The adult **wolf** returned to her lair.

_____ 4. Red didn't **pitch** after the fourth inning.

_____ 5. The Mather family had a **winding** driveway.

_____ 6. The young ball player **wolfed** down his lunch.

choke	1. to strangle
	2. to bring the hands up on the bat
hitch	1. obstacle
	2. to fasten or tie temporarily
wind-up	1. the swing of the pitcher's arm just before the pitch
	2. to close or conclude

_____ 1. We **hitched** the mule to the cart.

_____ 2. Skip would not **choke** up on his bat.

_____ 3. Paul wished to play, but there was just one **hitch**.

_____ 4. We wish to **wind-up** our program with more music.

_____ 5. Mom was afraid the dog would **choke** itself on its leash.

_____ 6. He has a great **wind-up** and curve ball.

Book Words

Use a spelling word to replace the bold words in the story. Write the replacement word on the corresponding numbered line below the story.

No Spelling Today

(1) **Throughout the time of** the afternoon Joan sat on a (2) **pad** near the babbling (3) **creek** that meandered through the pasture. She knew she (4) **ought to** have been studying the words for her spelling test, but instead she was doodling on the (5) **stack of paper** on her lap. Across the stream several sheep were grazing. Their soft (6) **fleece** was growing back after the spring shearing. Joan (7) **was able to** hear a chirping wren in the (8) **thicket** nearby. Suddenly, the peaceful scene was disturbed by a (9) **female** calling her name. "Joan, Joan," the voice called out. "Come eat some (10) **custard** I just cooked," continued the loud voice. Joan (11) **realized** she'd dozed off and her mom was calling her to the house. Tucking her list of spelling words under her arm, she walked back home in the late afternoon sun.

brook	notebook	wolf
bush	pudding	woman
could	should	wool
cushion	sugar	would
during	understood	yours

1. _____

2. _____

3. _____

4. _____

5. _____

6. _____

7. _____

8. _____

9. _____

10. _____

11. _____

Write two sentences using two of the four words not used above.

1. _____

2. _____

Weird Words

Use a dictionary to help you answer the questions using complete sentences.

1. Which would you use to treat a sore throat: a **gargoyle** or a **gargle**?

   _____

2. Which might be used on a gravestone: an **epiphyte** or an **epitaph**?

   _____

3. Which is an instrument: **calligraphy** or a **calliope**?

   _____

4. Would a building have a **gargoyle** or an **argyle** on it?

   _____

5. If you trick someone, do you **bamboozle** him or **barcarole** him?

   _____

6. If you studied handwriting, would you learn **calligraphy** or **cajolery**?

   _____

7. What would a gondolier sing: a **barcarole** or an **argyle**?

   _____

8. If you tried to coax someone, would you be using **cajolery** or **calamity**?

   _____

9. Which might you wear: **argyles** or **calliopes**?

   _____

10. In Venice, Italy, would you travel in a **gondola** or a **calamity**?

   _____

Double Negatives

Only use one negative word in a sentence. **Not**, **no**, **never**, and **none** are negative words.

Examples: Incorrect: No one nowhere was sad when it started to snow.
Correct: No one anywhere was sad when it started to snow.

Incorrect: There weren't no icicles hanging from the roof.
Correct: There weren't any icicles hanging from the roof.

Underline the word in parentheses to say no correctly.

1. There wasn't (no, any) snow on our grass this morning.

2. I couldn't find anyone (nowhere, anywhere) who wanted to build a snowman.

3. We couldn't believe that (no one, anyone) wanted to stay inside today with all the beautiful snow outside to play in.

4. We shouldn't ask (anyone, no one) to go ice skating with us.

5. None of the students could think of (nothing, anything) to do at recess except play in the newly fallen snow!

6. No one (never, ever) thought it was a waste of time to go ice skating on the pond.

7. Not a single student skiing (nowhere, anywhere) was unhappy yesterday!

Replace the negative in parentheses.

1. You shouldn't (never) _____ play catch with a snowball unless you like to be covered with snow.

2. Isn't (no one) _____ going to join me outside to eat icicles?

3. There wasn't (nothing) _____ wrong with using the clean, fresh snow to make our fruit drinks.

4. The snowman outside isn't (nowhere) _____ as large as the statue in front of our school.

5. Falling snow isn't (no) _____ fun if you can't go out and play in it.

Fractions

A **fraction** is a number that names part of a whole, such as $\frac{1}{2}$ or $\frac{1}{3}$.

A fraction is made up of two numbers—the **numerator** (top number) and the **denominator** (bottom number). The larger the denominator, the smaller each of the equal parts: $\frac{1}{16}$ is smaller than $\frac{1}{2}$.

Study the fractions below.

I whole.

2 equal parts or halves

One-half of the circle is shaded. $\frac{1}{2}$

3 equal parts or thirds

One-third of the circle is shaded. $\frac{1}{3}$

4 equal parts or fourths

One-fourth of the circle is shaded. $\frac{1}{4}$

5 equal parts or fifths

One-fifth of the circle is shaded. $\frac{1}{5}$

6 equal parts or sixths

One-sixth of the circle is shaded. $\frac{1}{6}$

8 equal parts or eighths

One-eighth of the circle is shaded. $\frac{1}{8}$

10 equal parts or tenths

One-tenth of the circle is shaded. $\frac{1}{10}$

12 equal parts or twelfths

One-twelfth of the circle is shaded. $\frac{1}{12}$

Fractions

Name the fraction that is shaded.

Examples:

3 of 4 equal parts are shaded.

12 of 16 equal parts are shaded.

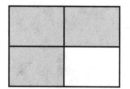

$$\frac{3}{4}$$

$$\frac{12}{16}$$

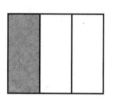

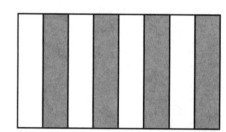

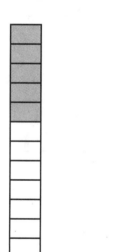

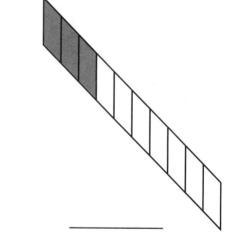

COMPLETE YEAR GRADE 4

What Fraction Am I?

Identify the fraction for each shaded section.

A. _____

B. _____

C. _____

D. _____

E. _____

F. _____

G. _____

H. _____

I. _____

J. _____

K. _____

L. _____

M. _____

Picture the Problem

Use the picture to solve the problem.

1. Andy had two ropes of the same length. He cut one rope into 2 equal parts and gave the 2 halves to Bill. The other rope he cut into fourths and gave 2 of the fourths to Sue. Circle who got the most rope.

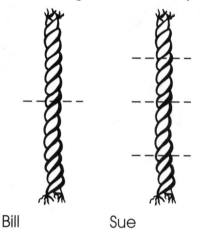

Bill   Sue

2. Henry cut an 8-foot log into 4 equal pieces and burned 2 of them in the fireplace. Joseph cut an 8-foot log into 8 equal pieces and put 3 of them in the fireplace. Circle who put the most wood in the fireplace.

Henry   Joseph

3. Mr. Johns built an office building with an aisle down the middle. He divided one side into 6 equal spaces. He divided the other side into 9 equal spaces. The Ace Company rented 5 of the ninths. The Best Company rented 4 of the sixths. Circle which company rented the larger space.

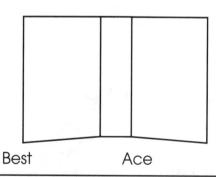

Best   Ace

4. The 4-H Club display area at the state fair was divided into 2 equal areas. One of these sections had 12 booths, the other had 9 booths. The flower display covered 2 of the ninths, and the melon display covered 4 of the twelfths. Circle which display had the most room.

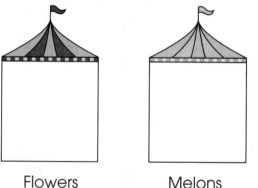

Flowers   Melons

COMPLETE YEAR GRADE 4

Second Quarter Check-Up

Reading and Language Arts

❑ I understand and can use adverbs, or words that describe verbs.

❑ I know synonyms and antonyms.

❑ I understand homophones, or words that sound the same but are spelled differently.

❑ I can recognize up to five-syllable words.

❑ I know how to classify words into similar groupings.

❑ I understand similes, metaphors, and idioms.

❑ I know to use the correct versions of frequently confused words.

❑ I can form contractions.

❑ I understand and can write analogies.

❑ I recognize words that are spelled the same but have two different meanings.

❑ I recognize double negatives and understand why they should be avoided.

Math

❑ I can multiply by powers of 10 and find the missing factor when given one factor and the product.

❑ I can divide two-digit dividends by one-digit divisors, divide with remainders, and divide with two-digit divisors.

❑ I can use multiplication to check answers of division problems.

❑ I can identify missing operations and complete number puzzles.

❑ I can create line graphs and work with ordered pairs.

❑ I can determine the average of a set of numbers.

❑ I can use spinners and coins to determine probability.

❑ I can identify fractions as parts of a whole.

Final Project

Eight planets orbit the Sun. With an adult, research to find the average distance in miles each planet is from the Sun. List the planets in order from the planet closest to the Sun to the one farthest from it. To help you remember the order of the planets, write a sentence using the first letter of each planet. Then, find the average of all planets' distance from the Sun.

Third Quarter Introduction

In the weeks after the winter or mid-year break, students are often ready to tackle new learning challenges. In many classrooms, brand-new concepts and skills are introduced during third quarter that may be difficult for your child. You can help at home by encouraging your child and providing positive learning support using resources found in *Complete Year*.

Third Quarter Skills

Practice pages in this book for Weeks 19–27 will help your child improve the following skills.

Reading and Language Arts
- Understand and identify prefixes and suffixes
- Identify complete sentences, fragments, and run-ons
- Identify simple and compound subjects and predicates
- Identify statements, questions, commands, and exclamations
- Use commas and connecting words to combine sentences
- Answer questions about texts to demonstrate reading comprehension

Math
- Add and subtract fractions
- Compare fractions and understand equivalent fractions
- Read and complete word problems using fractions
- Add and subtract mixed numbers
- Convert fractions to decimals
- Add and subtract decimals
- Build shapes and use tangrams
- Recognize and create patterns
- Identify polygons; lines; line segments; rays; right, acute, and obtuse angles; and the radius and diameter of a circle
- Determine the measurement of each angle in a triangle
- Identify three-dimensional shapes

Multi-Sensory Learning Activities

Try these fun activities for enhancing your child's learning and development during the third quarter of the school year. Be sure to choose activities that include speaking, listening, touching, and active movement.

Reading and Language Arts

Cut a sheet of paper into long strips. On each strip, write a run-on sentence. Ask your child to cut the paper into two to form two complete sentences. Make sure your child adds a period and a capital letter as needed.

Provide examples of sentence fragments and have your child identify what is missing. Then, have him or her turn the fragments into complete sentences.

Find or create 10 riddles. Write the questions from each riddle on index cards or construction paper squares. Omit the question marks. Write the answers from each riddle as complete sentences on different-colored index cards or construction paper squares. Omit the final punctuation. Scramble the cards. Then, ask your child to read the cards and match each question and answer to form the original riddle. He or she should add the final punctuation to each card with a marker or pen.

Ask your child to read an article from today's newspaper. Have him or her find examples of commas being used in compound sentences joined by **and**, **but**, or **or**.

Math

Practice mental fraction math. Say problems for your child to visualize such as "one-sixth plus four-sixths minus three-sixths." Have your child work the problem in his or her head, then state the answer.

Ask your child to draw circles that represent pizzas. How many different ways can the pizzas be divided so that four people would each get an equal number of slices? Have your child write an equivalent fraction to show each person's serving for each pizza drawn.

Ask your child to draw divided shapes to represent two fractions with the same denominator, such as $\frac{2}{3}$ and $\frac{1}{3}$. Your child should be able to see from the drawing which number is greater. Show the fractions in written form next to the models so that your child can see the comparison symbolically. Repeat this process with several different fractions, always comparing two fractions with the same denominator.

Draw base-ten squares for your child. Each 100-box square is

Third Quarter Introduction, cont.

considered a whole. Have your child shade in a given fraction, such as $\frac{70}{100}$. Ask the following questions: Is this fraction more or less than $\frac{1}{2}$? Is it closer to $\frac{1}{2}$ or $\frac{3}{4}$? What are some different ways to say this fraction using tenths and hundredths? Show your child that the quantity (which is less than the whole) can also be written as 0.7 (seven tenths) or 0.70 (seventy hundredths). Repeat this process with another square and a new fraction.

Have your child go "angling." First, divide a large sheet of paper into three columns, labeled **Obtuse**, **Right**, and **Acute**. Set a time limit and physical limits where your child may go. He or she should look for and list every angle he or she sees under the appropriate column. Have your child be specific. For example, if he or she sees a right angle on a table, he or she should not write "the table," but rather, "4 corners of the paint table."

 **Science**

Brainstorm ways that weather affects different people. What jobs depend on certain weather? How does weather affect feelings? Why do people listen to or read weather forecasts? Why do people talk about the weather? Ask how the weather affects your child personally.

 **Social Studies**

Read about the first settlers in your state. Talk about why they settled there. What were the natural resources that attracted them? What was going on in the country as a whole at the time? On large piece of paper, have your child draw a picture of an area of your state that would have been attractive to settlers. Ask your child to draw the area as it might have looked at the time.

 Seasonal Fun

Ask your child to write a short poem using lots of descriptive words about winter. Then, provide some magazines to look through for finding winter scenes. When your child finds an image, have him or her cut it from the magazine. Encourage him or her to cut as close to the outside edge of the object as possible. Then, ask your child to create a collage using the images and the poem.

Week 19 Skills

Subject	Skill	Multi-Sensory Learning Activities
Reading and Language Arts	Understand and identify prefixes and suffixes, or syllables at the beginning and ending of a word that change its meaning.	• Complete Practice Pages 206–210. • Copy the following lists of prefixes and suffixes. Help your child brainstorm a list of words containing these affixes. Prefixes: **anti, astro, auto, bi, con, de, dis, en, ex, fore, hemi, macro, micro, mono, non, pre, pro, re, sub, tri, un, uni**; Suffixes: **ance, en, ent, ese, ess, ful, lon, ish, ist, ite, itis, less, ment, ness, ly**.
Math	Add fractions.	• Complete Practice Pages 211 and 212. • Give your child a set of small objects such as pennies. Ask him or her to model and solve addition problems with fractions. For example, say, "You have 12 cookies to share with three of your friends. How many cookies does each person get? What fraction of the cookies do two friends get?"
	Subtract fractions.	• Complete Practice Pages 213 and 214. • Cut two apples into evenly sized wedges. Have your child model subtraction problems. For example, say, "Show me $\frac{4}{8}$ of the apple. If you eat $\frac{2}{8}$ of the apple, how much do you have left?"

Prefixes

A **prefix** is a syllable at the beginning of a word that changes its meaning.

Add a prefix to the beginning of each word in the box to make a word with the meaning given in each sentence below. The first one is done for you.

PREFIX	MEANING
bi	two or twice
en	to make
in	within
mis	wrong
non	not or without
pre	before
re	again
un	not

grown	information	cycle	school
write	large	usual	sense

1. Jimmy's foot hurt because his toenail was (growing within). __ingrown__

2. If you want to see what is in the background, you will have to (make bigger) the photograph. _____

3. I didn't do a very good job on my homework, so I will have to (write it again) it. _____

4. The newspaper article about the event has some (wrong facts). _____

5. I hope I get a (vehicle with two wheels) for my birthday. _____

6. The story he told was complete (words without meaning)! _____

7. Did you go to (school that comes before kindergarten) before you went to kindergarten? _____

8. The ability to read words upside down is most (not usual). _____

Prefixes

Circle the correct word for each sentence.

1. You will need to _____ the directions before you complete this page.

   reset   reread   repair

2. Since she is allergic to milk products she has to use

   _____ products.

   nondairy   nonsense   nonmetallic

3. That certainly was an _____ costume he selected for the Halloween party.

   untied   unusual   unable

4. The directions on the box said to _____ the oven before baking the brownies.

   preheat   preschool   prevent

5. "I'm sorry if I _____ you as to the cost of the trip," explained the travel agent.

   misdialed   misread   misinformed

6. You may use the overhead projector to _____ the picture so the whole class can see it.

   enlarge   enable   endanger

Suffixes

A **suffix** is a syllable at the end of a word that changes its meaning. In most cases, when adding a suffix that begins with a vowel, drop the final **e** of the root word. For example, **fame** becomes **famous**. Also, change a final **y** in the root word to **i** before adding any suffix except **ing**. For example, **silly** becomes **silliness**.

Add a suffix to the end of each word in the box to make a word with the meaning given (in parentheses) in each sentence below. The first one is done for you.

PREFIX	MEANING
ful	full of
ity	quality or degree
ive	have or tend to be
less	without or lacking
able	able to be
ness	state of
ment	act of
or	person that does something
ward	in the direction of

effect   like   thought   pay   beauty   thank   back   act   happy

1. Mike was (full of thanks) for a hot meal. thankful ___thankful___

2. I was (without thinking) for forgetting your birthday. _____

3. The mouse trap we put out doesn't seem to be (have an effect).

   _____

4. In spring, the flower garden is (full of beauty). _____

5. Sally is such a (able to be liked) girl! _____

6. Tim fell over (in the direction of the back) because he wasn't watching where he was going. _____

7. Jill's wedding day was one of great (the state of being happy).

   _____

8. The (person who performs) was very good in the play. _____

9. I have to make a (act of paying) for the stereo I bought. _____

Suffixes

Read the story. Choose the correct word from the box to complete the sentences.

beautiful	basement	director	backward
breakable	colorful	forward	agreement
careless	careful	payment	firmness

Colleen and Marj carried the boxes down to the _____

apartment. "Be _____ with those," cautioned Colleen's mother. "All

the things in that box are _____." As soon as the two girls helped carry

all the boxes from the moving van down the stairs, they would be able to go to

school for the play tryouts. That was the _____ made with Colleen's

mother earlier that day.

"It won't do any good to get _____ with your work. Just keep at it

and the job will be done quickly," she spoke with a _____ in her voice.

"It's hard to see where I'm going when I have to walk _____,"

groaned Marj. "Can we switch places with the next box?"

Colleen agreed to switch places, but they soon discovered that the last two

boxes were lightweight. Each girl had her own box to carry, so each of them got

to walk looking _____. "These are so light," remarked Marj. "What's in

them?"

"These have the _____, _____ hats I was telling you

about. We can take them to the play tryouts with us," answered Colleen. "I bet

we'll impress the _____. Even if we don't get parts in the play, I bet our

hats will!"

Colleen's mother handed each of the girls a 5-dollar bill. "I really appreciate

your help. Will this be enough?"

"Thanks, Mom. You bet!" Colleen shouted as the girls ran down the sidewalk.

Break It Up!

For each word given below, write the root word and the prefix and/or suffix. Remember, some root words' spellings have been changed before adding suffixes. Not all words will have a prefix and a suffix.

Word	Prefix	Root Word	Suffix
resourceful			
accomplishment			
numbness			
convincing			
merciless			
sturdiest			
disobeying			
unmistakable			
disinfecting			
disclaimed			
reopening			
inventive			
restless			
precaution			
imitating			

Fractions: Addition

When adding fractions with the same denominator, the denominator stays the same. Add only the numerators.

Example: numerator $\quad \dfrac{1}{8} \ + \ \dfrac{2}{8} \ = \ \dfrac{3}{8}$
denominator

Add the fractions on the flowers. Begin in the center of each flower and add each petal. The first one is done for you.

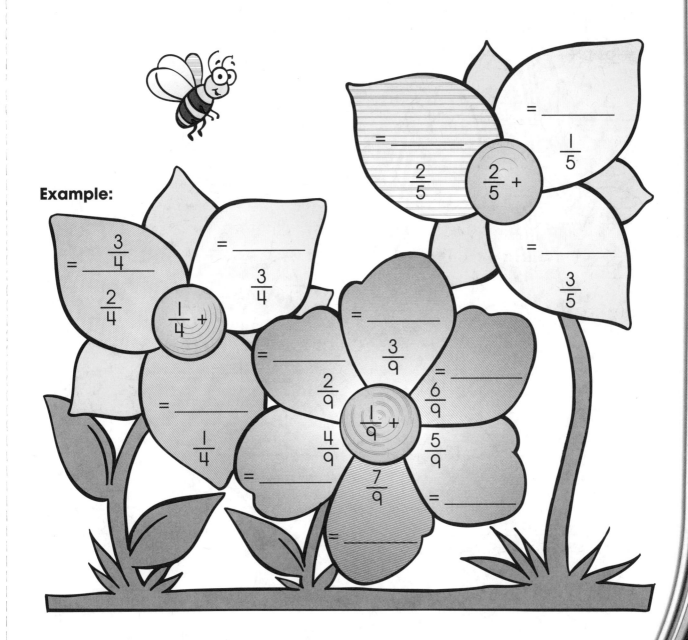

Bubble Math

Reduce each sum to a whole number or a mixed number in lowest terms.

$$\frac{6}{9} + \frac{6}{9}$$

$$\frac{5}{11} + \frac{8}{11}$$

$$\frac{3}{4} + \frac{2}{4}$$

$$\frac{8}{11} + \frac{8}{11}$$

$$\frac{2}{5} + \frac{3}{5}$$

$$\frac{4}{5} + \frac{6}{5}$$

$$\frac{5}{7} + \frac{6}{7}$$

$$\frac{5}{9} + \frac{5}{9}$$

$$\frac{8}{9} + \frac{3}{9}$$

$$\frac{2}{4} + \frac{2}{4}$$

$$\frac{4}{8} + \frac{4}{8}$$

$$\frac{4}{8} + \frac{6}{8}$$

$$\frac{5}{4} + \frac{2}{4}$$

$$\frac{3}{9} + \frac{7}{9}$$

$$\frac{3}{12} + \frac{10}{12}$$

$$\frac{6}{8} + \frac{6}{8}$$

$$\frac{3}{6} + \frac{3}{6}$$

$$\frac{8}{11} + \frac{3}{11}$$

$$\frac{7}{11} + \frac{7}{11}$$

$$\frac{13}{16} + \frac{7}{16}$$

$$\frac{7}{14} + \frac{8}{14}$$

$$\frac{6}{12} + \frac{8}{12}$$

$$\frac{4}{3} + \frac{2}{3}$$

$$\frac{5}{7} + \frac{6}{7}$$

$$\frac{8}{15} + \frac{14}{15}$$

$$\frac{4}{11} + \frac{9}{11}$$

$$\frac{7}{13} + \frac{6}{13}$$

Soap

$$\frac{7}{12} + \frac{7}{12}$$

$$\frac{5}{12} + \frac{10}{12}$$

$$\frac{5}{12} + \frac{8}{12}$$

Fractions: Subtraction

When subtracting fractions with the same denominator, the denominator stays the same. Subtract only the numerators.

Solve the problems, working from left to right. As you find each answer, copy the letter from the key into the numbered blanks. The answer is the name of a famous American. The first one is done for you.

1. $\frac{3}{8} - \frac{2}{8} = \frac{1}{8}$

2. $\frac{2}{4} - \frac{1}{4} = $ ___

3. $\frac{5}{9} - \frac{3}{9} = $ ___

4. $\frac{2}{3} - \frac{1}{3} = $ ___

5. $\frac{8}{12} - \frac{7}{12} = $ ___

6. $\frac{4}{5} - \frac{1}{5} = $ ___

7. $\frac{6}{12} - \frac{3}{12} = $ ___

8. $\frac{4}{9} - \frac{1}{9} = $ ___

9. $\frac{11}{12} - \frac{7}{12} = $ ___

10. $\frac{7}{8} - \frac{3}{8} = $ ___

11. $\frac{4}{7} - \frac{2}{7} = $ ___

12. $\frac{14}{16} - \frac{7}{16} = $ ___

13. $\frac{18}{20} - \frac{13}{20} = $ ___

14. $\frac{13}{15} - \frac{2}{15} = $ ___

15. $\frac{5}{6} - \frac{3}{6} = $ ___

Key:
T $\frac{1}{8}$ P $\frac{5}{24}$ H $\frac{1}{4}$
F $\frac{4}{12}$ E $\frac{2}{7}$ J $\frac{3}{12}$
E $\frac{3}{9}$ O $\frac{2}{9}$ F $\frac{4}{8}$
R $\frac{7}{16}$ O $\frac{2}{8}$ Y $\frac{8}{20}$
Q $\frac{1}{32}$ M $\frac{1}{3}$ S $\frac{5}{20}$
A $\frac{1}{12}$ R $\frac{12}{15}$ S $\frac{3}{5}$
H $\frac{2}{6}$ O $\frac{11}{15}$

Who helped write the Declaration of Independence?

T __ __ __ __ __
1 2 3 4 5 6

__ __ __ __ __ __ __ __ __
7 8 9 10 11 12 13 14 15

Crazy Quilts

Toni and her mother made a crazy quilt. It doesn't have a set pattern; the pieces are many colors and sizes. Read each story problem. Circle the correct problem, and write the answer on the line.

1. Toni had $\frac{6}{8}$ of a yard of yellow gingham. She used $\frac{3}{8}$ of a yard to make two triangles for the quilt. How much yellow gingham did she have left?

   $$\frac{3}{8} - \frac{2}{8} \qquad \frac{6}{8} - \frac{3}{8} \qquad \frac{6}{8} + \frac{2}{8}$$ _____

2. Toni's mother found $\frac{5}{10}$ of a yard of red velvet material. She made a rectangle from $\frac{2}{10}$ of a yard. How much red velvet did she have left?

   $$\frac{5}{10} - \frac{2}{10} \qquad \frac{5}{10} + \frac{2}{10} \qquad \frac{5}{10} + \frac{5}{10}$$ _____

3. Mother and Toni liked to sew black satin between the red and yellow pieces. They had $\frac{3}{4}$ of a yard of black satin. They used $\frac{1}{4}$ of a yard to place between the red and yellow pieces. How much black satin did they have left?

   $$\frac{3}{4} - \frac{1}{4} \qquad \frac{3}{4} - \frac{3}{4} \qquad \frac{2}{4} + \frac{3}{4}$$ _____

4. Toni had $\frac{2}{3}$ of an hour before her piano lesson. She wanted to make one more blue piece. It took her $\frac{1}{3}$ of an hour to make the blue piece. What fraction of an hour did she have left to get ready for her piano lesson?

   $$\frac{1}{3} + \frac{1}{3} \qquad \frac{2}{3} - \frac{1}{3} \qquad \frac{2}{4} + \frac{3}{4}$$ _____

5. Mother and Toni finished $\frac{4}{8}$ of the quilt. Toni did $\frac{1}{8}$ of it herself. How much did Mother do?

   $$\frac{1}{8} + \frac{4}{8} \qquad \frac{3}{8} + \frac{4}{8} \qquad \frac{4}{8} - \frac{1}{8}$$ _____

6. Toni and her mother wanted to give the quilt to Grandmother for her birthday. They used purple cotton to make the edging. They had $\frac{6}{8}$ of a yard of the purple cloth. They used $\frac{5}{8}$ of a yard to make the edging. How much purple cloth did they have left?

   $$\frac{6}{8} + \frac{5}{8} \qquad \frac{6}{8} - \frac{5}{9} \qquad \frac{6}{8} - \frac{5}{8}$$ _____

Week 20 Skills

Subject	Skill	Multi-Sensory Learning Activities
Reading and Language Arts	Review prefixes and suffixes.	• Complete Practice Pages 216–220. • Read *Pippi Longstocking* by Astrid Lindgren. Read words that contain prefixes and suffixes and discuss the meaning of each. Recognizing affixes will help your child decode unfamiliar words.
Math	Compare fractions as greater than or less than.	• Complete Practice Page 221. • Ask your child if he or she would rather have $\frac{2}{10}$ or $\frac{2}{6}$ of a favorite candy bar. Ask for an explanation to assess your child's understanding. Then, use two candy bars to show $\frac{2}{10}$ and $\frac{2}{6}$ and give your child the fraction he or she chose.
	Understand equivalent fractions.	• Complete Practice Pages 222 and 223. • Make two sets of fraction flash cards. On the first deck, write one fraction per card. On the second deck, write an equivalent fraction for each fraction of the first deck. Then, hide cards from the second deck around your home. Hold up one flash card for your child and encourage him or her to find the card with the equivalent fraction.
	Read and complete word problems using fractions.	• Complete Practice Page 224. • Find a recipe that uses fractions. Read the recipe together. Follow the recipe to make the food.

The Beginning

Add a prefix to each word in the list to make a new word. Write the new word on the trunk that has that prefix.

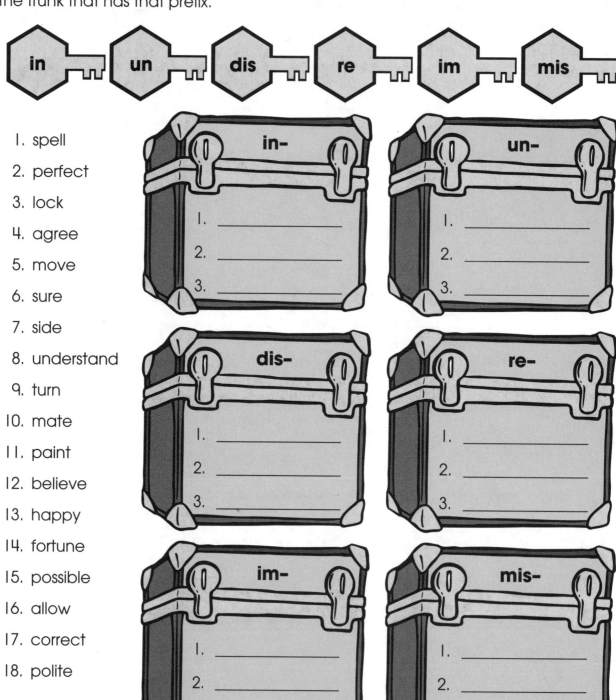

1. spell
2. perfect
3. lock
4. agree
5. move
6. sure
7. side
8. understand
9. turn
10. mate
11. paint
12. believe
13. happy
14. fortune
15. possible
16. allow
17. correct
18. polite

in-
1. _____
2. _____
3. _____

un-
1. _____
2. _____
3. _____

dis-
1. _____
2. _____
3. _____

re-
1. _____
2. _____
3. _____

im-
1. _____
2. _____
3. _____

mis-
1. _____
2. _____
3. _____

The End

Add a suffix from the box to each word in parentheses to make a new word. The new word must make sense in the sentence. Write the new word in the blank.

ly	less	ion
ful	ing	ed

1. The snow fell _____ and covered the trees.
   (quick)

2. We _____ our dog Duke to roll over.
   (train)

3. It's fun to go _____ in a tent.
   (camp)

4. Who will be running for president in the next _____?
   (elect)

5. Be extra _____ with that knife.
   (care)

6. My mom was so excited that she was _____.
   (speech)

7. We _____ for hours but caught nothing.
   (fish)

8. It is my _____ that it will rain tomorrow.
   (predict)

9. Jack is _____ on a hunting trip.
   (go)

10. Grandma's homemade chocolate cake tastes _____.
    (wonder)

11. The opera star sang _____.
    (loud)

Fore and Aft

Fill in the blanks with the appropriate affixes. Some will be used more than once.

Prefixes: dis im re un mis   Suffixes: ful ish ist less ly ness ward

Meaning	Root Word + Affix	New Word
1. having no fear	fear __ __ __ __	_____
2. to vanish	__ __ __ appear	_____
3. toward a lower level	down __ __ __ __	_____
4. having no friends	friend __ __ __ __	_____
5. an error in action	__ __ __ take	_____
6. to enter again	__ __ enter	_____
7. too many to count	count __ __ __ __	_____
8. not happy	__ __ happy	_____
9. perfection seeker	perfection __ __ __	_____
10. quality of being dark	dark __ __ __ __	_____
11. not possible	__ __ possible	_____
12. having doubts	doubt __ __ __	_____
13. without a care	care __ __ __ __	_____
14. sad from being alone	lone __ __	_____
15. not thinking	__ __ thinking	_____
16. without shoes	shoe __ __ __ __	_____
17. in a mysterious way	mysterious __ __	_____
18. appear again	__ __ appear	_____
19. in a quiet manner	quiet __ __	_____
20. call by wrong name	__ __ __ call	_____
21. somewhat yellow	yellow __ __ __	_____
22. cautious	care __ __ __	_____
23. to release	__ __ __ engage	_____

Using Prefixes

prearrange
predict
preface
prepay
preview
reappear
rebuild
recover
redecorate
refill
reform
reload
remodel
repaint
restore

Fill in the blanks.

1. After the tornado destroyed the barn, the neighbors helped us _____.

2. If you try to guess what a story is about by looking at the pictures, you are trying to _____.

3. When Dad decided to _____ the family room he had to tear down walls and install new windows.

4. My folks selected new wallpaper and drapes when they decided to _____.

5. You have to _____ the photographer for your school pictures before he will take them.

6. We had to _____ the chair because my cat clawed the fabric.

7. It's difficult to _____ a bicycle to its original condition if a truck runs over it.

8. The room parents worked with the teacher to _____ the details of the field trip.

9. We helped to _____ the ice-cream machine when it ran out of ingredients.

10. The _____ of the book gives an introduction.

11. The magician hid the coin and then made it _____.

12. I was so thirsty that I asked for a _____ of lemonade.

13. When my brother's new car got scratched, he wanted to _____ it immediately.

14. Before watching the afternoon movie, we saw a _____ of coming attractions.

15. My clay project in art class started to fall apart, so I had to _____ it.

A Little More

Draw a box around the root part of each word below.

1. moved	3. pushes	5. invited	7. jumpy	9. slapped
2. finally	4. reported	6. softly	8. privately	10. parents

Circle all the prefixes and suffixes in the words below.

1. signed	3. bushes	5. invisible	7. thinking	9. Saturdays
2. handful	4. asleep	6. running	8. wooden	10. spying

Add a prefix or suffix to each word below to make a new word. The new word may be one already used on this worksheet.

1. _____ report _____

2. _____ visible _____

3. _____ wood _____

4. _____ soft _____

5. _____ run _____

6. _____ jump _____

Circle the words that have prefixes.

1. He will recover by next week.

2. Go ahead and say what you're thinking.

3. It's not always easy to fall asleep.

4. Iggie's house was almost invisible through the trees.

Circle the words that have suffixes.

1. Winnie went running toward her house.

2. The treehouse floor was made of wooden planks.

3. Her binoculars were really powerful.

4. Glenn's voice was whispery as he read the sign.

A Little More

Compare the fractions below. Use **>**, **<**, and **=**.

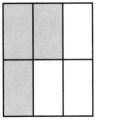 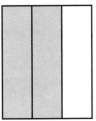 $\frac{3}{6}$ ◯ $\frac{2}{3}$

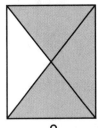  $\frac{3}{4}$ ◯ $\frac{3}{4}$

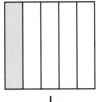 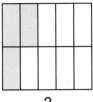 $\frac{1}{5}$ ◯ $\frac{3}{10}$

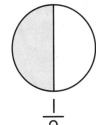 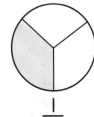 $\frac{1}{2}$ ◯ $\frac{1}{3}$

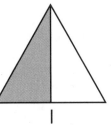 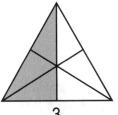 $\frac{1}{2}$ ◯ $\frac{3}{6}$

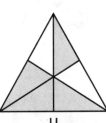 $\frac{4}{6}$ ◯ $\frac{4}{6}$

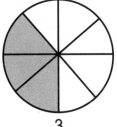 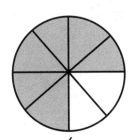 $\frac{3}{8}$ ◯ $\frac{6}{8}$

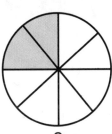 $\frac{3}{8}$ ◯ $\frac{2}{8}$

 $\frac{3}{4}$ ◯  $\frac{1}{2}$

Equivalent Fractions

Equivalent fractions are two different fractions that represent the same number.

Example: $\dfrac{1}{2}$ = $\dfrac{3}{6}$

Complete these equivalent fractions.

$\dfrac{1}{3} = \dfrac{}{6}$ $\dfrac{1}{2} = \dfrac{}{4}$ $\dfrac{3}{4} = \dfrac{}{8}$ $\dfrac{1}{3} = \dfrac{}{9}$

Circle the figures that show a fraction equivalent to figure a. Write the fraction for the shaded area under each figure.

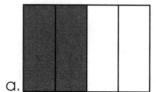   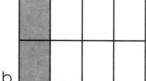   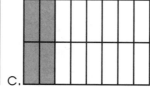   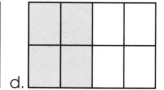

a. _____   b. _____   c. _____   d. _____

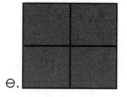   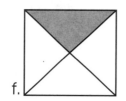   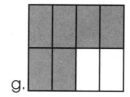   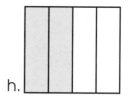

e. _____   f. _____   g. _____   h. _____

To find an equivalent fraction, multiply both parts of the fraction by the same number.

Example: $\dfrac{2}{3} \times \dfrac{3}{3} = \dfrac{6}{9}$

Find an equivalent fraction.

$\dfrac{1}{4} = \dfrac{}{8}$ $\dfrac{3}{4} = \dfrac{}{16}$ $\dfrac{4}{5} = \dfrac{8}{}$ $\dfrac{3}{8} = \dfrac{}{24}$

Match the Fractions

Above each bar, write a fraction for the shaded part. Then, match each fraction on the left with its equivalent fraction on the right.

1. _____

a. _____

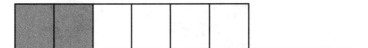

2. _____

b. _____

3. _____

c. _____

4. _____

d. _____

5. _____

e. _____

6. _____

f. _____

7. _____

g. _____

The Mystery of the Missing Sweets

Some mysterious person is sneaking away with pieces of desserts from Sam Sillicook's Diner. Help him figure out how much is missing.

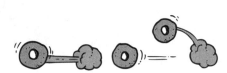

1. What fraction of Sam's Super Sweet Chocolate Cream Cake is missing?

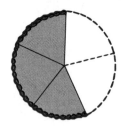

_____

2. What fraction of Sam's Tastee Toffee Coffee Cake is missing?

_____

3. What fraction of Sam's Tasty Tidbits of Chocolate Ice Cream is missing?

_____

4. What fraction of Sam's Heavenly Tasting Cherry Cream Tart is missing?

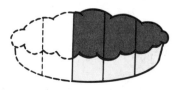

_____

5. Sam's Upside-Down Ice-Cream Cake is very famous. What fraction has vanished?

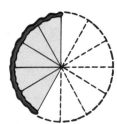

_____

6. What fraction of Sam's Luscious Licorice Candy Cake is missing?

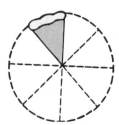

_____

Week 21 Skills

Subject	Skill	Multi-Sensory Learning Activities
Reading and Language Arts	Identify complete sentences, fragments, and run-ons.	• Complete Practice Pages 226–228. • Use your imagination to tell a story with your child. The two of you should go back and forth supplying part of a sentence. The trick is to identify when to add a period to the sentence. For example, your child might say, "Once upon a time…" and then you say, "…there lived a fairy princess." Then, your child should say "period" to avoid a run-on sentence.
	Identify sentence subjects, or nouns or pronouns that tell who or what a sentence is about.	• Complete Practice Page 229. • Have your child write 10 original sentences about zoo animals, then underline the complete subject in each.
	Identify sentence predicates, or verbs that tell what the subject does.	• Complete Practice Page 230. • Find one of your child's favorite picture books from when he or she was younger. Read a few sentences and ask your child to name the predicate of each.
Math	Add and subtract mixed numbers.	• Complete Practice Pages 231–234. • Ask your child to name three items he or she would like to receive as birthday gifts. Have your child research the price of each, round it to the nearest ten cents, and write it as a mixed number (for example, $12.68 = 12\frac{7}{10}$). What is the sum of the prices?

Sentences

A **sentence** is a group of words that expresses a complete thought.

Write **S** by each group of words that is a sentence and **NS** by those that are not a complete sentence.

Examples:

__NS__   A pinch of salt in the soup.

__S__   Grandmother was fond of her flower garden.

_____ 1. Tigers blend in with their surroundings.

_____ 2. Our crop of vegetables for this summer.

_____ 3. Don't forget to put the plug in the sink.

_____ 4. Usually older people in good health.

_____ 5. Fond of lying in the sun for hours.

_____ 6. Will ducks hatch a swan egg?

_____ 7. I hope he won't insist on coming with us.

_____ 8. Regular exercise will pump up your muscles.

_____ 9. A fact printed in all the newspapers.

_____ 10. Did you pinch the baby?

_____ 11. Plug the hole with your finger.

_____ 12. A new teacher today in health class.

_____ 13. I insist on giving you some of my candy.

_____ 14. A blend of peanut butter and honey.

_____ 15. As many facts as possible in your report.

Run-On Sentences

A **sentence** expresses a clear thought. But if two or more sentences are written together without punctuation, their meaning is confusing. This is called a **run-on sentence**.

Example: The artist has painted twenty portraits the paintings will be displayed in the new museum.
The artist has painted twenty portraits.
The paintings will be displayed in the new museum.

Read each diary entry below. Rewrite each run-on sentence as two or more good sentences.

Dear Diary,
    After lunch we went to the animal shelter the cages were full of adorable pets to adopt we chose a frisky two-year-old brown dog.

_____

_____

_____

_____

Dear Diary,
    While we were on our field trip my friend, Joe, found an animal fossil Mrs. Roberts is taking it to the university tomorrow.

_____

_____

_____

_____

Run-On Sentences

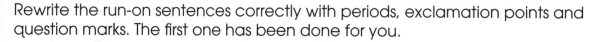

A **run-on sentence** occurs when two or more sentences are joined together without punctuation.

Examples: **Run-on sentence:** I lost my way once did you?
Two sentences with correct punctuation: I lost my way once. Did you?
Run-on sentence: I found the recipe it was not hard to follow.
Two sentences with correct punctuation: I found the recipe. It was not hard to follow.

Rewrite the run-on sentences correctly with periods, exclamation points and question marks. The first one has been done for you.

1. Did you take my umbrella I can't find it anywhere!

   <u>Did you take my umbrella? I can't find it anywhere!</u>

2. How can you stand that noise I can't!

   _____

3. The cookies are gone I see only crumbs.

   _____

4. The dogs were barking they were hungry.

   _____

5. She is quite ill please call a doctor immediately!

   _____

6. The clouds came up we knew the storm would hit soon.

   _____

7. You weren't home he stopped by this morning.

   _____

Subjects

The **subject** of a sentence tells you who or what the sentence is about. A subject is either a common noun, a proper noun or a pronoun.

Examples: Sue went to the store.
Sue is the subject of the sentence.

The tired boys and girls walked home slowly.
The tired boys and girls is the subject of the sentence.

Underline the subject of each sentence. The first one has been done for you.

1. The birthday cake was pink and white.

2. Anthony celebrated his fourth birthday.

3. The tower of building blocks fell over.

4. On Saturday, our family will go to a movie.

5. The busy editor was writing sentences.

6. Seven children painted pictures.

7. Two happy dolphins played cheerfully on the surf.

8. A sand crab buried itself in the dunes.

9. Blue waves ran peacefully ashore.

10. Sleepily, she went to bed.

Write a subject for each sentence.

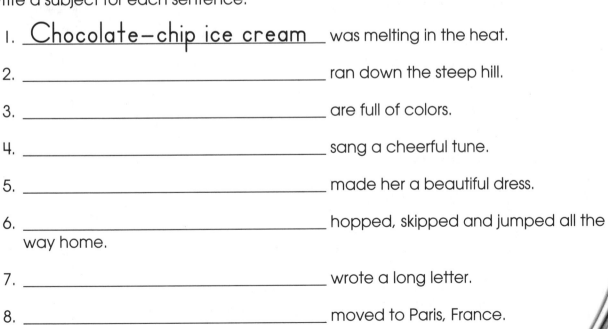

1. Chocolate-chip ice cream was melting in the heat.

2. _____ ran down the steep hill.

3. _____ are full of colors.

4. _____ sang a cheerful tune.

5. _____ made her a beautiful dress.

6. _____ hopped, skipped and jumped all the way home.

7. _____ wrote a long letter.

8. _____ moved to Paris, France.

Predicates

The **predicate** of a sentence tells what the subject is doing. The predicate contains the action, linking and/or helping verb.

Examples: Sue went to the store.
Went to the store is the predicate.

The tired boys and girls walked home slowly.
Walked home slowly is the predicate.

Hint: When identifying the predicate, look for the verb. The verb is usually the first word of the predicate.

Underline the predicate in each sentence with two lines. The first one has been done for you.

1. The choir sang joyfully.

2. Their song had both high and low notes.

3. Sal played the piano while they sang.

4. This Sunday the orchestra will have a concert in the park.

5. John is working hard on his homework.

6. He will write a report on electricity.

7. The report will tell about Ben Franklin's kite experiment.

8. Jackie, Mary and Amy played on the swings.

9. They also climbed the rope ladder.

10. Before the girls went home, they slid down the slide.

Write a predicate for each sentence.

1. Sam and Libby_____.

2. At school, the children _____.

3. The football team _____.

4. Seven silly serpents _____.

5. At the zoo, the animals _____.

Fractions: Mixed Numbers

A **mixed number** is a number written as a whole number and a fraction, such as $6\frac{5}{8}$.

To change a fraction into a mixed number, divide the denominator (bottom number) into the numerator (top number). Write the remainder over the denominator.

Example:

$$\frac{14}{6} = 2\frac{2}{6}$$

$$6\overline{)14} \quad \begin{array}{r} 2 \ R2 \\ \end{array}$$
$$\underline{-12}$$
$$2$$

To change a mixed number into a fraction, multiply the denominator by the whole number, add the numerator and write it on top of the denominator.

Example:

$$3\frac{1}{7} = \frac{22}{7} \quad (7 \times 3) + 1 = \frac{22}{7}$$

Write each fraction as a mixed number. Write each mixed number as a fraction.

$\frac{21}{6} = $ _____ $\frac{24}{5} = $ _____ $\frac{10}{3} = $ _____ $\frac{21}{4} = $ _____

$\frac{11}{6} = $ _____ $\frac{13}{4} = $ _____ $\frac{12}{5} = $ _____ $\frac{10}{9} = $ _____

$4\frac{3}{8} = \dfrac{\Box}{8}$ $2\frac{1}{3} = \dfrac{\Box}{3}$ $4\frac{3}{5} = \dfrac{\Box}{5}$ $3\frac{4}{6} = \dfrac{\Box}{6}$

$7\frac{1}{4} = \dfrac{\Box}{4}$ $2\frac{3}{5} = \dfrac{\Box}{5}$ $7\frac{1}{2} = \dfrac{\Box}{2}$ $6\frac{5}{7} = \dfrac{\Box}{7}$

$\frac{11}{8} = $ _____ $\frac{21}{4} = $ _____ $\frac{33}{5} = $ _____ $\frac{13}{6} = $ _____

$\frac{23}{7} = $ _____ $8\frac{1}{3} = $ _____ $9\frac{3}{7} = $ _____ $\frac{32}{24} = $ _____

Fractions: Adding Mixed Numbers

When adding mixed numbers, add the fractions first, then the whole numbers.

Examples:

$$9\frac{1}{3}$$
$$+3\frac{1}{3}$$
$$\overline{12\frac{2}{3}}$$

$$2\frac{3}{6}$$
$$+1\frac{1}{6}$$
$$\overline{3\frac{4}{6}}$$

Add the number in the center to the number in each surrounding section.

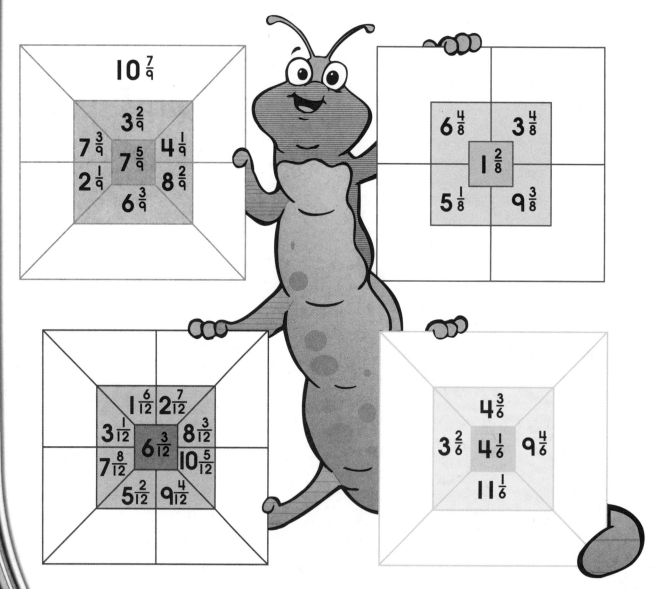

Square 1 (center $7\frac{5}{9}$):
- $10\frac{7}{9}$
- $3\frac{2}{9}$
- $7\frac{3}{9}$
- $4\frac{1}{9}$
- $2\frac{1}{9}$
- $8\frac{2}{9}$
- $6\frac{3}{9}$

Square 2 (center $1\frac{2}{8}$):
- $6\frac{4}{8}$
- $3\frac{4}{8}$
- $5\frac{1}{8}$
- $9\frac{3}{8}$

Square 3 (center $6\frac{3}{12}$):
- $1\frac{6}{12}$
- $2\frac{7}{12}$
- $3\frac{1}{12}$
- $8\frac{3}{12}$
- $7\frac{8}{12}$
- $10\frac{5}{12}$
- $5\frac{2}{12}$
- $9\frac{4}{12}$

Square 4 (center $4\frac{1}{6}$):
- $4\frac{3}{6}$
- $3\frac{2}{6}$
- $9\frac{4}{6}$
- $11\frac{1}{6}$

Fractions: Subtracting Mixed Numbers

When subtracting mixed numbers, subtract the fractions first, then the whole numbers.

Subtract the mixed numbers. The first one is done for you.

$$7\frac{3}{8}$$
$$-4\frac{2}{8}$$
$$\overline{3\frac{1}{8}}$$

$$4\frac{5}{6}$$
$$-3\frac{1}{6}$$

$$4\frac{1}{2}$$
$$-3$$

$$7\frac{5}{8}$$
$$-6\frac{3}{8}$$

$$6\frac{6}{8}$$
$$-1\frac{1}{8}$$

$$5\frac{3}{4}$$
$$-1\frac{1}{4}$$

$$5\frac{2}{3}$$
$$-3\frac{1}{3}$$

$$4\frac{8}{10}$$
$$-3\frac{3}{10}$$

$$9\frac{8}{9}$$
$$-4\frac{3}{9}$$

$$7\frac{2}{3}$$
$$-6\frac{1}{3}$$

$$7\frac{2}{3}$$
$$-5$$

$$9\frac{8}{10}$$
$$-6\frac{3}{10}$$

$$4\frac{7}{9}$$
$$-2$$

$$6\frac{7}{8}$$
$$-5\frac{3}{8}$$

$$6\frac{3}{4}$$
$$-3\frac{1}{4}$$

$$5\frac{6}{7}$$
$$-3\frac{1}{7}$$

$$7\frac{6}{7}$$
$$-2\frac{4}{7}$$

Sally needs $1\frac{3}{8}$ yards of cloth to make a dress. She has $4\frac{5}{8}$ yards. How much cloth will be left over?

_____

Review

Add or subtract the fractions and mixed numbers. Reduce, if possible.

$$4\frac{7}{8} \qquad 8\frac{3}{9} \qquad 3\frac{1}{8} \qquad 4\frac{5}{6} \qquad 7\frac{5}{11}$$
$$-2\frac{5}{8} \qquad +2\frac{5}{9} \qquad +1\frac{3}{8} \qquad -3\frac{1}{6} \qquad +3\frac{3}{11}$$

$\dfrac{4}{12} + \dfrac{3}{12} = $ _____ $\dfrac{3}{5} + \dfrac{1}{5} = $ _____

$\dfrac{3}{8} - \dfrac{1}{8} = $ _____ $\dfrac{3}{9} + \dfrac{1}{9} = $ _____

$\dfrac{3}{4} - \dfrac{2}{4} = $ _____

Reduce the fractions.

$\dfrac{4}{6} = $ _____ $\dfrac{7}{21} = $ _____

$\dfrac{9}{12} = $ _____ $\dfrac{2}{4} = $ _____

$\dfrac{6}{24} = $ _____ $\dfrac{8}{32} = $ _____

Change the mixed numbers to fractions and the fractions to mixed numbers.

$3\dfrac{1}{3} = \dfrac{\boxed{}}{3}$ $\dfrac{14}{4} = $ _____ $\dfrac{26}{6} = $ _____ $3\dfrac{7}{12} = \dfrac{\boxed{}}{12}$ $\dfrac{22}{7} = $ _____

Week 22 Skills

Subject	Skill	Multi-Sensory Learning Activities
Reading and Language Arts	Review subjects and predicates.	• Complete Practice Pages 236–240. • Write a sentence on a piece of paper, such as "The porcupine makes its home in many parts of the world." Have your child draw a line dividing the subject from the predicate in each sentence you write.
Math	Convert fractions to decimals.	• Complete Practice Pages 241–243. • Place a meter stick on top of a long sheet of butcher paper. Have your child think of the meter stick as one whole. Then, have him or her divide the meter stick into tenths, making marks on the paper. Have your child write the tenths as $\frac{1}{10}$ and 0.1, $\frac{2}{10}$ and 0.2, and so on. Repeat this process with hundredths.
	Add and subtract decimals.	• Complete Practice Page 244. • Shuffle a deck of playing cards, with face cards and 10s removed. Write the decimals **0.01**, **0.1**, and **1.0** on the sides of three small boxes, one number per box. Ask your child to throw three cards into the boxes. For each card that makes it inside a box, multiply it by the value of the box. For example, if a 3 is thrown into the 0.01 box, your child would receive 0.03 points. After 10 rounds, ask your child to add up his or her total score.

Changing the Predicate

Circle the predicate in each sentence. Change the predicate to make a new sentence. The words you add must make sense with the rest of the sentence. The first one has been done for you.

1. Twelve students (signed up for the student council elections.)

   Twelve students were absent from my class today!

2. Our whole family went to the science museum last week.

   _____

   _____

3. The funny story made us laugh.

   _____

   _____

4. The brightly colored kites drifted lazily across the sky.

   _____

   _____

5. My little brother and sister spent the whole day at the amusement park.

   _____

   _____

6. The tiny sparrow made a tapping sound at my window.

   _____

   _____

Subjects and Predicates

The **subject** tells who or what the sentence is about. The **predicate** tells what the subject does, did, is doing, or will do. A complete sentence must have a subject and a predicate.

Examples:	**Subject**	**Predicate**
	Sharon	writes to her grandmother every week.
	The horse	ran around the track quickly.
	My mom's car	is bright green.
	Denise	will be here after lunch.

Circle the subject of each sentence. Underline the predicate.

1. My sister is a very happy person.

2. I wish we had more holidays in the year.

3. Laura is one of the nicest girls in our class.

4. John is fun to have as a friend.

5. The rain nearly ruined our picnic!

6. My birthday present was exactly what I wanted.

7. Your bicycle is parked beside my skateboard.

8. The printer will need to be filled with paper before you use it.

9. Six dogs chased my cat home yesterday!

10. Anthony likes to read anything he can get his hands on.

11. Twelve students signed up for the dance committee.

12. Your teacher seems to be a reasonable person.

Subjects and Predicates

Write subjects to complete the following sentences.

1. _____ went to school last Wednesday.

2. _____ did not understand the joke.

3. _____ barked so loudly that no one could sleep a wink.

4. _____ felt unhappy when the ball game was rained out.

5. _____ wonder what happened at the end of the book.

6. _____ jumped for joy when she won the contest.

Write predicates to complete the following sentences.

7. Everyone _____ .

8. Dogs _____ .

9. I _____ .

10. Justin _____ .

11. Jokes _____ .

12. Twelve people _____ .

Subjects and Predicates

A **sentence** is a group of words that expresses a complete thought. It must have at least one subject and one verb.

Examples: **Sentence:** John felt tired and went to bed early.

Not a sentence: Went to bed early.

Write **S** if the group of words is a complete sentence. Write **NS** if the group of words is not a sentence.

_____ 1. Which one of you?

_____ 2. We're happy for the family.

_____ 3. We enjoyed the program very much.

_____ 4. Felt left out and lonely afterwards.

_____ 5. Everyone said it was the best party ever!

_____ 6. No one knows better than I what the problem is.

_____ 7. Seventeen of us!

_____ 8. Quickly before they.

_____ 9. Squirrels are lively animals.

_____ 10. Not many people believe it really happened.

_____ 11. Certainly, we enjoyed ourselves.

_____ 12. Tuned her out.

Subjects and Predicates

On the previous page, some of the groups of words are not sentences. Rewrite them to make complete sentences.

1. _____

_____

2. _____

_____

3. _____

_____

4. _____

_____

5. _____

_____

Fractions to Decimals

When a figure is divided into 10 equal parts, the parts are called tenths. Tenths can be written two ways—as a fraction or a decimal. A **decimal** is a number with one or more places to the right of a decimal point, such as 6.5 or 2.25. A **decimal point** is the dot between the ones place and the tenths place.

Examples:

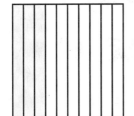

ones	tenths
0 •	3

$\frac{3}{10}$ or 0.3 of the square is shaded.

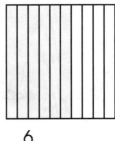

$\frac{6}{10}$ 0.6

Write the decimal and fraction for the shaded parts of the following figures. The first one is done for you.

      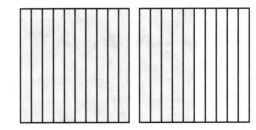

____ ____   ____ ____   ____ ____   ____ ____

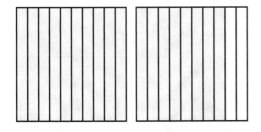   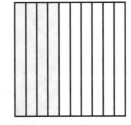   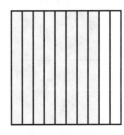

____ ____   ____ ____   ____ ____   ____ ____

Fractions to Decimals

Compare the fraction to the decimal in each box. Circle the larger number.

Example:

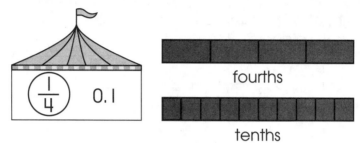

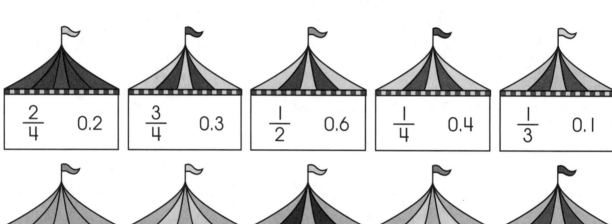

$\frac{2}{4}$ 0.2 $\frac{3}{4}$ 0.3 $\frac{1}{2}$ 0.6 $\frac{1}{4}$ 0.4 $\frac{1}{3}$ 0.1

$\frac{1}{4}$ 0.7 $\frac{2}{4}$ 0.8 $\frac{3}{4}$ 0.9 $\frac{5}{6}$ 0.5 $\frac{2}{5}$ 0.6

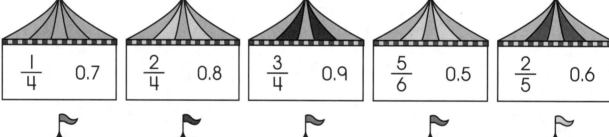

$\frac{3}{12}$ 0.9 $\frac{1}{6}$ 0.2 $\frac{2}{3}$ 0.8 $\frac{1}{5}$ 0.3 $\frac{2}{5}$ 0.7

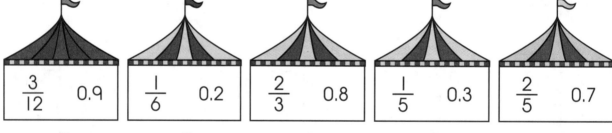

$\frac{3}{10}$ 0.5 $\frac{1}{9}$ 0.4 $\frac{4}{5}$ 0.7 $\frac{1}{3}$ 0.7 $\frac{6}{12}$ 0.1

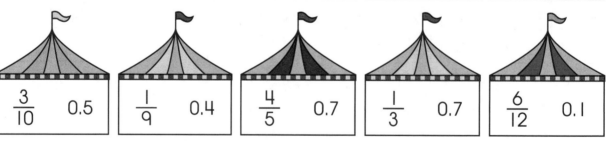

Decimals: Hundredths

The next smallest decimal unit after a tenth is called a hundredth. One hundredth is one unit of a figure divided into 100 units. Written as a decimal, it is one digit to the right of the tenths place.

Example:

One square divided into hundredths, 34 hundredths are shaded. Write: 0.34.

ones	tenths	hundredths
0	3	4

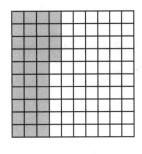

0.34

Write the decimal for the shaded parts of the following figures.

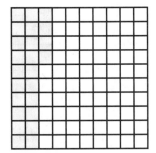 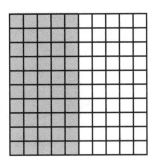 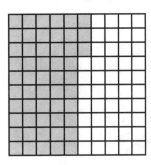 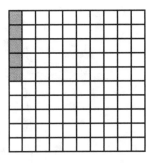

_____ _____ _____

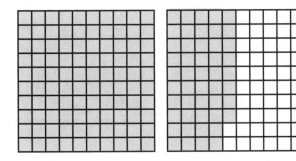 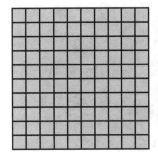 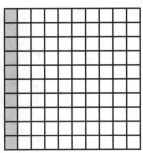

_____ _____

Decimals

Add or subtract. Remember to include the decimal point in your answers.

Example:

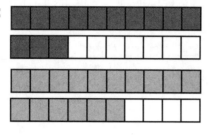

$1\frac{3}{10} = 1.3$

$1\frac{6}{10} = 1.6$

$$\begin{array}{r} 1.3 \\ +\,1.6 \\ \hline 2.9 \end{array}$$

8.1 + 1.7	4.1 + 6.2	0.5 + 1.6	7.6 − 6.5	7.2 − 2.6	1.2 + 5.0	8.7 − 3.9	6.8 − 3.7

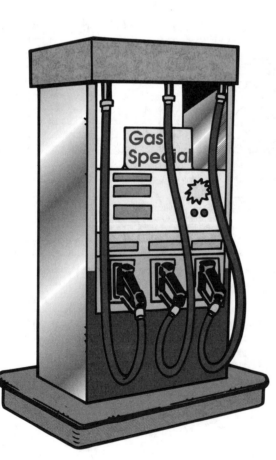

7.8 − 6.8	16.5 − 7.3	6.4 + 5.3	10.0 + 3.5
0.42 + 0.35	0.98 − 0.87	0.78 − 0.13	0.83 + 0.12
0.95 − 0.14	3.23 + 2.48	4.68 − 2.65	5.86 − 2.73
6.98 + 1.40	3.27 + 1.82	4.65 − 1.32	5.97 + 2.77

Mr. Martin went on a car trip with his family. Mr. Martin purchased gas 3 times. He bought 6.7 gallons, 7.3 gallons, then 5.8 gallons of gas. How much gas did he purchase in all?

_____

Week 23 Skills

Subject	Skill	Multi-Sensory Learning Activities
Reading and Language Arts	Identify simple subjects and predicates.	• Complete Practice Page 246. • Have your child write five original sentences about personal interests or hobbies. Then, have him or her circle the simple subjects and simple predicates in each.
	Identify compound subjects and predicates, or sentences with more than one simple subject or predicate.	• Complete Practice Pages 247–250. • Write a sentence with a compound subject, such as "Mary and her mother went shopping for a birthday present." Have your child give some examples of compound subjects in oral sentences.
Math	Build shapes and use tangrams.	• Complete Practice Pages 251–253. • Have your child keep a glossary of geometry terms. Have your child define and illustrate the following terms: **triangle**, **square**, **rectangle**, **parallelogram**, **trapezoid**, **pentagon**, and **hexagon**.
Bonus: Science		• With your child, talk about weather. Brainstorm familiar expressions containing weather words, such as "razor-sharp winds," "fair-weather friend," and "head in the clouds." Have your child draw literal interpretations of a few of the expressions.

Simple Subjects and Predicates

The **simple subject** is the most important word in the complete subject. It is a **noun** or **pronoun** that tells who or what the sentence is about. The **simple predicate** is the most important word in the complete predicate. It is a **verb** that tells what the subject is or does.

Example:

simple subject   simple predicate

Handmade pottery can be very beautiful.

complete subject   complete predicate

Underline the complete subject once and the complete predicate twice.

1. The science of pottery making is called ceramics.

2. Humans have been making pottery for thousands of years.

3. Early people made household utensils out of pottery.

4. Pottery has been made many different ways.

5. The earliest pottery making method was probably the hand-building method.

6. Clay coils were wound on top of one another.

7. Another method utilized the potter's wheel.

8. The Egyptians used the potter's wheel at least three thousand years ago

9. The ancient Greeks used the potter's wheel when making pottery.

10. Their vases are excellent examples of simplicity of color and shape.

Write the simple subjects and the simple predicates from the sentences above.

Simple Subject	Simple Predicate		Simple Subject	Simple Predicate
1. _____	_____	6. _____	_____
2. _____	_____	7. _____	_____
3. _____	_____	8. _____	_____
4. _____	_____	9. _____	_____
5. _____	_____	10. _____	_____

Compound Subjects

A **compound subject** is a subject with two parts joined by the word **and** or another conjunction. Compound subjects share the same predicate.

Example: Her shoes were covered with mud. Her ankles were covered with mud, too.

> **Compound subject:** Her shoes and ankles were covered with mud.

The predicate in both sentences is **were covered with mud**.

Combine each pair of sentences into one sentence with a compound subject.

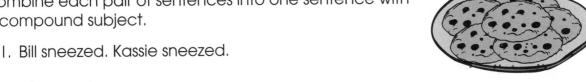

1. Bill sneezed. Kassie sneezed.

_____

2. Kristin made cookies. Joey made cookies.

_____

3. Fruit flies are insects. Ladybugs are insects.

_____

4. The girls are planning a dance. The boys are planning a dance.

_____

5. Our dog ran after the ducks. Our cat ran after the ducks.

_____

6. Joshua got lost in the parking lot. Daniel got lost in the parking lot.

_____

Compound Subjects

If sentences do not share the same predicate, they cannot be combined to write a sentence with a compound subject.

Example: Mary laughed at the story.
Tanya laughed at the television show.

Combine the pairs of sentences that share the same predicate. Write new sentences with compound subjects.

1. Pete loves swimming. Jake loves swimming.

   _____

2. A bee stung Elizabeth. A hornet stung Elizabeth.

   _____

3. Sharon is smiling. Susan is frowning.

   _____

4. The boys have great suntans. The girls have great suntans.

   _____

5. Six squirrels chased the kitten. Ten dogs chased the kitten.

   _____

6. The trees were covered with insects. The roads were covered with ice.

   _____

Compound Predicates

A **compound predicate** is a predicate with two parts joined by the word **and** or another conjunction. Compound predicates share the same subject.

Example: The baby grabbed the ball. The baby threw the ball.

> **Compound predicate:** The baby grabbed the ball and threw it.

> The subject in both sentences is **the baby**.

Combine each pair of sentences into one sentence to make a compound predicate.

1. Leah jumped on her bike. Leah rode around the block.

_____

2. Father rolled out the pie crust. Father put the pie crust in the pan.

_____

3. Anthony slipped on the snow. Anthony nearly fell down.

_____

4. My friend lives in a green house. My friend rides a red bicycle.

_____

5. I opened the magazine. I began to read it quietly.

_____

6. My father bought a new plaid shirt. My father wore his new red tie.

_____

Compound Predicates

Combine the pairs of sentences that share the same subject. Write new sentences with compound predicates.

1. Jenny picked a bouquet of flowers. Jenny put the flowers in a vase.

   _____

   _____

2. I really enjoy ice cream. She really enjoys ice cream.

   _____

   _____

3. Everyone had a great time at the pep rally. Then everyone went out for a pizza.

   _____

   _____

4. Cassandra built a model airplane.
   She painted the airplane bright yellow.

   _____

   _____

5. Her brother was really a hard person to get to know. Her sister was very shy, too.

   _____

   _____

Figure Finding

Find Figure 1 in Design 1 and shade it. Do this for each shape. The figure may be turned, and it may not be the same size.

Connect the Dots

Connect the dots to make each shape.
Note: not all dots will be used.

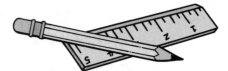

a rectangle

a kite

a different 4-sider

a different 4-sider

a triangle

a different triangle

a different triangle

a different triangle

a 5-sider

a 6-sider

a different 6-sider

a 7-sider

COMPLETE YEAR GRADE 4

The Rocket Puzzle

The rocket has four parts. Cut them apart.
The rocket can change itself into many shapes.

Use all 4 pieces to make each shape below.

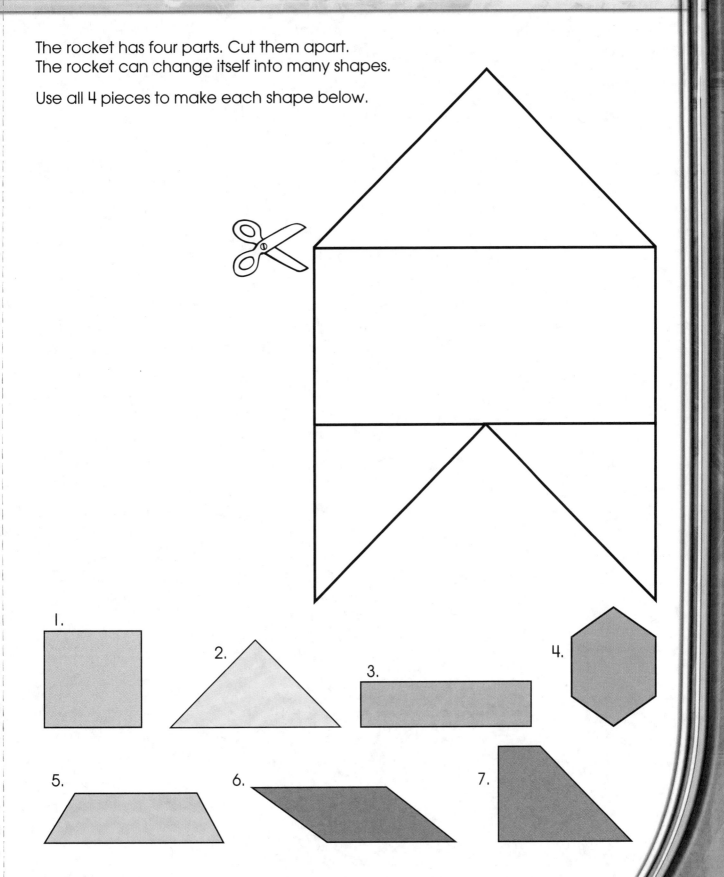

1.

2.

3.

4.

5.

6.

7.

Week 24 Skills

Subject	Skill	Multi-Sensory Learning Activities
Reading and Language Arts	Identify statements, questions, commands, and exclamations.	• Complete Practice Pages 256–260. • Give your child an example of each sentence type. Then, have your child write an example of each kind of sentence. Read various sentences from his or her favorite book, and ask your child to identify the type of each.
Math	Use tangrams to create shapes.	• Complete Practice Page 261. • Show your child cutouts of different geometric shapes in varying colors and sizes. Ask him or her to identify each shape. Then, have your child create a picture of an object or a scene using only geometric shapes.
	Recognize and create patterns.	• Complete Practice Pages 263 and 264. • Create a grid with five rows and eight columns. In the first row, write 1-, 2-, 3- and 4-digit numbers (two of each). In the second row, have your child write the product of each number x 1; in the third row, x 10; in the fourth, x 100; and in the fifth, x 1,000. Then, ask your child to examine the grid for patterns.

Statements and Questions

A **statement** tells some kind of information. It is followed by a period (.).

Examples: It is a rainy day. We are going to the beach next summer.

A **question** asks for a specific piece of information. It is followed by a question mark (?).

Examples: What is the weather like today? When are you going to the beach?

Write whether each sentence is a statement or question. The first one has been done for you.

1. Jamie went for a walk at the zoo. _____statement_____

2. The leaves turn bright colors in the fall. _____

3. When does the Easter Bunny arrive? _____

4. Madeleine went to the new art school. _____

5. Is school over at 3:30? _____

6. Grandma and Grandpa are moving. _____

7. Anthony went home. _____

8. Did Mary go to Amy's house? _____

9. Who went to work late? _____

10. Ms. McDaniel is a good teacher. _____

Write two statements and two questions below.

Statements:

_____

_____

Questions:

_____

_____

Commands and Exclamations

A **command** tells someone to do something. It is followed by a period (.).

Examples: Get your math book. Do your homework.

An **exclamation** shows strong feeling or excitement.
It is followed by an exclamation mark (!).

Examples: Watch out for that car! Oh, no! There's a snake!

Write whether each sentence is a command or exclamation. The first one has been done for you.

1. Please clean your room. _____command_____

2. Wow! Those fireworks are beautiful! _____

3. Come to dinner now. _____

4. Color the sky and water blue. _____

5. Trim the paper carefully. _____

6. Hurry, here comes the bus! _____

7. Isn't that a lovely picture! _____

8. Time to stop playing and clean up. _____

9. Brush your teeth before bedtime. _____

10. Wash your hands before you eat! _____

Write two commands and two exclamations below.

Commands:

_____

_____

Exclamations:

_____

_____

Four Kinds of Sentences

Write **S** for statement, **Q** for question, **C** for command or **E** for exclamation. End each sentence with a period, question mark, or exclamation mark.

Example:

__E__   You better watch out!

_____ 1. My little brother insists on coming with us

_____ 2. Tell him movies are bad for his health

_____ 3. He says he's fond of movies

_____ 4. Does he know there are monsters in this movie

_____ 5. He says he needs facts for his science report

_____ 6. He's writing about something that hatched from an old egg

_____ 7. Couldn't he just go to the library

_____ 8. Could we dress him like us so he'll blend in

_____ 9. Are you kidding

_____ 10. Would he sit by himself at the movie

_____ 11. That would be too dangerous

_____ 12. Mom said she'd give us money for candy if we took him with us

_____ 13. Why didn't you say that earlier

_____ 14. Get your brother and let's go

Four Kinds of Sentences

For each pair of words, write two kinds of sentences (any combination of question, command, statement, or exclamation). Use one or both words in each sentence. Name each kind of sentence you wrote.

Example: pump   crop

Question: <u>What kind of crops did you plant?</u>

Command: <u>Pump the water as fast as you can.</u>

1. pinch   health

   _____ : _____

   _____ : _____

2. fond   fact

   _____ : _____

   _____ : _____

3. insist   hatch

   _____ : _____

   _____ : _____

exclamation   command   statement   question

End Punctuation

A **statement** ends with a period. (.)
A **question** ends with a question mark. (?)
A **command** ends with a period. (.)
An **exclamation** ends with an exclamation point. (!)

Write the correct punctuation in each box.

1. Every Saturday morning we help an elderly person ☐

2. Would you like to help us this Saturday ☐

3. Be at my house at 8:00 ☐

4. You can help me gather the supplies we will need ☐

5. I won't be late ☐

6. Today, we are raking Mrs. Ray's yard ☐

7. That elm tree is huge ☐

8. Take these lawn bags to Bob and Eric ☐

9. Tell Jan and Pat to mow the backyard ☐

10. Will you help them rake the backyard ☐

11. Don't mow too close to the flowers ☐

12. Look at that big gazebo ☐

13. Mrs. Ray has left lemonade there for us ☐

14. I will mow the front yard ☐

15. Will you sweep the front walks ☐

16. Go ask Mrs. Ray to come see her clean yard ☐

17. She thinks the yard looks super ☐

18. What will we do next Saturday ☐

19. We are helping Mr. Scott shop for groceries ☐

20. Would you like to work with us again ☐

Tangram

Cut out the tangram below. Use the shapes to make a cat, a chicken, a boat and a large triangle.

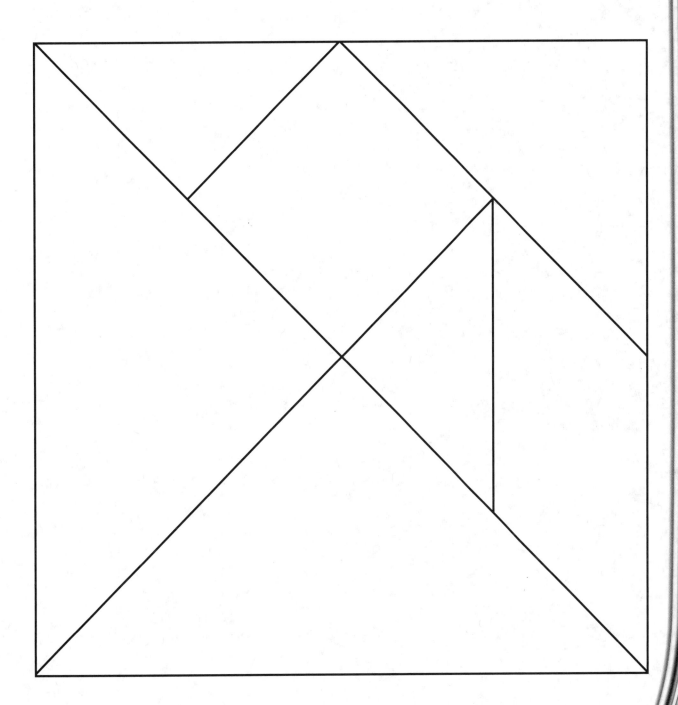

Circles and Squares

Shade the correct shapes to keep each pattern going.

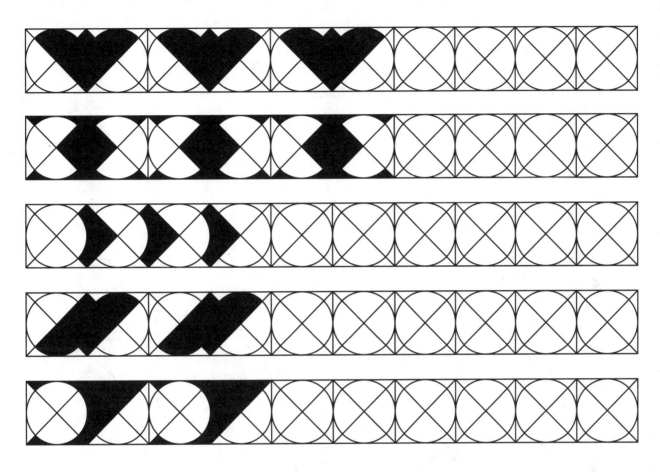

Make your own patterns using two colors.

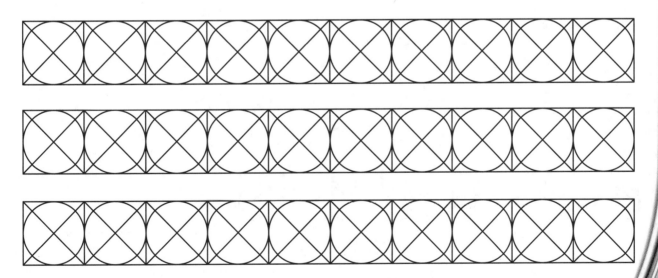

Patterns

Write the one that would come next in each pattern.

0   2   0   4   0   6   _____

1   3   5   7   9   11   _____

5   10   20   40   80   _____

                                    _____

   _____

     _____

1   A   2   B   3   C   _____

A   B   C   1   2   3   _____

        _____

Week 25 Skills

Subject	Skill	Multi-Sensory Learning Activities
Reading and Language Arts	Use commas and connecting words to combine sentences.	• Complete Practice Pages 266–270. • Send your child an e-mail or text message with a compound sentence that is missing a comma. Have your child correct the message and send it back to you.
Math	Identify polygons.	• Complete Practice Page 271. • Provide your child with a series of shape riddles. Give your child three or four clues describing a polygon. Try to incorporate as many geometric terms as you can for your clues. Then, see if your child can guess the correct shape.
	Identify lines, line segments, and rays.	• Complete Practice Page 272. • Draw several lines, line segments, and rays. Ask your child to correctly identify each one.
	Identify right, acute, and obtuse angles.	• Complete Practice Page 273. • Draw a series of angles. Ask your child to use a protractor to measure the angles, and to then determine if they are right, acute, or obtuse.
	Identify the radius and diameter of a circle.	• Complete Practice Page 274. • Have your child draw several circles by tracing objects such as lids or drinking glasses. Then, have him or her find the radius and diameter of each circle.

Conjunctions

Choose the best conjunction from the box to combine the pairs of sentences. Then rewrite the sentences, using a comma as needed.

| and | but | or | because | when | after | so |

1. I like Leah. I like Ben.

   _____

2. Should I eat the orange? Should I eat the apple?

   _____

3. You will get a reward. You turned in the lost item.

   _____

4. I really mean what I say! You had better listen!

   _____

5. I like you. You're nice, friendly, helpful and kind.

   _____

6. You can have dessert. You ate all your peas.

   _____

7. I like your shirt better. You should decide for yourself.

   _____

8. We walked out of the building. We heard the fire alarm.

   _____

9. I like to sing folk songs. I like to play the guitar.

   _____

COMPLETE YEAR GRADE 4

Using Conjunctions

Combine each pair of sentences using the conjunctions **or, and, but, after,** or **when**. You may need to change the word order in the sentences.

Example: My stomach hurts.   I still want to go to the movies.

My stomach hurts, but I still want to go to the movies.

1. He accused me of peeking.   I felt very angry.

   _____

2. The accident was over.   I started shaking.

   _____

3. Is that a freckle?   Is that dirt?

   _____

4. I forgot my jacket.   I had to go back and get it.

   _____

5. I like Christmas.   I don't like waiting for it.

   _____

6. Would you like to live in a castle?   Would you like to live on a houseboat?

   _____

7. The general gave the command.   The army marched.

   _____

8. The trees dropped all their leaves.   We raked them up.

   _____

Combining Sentences

Two sentences can be written as one sentence by using **connecting words**.

Choose one of the words in the box to combine the two sentences into one sentence.

1. We can eat now. We can eat after the game.

while or because	_____

2. We stood on the cabin's deck. The sun rose over the deck.

as or but	_____

3. Sarah wanted to watch TV. She had lots of homework to finish.

because when but	_____

4. The concert did not begin on time. The conductor was late arriving.

until because while	_____

5. The spectators cheered and applauded. The acrobats completed their performances.

when if but	_____

6. The baseball teams waited in their dugouts. The rain ended and the field was uncovered.

or until after	_____

Commas With Compound Sentences

A **compound sentence** contains two simple sentences joined by a comma and a connecting word such as "and." The simple sentences must be about the same topic.

Example: Jane helps prepare dinner, and Pat sets the table.

Write **compound** on the line if it is a compound sentence and add the needed comma. Write **no** on the line if it is not a compound sentence.

1. The porpoise looks very much like a fish. _____

2. It is a mammal and it bears its young alive. _____

3. The porpoise resembles and is closely related to the dolphin. _____

4. The top of a porpoise is mostly black and its underside is white. _____

5. It searches out and eats small fish and shellfish. _____

6. A mother porpoise has just one baby and that baby is large. _____

7. The mother nurses the baby while swimming through the water. _____

8. Porpoises seem to like humans and they have saved people who were drowning. _____

9. Porpoises are social animals and swim in large groups. _____

10. Porpoises often travel with tuna and they are sometimes caught in the tuna nets. _____

Use a comma and the word *and* to combine each pair of sentences.

1. Most species of dolphins live only in salt water. They can be found in almost all

   the oceans. _____

   _____

2. The word "dolphin" also refers to a big game fish. This fish is good to eat.

   _____

   _____

Combining Sentences

Some simple sentences can be easily combined into one sentence.

Examples: **Simple sentences:** The bird sang. The bird was tiny. The bird was in the tree.

Combined sentence: The tiny bird sang in the tree.

Combine each set of simple sentences into one sentence. The first one has been done for you.

1. The big girls laughed. They were friendly. They helped the little girls.

   The big, friendly girls laughed as they helped the little girls.

2. The dog was hungry. The dog whimpered. The dog looked at its bowl.

   _____

3. Be quiet now. I want you to listen. You listen to my joke!

   _____

4. I lost my pencil. My pencil was stubby. I lost it on the bus.

   _____

5. I see my mother. My mother is walking. My mother is walking down the street.

   _____

6. Do you like ice cream? Do you like hot dogs? Do you like mustard?

   _____

7. Tell me you'll do it! Tell me you will! Tell me right now!

   _____

Geometry: Polygons

A **polygon** is a closed figure with three or more sides.

Examples:

triangle
3 sides

square
4 equal
sides

rectangle
4 sides

pentagon
5 sides

hexagon
6 sides

octagon
8 sides

Identify the polygons.

_____

_____

_____

_____

_____

_____

Geometry: Line, Ray, Segment

A **line segment** has two end points.

Write: $\overline{AB}$

A **line** has no end points and goes on in both directions.

Write: $\overleftrightarrow{CD}$

A **ray** is part of a line and goes on in one direction. It has one end point.

Write: $\overrightarrow{EF}$

Identify each of the following as a line, line segment, or ray.

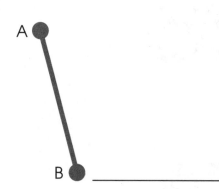

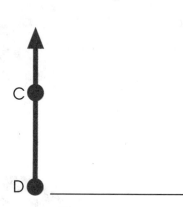

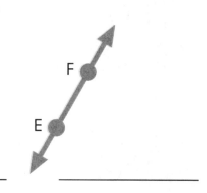

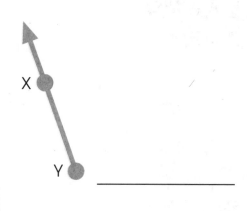

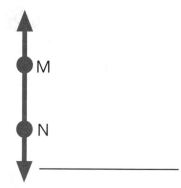

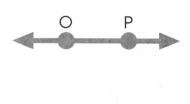

Geometry: Angles

The point at which two line segments meet is called an **angle**. There are three types of angles — right, acute, and obtuse.

 A **right angle** is formed when the two lines meet at 90°.

 An **acute angle** is formed when the two lines meet at less than 90°.

An **obtuse angle** is formed when the two lines meet at greater than 90°.

Angles can be measured with a protractor or index card. With a protractor, align the bottom edge of the angle with the bottom of the protractor, with the angle point at the circle of the protractor. Note the direction of the other ray and the number of degrees of the angle.

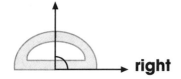 right   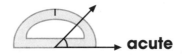 acute    obtuse

Place the corner of an index card in the corner of the angle. If the edges line up with the card, it is a right angle. If not, the angle is acute or obtuse.

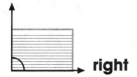 right   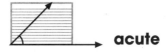 acute   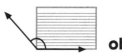 obtuse

Use a protractor or index card to identify the following angles as right, obtuse, or acute.

_____   _____   _____

 _____    _____    _____

Geometry: Circles

A **circle** is a round figure. It is named by its center. A **radius** is a line segment from the center of a circle to any point on the circle. A **diameter** is a line segment with both end points on the circle. The diameter always passes through the center of the circle.

Name the radius, diameter and circle.

Example:

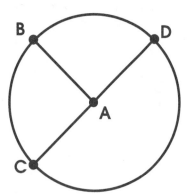

Circle   A

Radius   AB

Diameter   DC

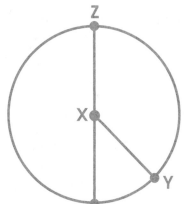

Circle   _____

Radius   _____

Diameter   _____

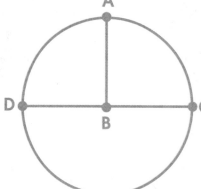

Circle   _____

Radius   _____

Diameter   _____

Week 26 Skills

Subject	Skill	Multi-Sensory Learning Activities
Reading and Language Arts	Answer questions about texts to demonstrate reading comprehension.	• Complete Practice Pages 276–280. • Cut out a newspaper or magazine article that is of interest to your child. Black out every tenth word. Have him or her read the article aloud, filling in the missing words with words that fit the context. • Share one of your own vivid childhood memories with your child. Encourage your child to ask you questions about the event, take notes, and write it as a story.
Math	Review geometry terms and definitions.	• Complete Practice Pages 281 and 283. • Ask your child to go on a hunt around your home for geometric shapes, such as cubes, cylinders, and spheres. Make a list of everything he or she finds.
Bonus: Social Studies		• Talk with your child about the state you live in. Discuss the state's capital, nickname, and motto, as well as the state symbols, such as the flag, flower, and bird. Have your child draw each symbol and explain why each one was selected. Are there any symbols that your child feels do not accurately represent the state? What would your child suggest as an alternative?

Spinning Top

Whir-r-r-ling! Matt's top is spinning very fast. Just like Matt's top, the Earth is also spinning. The Earth spins around an imaginary line that is drawn from the North **Pole** to the South Pole through the center of the Earth. This line is called Earth's **axis**. Instead of using the word "spin," though, we say that the Earth **rotates** on its axis. The Earth rotates **one** time every 24 hours. The part of the Earth facing the sun experiences **day**. The side that is away from the sun's light experiences **night**.

Draw a line from each picture of Matt to the correct picture of the Earth.

Matt lives here.

Matt lives here.

Use some of the words in bold above to fill in the puzzle.

1. The part of the Earth not facing the Sun experiences _____.

2. Earth's axis goes from the North to the South _____.

3. The Earth spins.

4. Number of times the Earth rotates in 24 hours.

5. Imaginary line on which the Earth rotates.

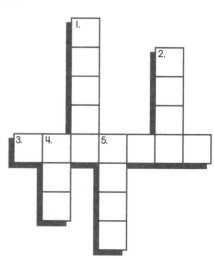

Lo-o-o-o-ong Trip

What is the longest trip you have ever taken? Was it 100 miles? 500 miles? Maybe it was more than 1,000 miles. You probably didn't know it, but last year you traveled 620 million miles.

The Earth travels in a path around the Sun called its orbit. Earth's **orbit** is almost 620 million miles. It takes 1 year, or 365 days, for the Earth to orbit or **revolve** around the Sun.

Look at the picture of Earth's orbit. It is not a perfect circle. It is a shape called an **ellipse**.

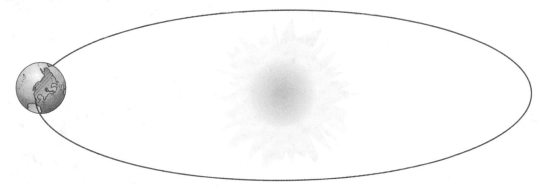

1. How long does it take for the Earth to revolve around the Sun?

   _____

2. How many times has the Earth revolved around the Sun since you were born?

   _____

3. How many miles has the Earth traveled in orbit since you were born?

   _____

4. Draw an **X** on Earth's orbit to show where it will be in 6 months.

Experiment: To draw an ellipse, place two straight pins about 3 inches apart in a piece of cardboard. Tie the ends of a 10 inch piece of string to the pins. Place your pencil inside the string. Keeping the string tight, draw an ellipse.

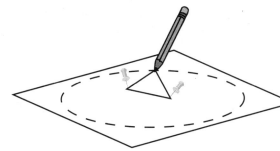

Make four different ellipses by changing the length of the string and the distance between the pins. How do the ellipses change?

A Funnel Cloud-Danger!

Did you know that a tornado is the most violent windstorm on Earth? A **tornado** is a whirling, twisting storm that is shaped like a funnel.

A tornado usually occurs in the spring on a hot day. It begins with thunderclouds and thunder. A cloud becomes very dark. The bottom of the cloud begins to twist and form a funnel. Rain and lightning begin. The funnel cloud drops from the dark storm clouds. It moves down toward the ground.

A tornado is very dangerous. It can destroy almost everything in its path.

Circle:
A (thunder, tornado) is the most vicious windstorm on Earth.

Check:
Which words describe a tornado?

☐ whirling   ☐ twisting   ☐ icy   ☐ funnel-shaped   ☐ dangerous

Underline:
A funnel shape is: ○   ▢   ⬭   ▽   〰

Write and Circle:
A tornado usually occurs in the _____ on a (hot, cool) day.

Write 1 - 2 - 3 below and in the picture above.

◯ The funnel cloud drops down to the ground.

◯ A tornado begins with dark thunder clouds.

◯ The dark clouds begin to twist and form a funnel.

Fire Mountains

Magma

Deep within Earth, molten rock, called magma, mixes with gases, making it lighter than the surrounding solid rock. The magma begins to rise toward Earth's surface and erupts through a weak area in the crust. The eruption can occur as a violent explosion, propelling lava hundreds of feet into the air. Or, it can gently ooze out the top and side vents of the volcano. There are two kinds of magma, rhyolite and basalt. Rhyolitic magma is thick and slow-moving. It often traps gases and produces explosive eruptions. Basaltic magma is fluid and faster-flowing. Gases easily escape from it as it gently flows from the vent.

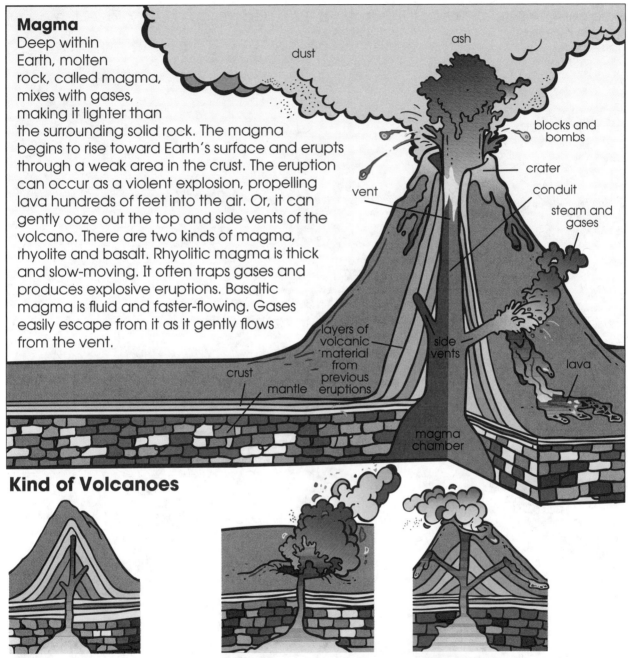

Kind of Volcanoes

Cinder Cone

Cinder cone volcanoes are formed from cinder and ash that are deposited around the vent after violent explosions. The layers of ash and cinder gradually build a cone-shaped mountain. The Paricutín Volcano in Mexico is a cinder cone volcano that grew to a height of over 1,300 feet in a cornfield.

Shield

Shield volcanoes are formed when lava flows gently from the vent, spreads, and builds on a broad, gently sloping mountain. The Hawaiian Islands form a chain of shield volcanoes and include the famous Kilauea and Mauna Loa.

Composite

Composite volcanoes are some of the most spectacular mountains on Earth. These steep-sided, cone-shaped mountains can rise over 10,000 feet. They are made from alternating layers of gently flowing lava, ash, cinder, blocks, and bombs. Some of the most beautiful mountains in the world, such as Mount Fuji in Japan and Vesuvius in Italy, are composite volcanoes.

Volcanoes

Using the **Fire Mountains** activity sheet (p. 279) and the box below, label the parts of the volcano.

Earth's crust	lava	side vent
Earth's mantle	crater	vent
magma chamber	ash and dust	conduit

Geometry Game

1. Cut out the cards at the bottom of the page. Put them in a pile.

2. Cut out the game boards on the next page.

3. Take turns drawing cards.

4. If you have the figure that the card describes on your gameboard, cover it.

5. The first one to get three in a row, wins.

cube	point	angle
line	square	cone
triangle	segment	rectangle
cylinder	circle	tangram
rectangular prism	sphere	ray

Geometry Game

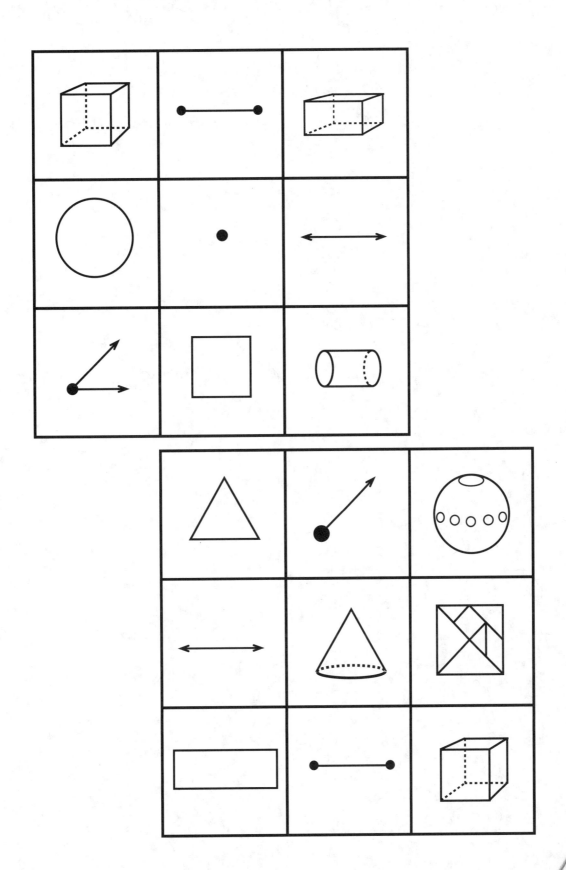

Week 27 Skills

Subject	Skill	Multi-Sensory Learning Activities
Reading and Language Arts	Answer questions about texts to demonstrate reading comprehension.	• Complete Practice Pages 286–290. • Read a nonfiction book with your child. Ask questions to assess comprehension and challenge your child to research more information on a topic related to the book.
Math	Review geometry terms and definitions.	• Complete Practice Pages 291 and 292. • Ask your child to use a ruler to create a geometric drawing made from straight lines. Have your child label a line, a line segment, and a ray in the drawing.
	Determine the measurement of each angle in a triangle.	• Complete Practice Page 293. • Ask your child to look for real-world examples of right, acute, and obtuse triangles. What are the approximate angle measurements of these objects?
	Identify three-dimensional shapes.	• Complete Practice Page 294. • Create a 3-D cube. On a piece of paper, draw five squares in the shape of a plus sign, and then add an extra square to the bottom. Cut out the entire shape. Fold the left and right sides of the shape in to form right angles. Fold the longest part of the shape (the two squares) in to form a right angle. Then, fold the top square of the longest part of the shape over to make the top of the cube. Tape all six sides of the cube together.

The Princess and the Pea

Fairy tales are short stories written for children involving magical characters.

Read the story. Then answer the questions.

Once there was a prince who wanted to get married. The catch was, he had to marry a real princess. The Prince knew that real princesses were few and far between. When they heard he was looking for a bride, many young women came to the palace. All claimed to be real princesses.

"Hmmm," thought the Prince. "I must think of a way to sort out the real princesses from the fake ones. I will ask the Queen for advice."

Luckily, since he was a prince, the Queen was also his mother. So of course she had her son's best interests at heart. "A real princess is very delicate," said the Queen. "She must sleep on a mattress as soft as a cloud. If there is even a small lump, she will not be able to sleep."

"Why not?" asked the Prince. He was a nice man but not as smart as his mother.

"Because she is so delicate!" said the Queen impatiently. "Let's figure out a way to test her. Better still, let me figure out a test. You go down and pick a girl to try out my plan."

The Prince went down to the lobby of the castle. A very pretty but humble-looking girl caught his eye. He brought her back to his mother, who welcomed her.

"Please be our guest at the castle tonight," said the Queen. "Tomorrow we will talk with you about whether you are a real princess."

The pretty but humble girl was shown to her room. In it was a pile of five mattresses, all fluffy and clean. "A princess is delicate," said the Queen. "Sweet dreams!"

The girl climbed to the top of the pile and laid down, but she could not sleep. She tossed and turned and was quite cross the next morning.

"I found this under the fourth mattress when I got up this morning," she said. She handed a small green pea to the Queen. "No wonder I couldn't sleep!"

The Queen clapped her hands. The Prince looked confused. "A real princess is delicate. If this pea I put under the mattress kept you awake, you are definitely a princess."

"Of course I am," said the Princess. "Now may I please take a nap?"

1. Why does the Prince worry about finding a bride? _____

   _____

2. According to the Queen, how can the Prince tell who is a real princess? _____

   _____

3. Who hides something under the girl's mattress? _____

The Princess and the Pea

Review the story "The Princess and the Pea." Then answer the questions.

1. Why does the Prince need a test to see who is a real princess?

   _____

   _____

   _____

2. Why does the Princess have trouble sleeping? _____

   _____

3. In this story, the Queen puts a small pea under a pile of mattresses to see if the girl is delicate. What else could be done to test a princess for delicacy?

   _____

   _____

   _____

The story does not tell whether or not the Prince and Princess get married and live happily ever after, only that the Princess wants to take a nap.

Write a new ending to the story.

4. What do you think happens after the Princess wakes up?

   _____

   _____

   _____

   _____

   _____

   _____

   _____

   _____

Oceans

If you looked at Earth from up in space, you would see a planet that is mostly blue. This is because more than two-thirds of Earth is covered with water. You already know that this is what makes our planet different from the others, and what makes life on Earth possible. Most of this water is in the four great oceans: Pacific, Atlantic, Indian and Arctic. The Pacific is by far the largest and the deepest. It is more than twice as big as the Atlantic, the second largest ocean.

The water in the ocean is salty. This is because rivers are always pouring water into the oceans. Some of this water picks up salt from the rocks it flows over. It is not enough salt to make the rivers taste salty. But the salt in the oceans has been building up over millions of years. The oceans get more and more salty every century.

The ocean provides us with huge amounts of food, especially fish. There are many other things we get from the ocean, including sponges and pearls. The oceans are also great "highways" of the world. Ships are always crossing the oceans, transporting many goods from country to country.

The science of studying the ocean is called oceanography. Today, oceanographers have special equipment to help them learn about the oceans and seas. Electronic instruments can be sent deep below the surface to make measurements. The newest equipment uses sonar or echo-sounding systems that bounce sound waves off the sea bed and use the echoes to make pictures of the ocean floor.

Answer these questions about the oceans.

1. How much of the Earth is covered by water? _____

2. Which is the largest and deepest ocean? _____

3. What is the science of studying the ocean? _____

4. What new equipment do oceanographers use? _____

Whales

The biggest animal in the world is the whale. The blue whale is the largest animal that ever lived. It is even bigger than the great dinosaurs of long ago. Whales are close cousins to dolphins and porpoises, but these animals are fewer than 13 feet in length.

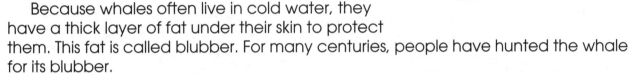

Whales spend their entire lives in water, usually in the ocean. Because of this, many people think that whales are fish. They are not. They are mammals. There are four things that prove that whales are mammals instead of fish: 1) Whales breathe with lungs instead of gills. A whale must come to the surface to breathe. It blows the old air from its lungs out of a hole in the top of its head. 2) They are warm-blooded. 3) They have hair—though not very much! 4) Baby whales are born alive and get milk from their mothers.

Because whales often live in cold water, they have a thick layer of fat under their skin to protect them. This fat is called blubber. For many centuries, people have hunted the whale for its blubber.

Whales are very sociable animals and "talk" with each other by making different noises, including clicks, whistles, squeaks, thumps and low moans. Because sound waves travel well in water, the "song" of some whales can be heard more than 100 miles away.

Answer these questions about whales.

1. Which whale is the biggest animal that has ever lived? _____

2. List four things proving that whales are mammals and not fish.

   a. _____

   b. _____

   c. _____

   d. _____

3. What are two "cousins" to the whale? _____

4. What is the thick layer of fat under a whale's skin called? _____

Dolphins and Porpoises

Dolphins and porpoises are members of the whale family. In fact, they are the most common whales. If they have pointed or "beaked" faces, they are dolphins. If they have short faces, they are porpoises. Sometimes large groups of more than 1,000 dolphins can be seen.

Dolphins and porpoises swim in a special way called "porpoising." They swim through the surface waters, diving down and then leaping up—sometimes into the air. As their heads come out of the water, they breathe in air. Dolphins are acrobatic swimmers, often spinning in the air as they leap.

Humans have always had a special relationship with dolphins. Stories dating back to the ancient Greeks talk about dolphins as friendly, helpful creatures. There have been reports over the years of people in trouble on the seas who have been rescued and helped by dolphins.

Answer these questions about dolphins and porpoises.

1. The small members of the whale family with the pointed faces are _____.

2. Those members of the whale family with short faces are _____.

3. What do you call the special way dolphins and porpoises swim? _____

4. Do dolphins breathe with lungs or gills? _____

5. How did ancient Greeks describe dolphins? _____

6. Where have dolphins been reported to help people? _____

Geometry

Geometry is the branch of mathematics that has to do with points, lines, and shapes.

Write the word from the box that is described below.

> triangle   square   cube   angle
> line   ray   segment   rectangle

a collection of points on a straight path that goes on and on in opposite directions

_____

a figure with three sides and three corners

_____

a figure with four equal sides and four corners

_____

part of a line that has one end point and goes on and on in one direction

_____

part of a line having two end points

_____

a space figure with six square faces

_____

two rays with a common end point

_____

a figure with four corners and four sides

_____

Geometry

Review the definitions on the previous page before completing the problems below.

Identify the labeled section of each of the following diagrams.

AB = _____

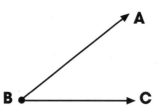

ABC = _____

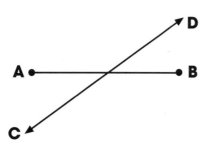

AB = _____

CD = _____

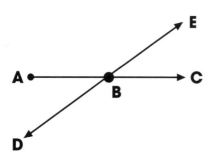

AC = _____

AB = _____

EBC = _____

BC = _____

Triangle Angles

A **triangle** is a figure with three corners and three sides. Every triangle contains three angles. The sum of the angles is always 180°, regardless of the size or shape of the triangle.

If you know two of the angles, you can add them together and then subtract the total from 180 to find the number of degrees in the third angle.

Find the number of degrees in the third angle of each triangle.

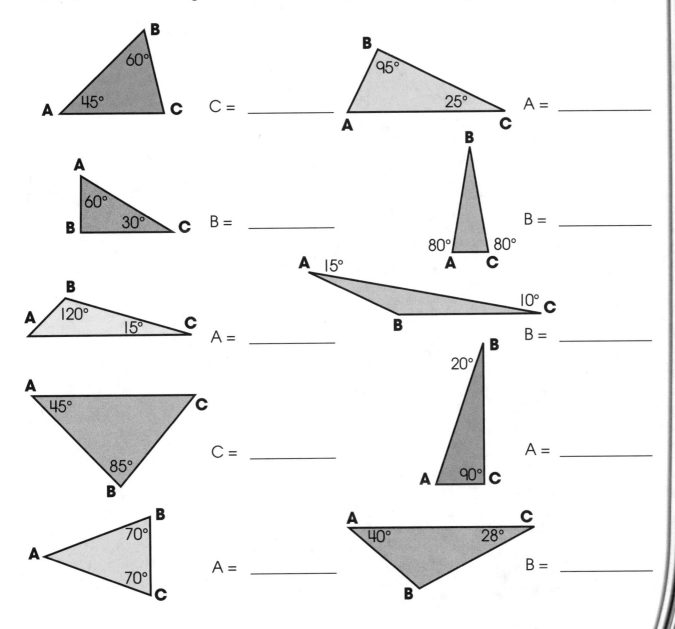

C = _____

A = _____

B = _____

B = _____

A = _____

B = _____

C = _____

A = _____

A = _____

B = _____

Space Figures

Space figures are figures whose points are in more than one plane. Cubes and cylinders are space figures.

  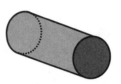 

| rectangular prism | cone | cube | cylinder | sphere | pyramid |

A **prism** has two identical, parallel bases.

All of the faces on a **rectangular prism** are rectangles.

A **cube** is a prism with six identical, square faces.

A **pyramid** is a space figure whose base is a polygon and whose faces are triangles with a common vertex—the point where two rays meet.

A **cylinder** has a curved surface and two parallel bases that are identical circles.

A **cone** has one circular, flat face and one vertex.

A **sphere** has no flat surface. All points are an equal distance from the center.

Circle the name of the figure you see in each of these familiar objects

	cone	sphere	cylinder
	cone	sphere	cylinder
	cube	rectangular prism	pyramid
	cone	pyramid	cylinder

Third Quarter Check-Up

Reading and Language Arts

❑ I understand and can identify prefixes and suffixes.

❑ I can identify complete sentences, fragments, and run-ons.

❑ I can identify simple and compound subjects and predicates.

❑ I can identify statements, questions, commands, and exclamations.

❑ I know how to use commas and connecting words to combine sentences.

❑ I can answer questions about texts to demonstrate reading comprehension.

Math

❑ I can add and subtract fractions.

❑ I can compare fractions and understand equivalent fractions.

❑ I can read and complete word problems using fractions.

❑ I can add and subtract mixed numbers.

❑ I can convert fractions to decimals.

❑ I can add and subtract decimals.

❑ I can build shapes and use tangrams.

❑ I can recognize and create patterns.

❑ I can identify polygons; lines; line segments; rays; right, acute, and obtuse angles; and the radius and diameter of a circle.

❑ I can determine the measurement of each angle in a triangle.

❑ I can identify three-dimensional shapes.

Final Project

Write several sentences on a piece of paper, including statements, questions, commands, and exclamations. Ask your child to identify each type of sentence. Then, practice fractions by asking your child questions about sentence punctuation. For example, ask, "What fraction of the sentences end with a period? What fraction of the sentences are questions? What fraction of the sentences begin with the word **will**?"

Fourth Quarter Introduction

As the school year nears its end, many students are feeling confident about the new skills they have learned as fourth graders. This may be evident in their fluency with multiplication, division, and fractions, or in their increasing comprehension of what they're reading. As the days get warmer and children play outside in the evenings, don't forget to maintain school day routines and continue to support your child's academic growth at home.

Fourth Quarter Skills

Practice pages in this book for Weeks 28–36 will help your child improve the following skills.

Reading and Language Arts
- Understand and identify the main idea of a text
- Follow step-by-step directions
- Understand and identify cause and effect situations
- Use context clues to interpret meaning
- Draw conclusions from a reading passage
- Use quotation marks around song titles, poems, and dialogue
- Use correct capitalization and punctuation
- Identify and write topic sentences and supporting sentences
- Determine purpose and point of view
- Write a friendly letter, outline ideas, and write a fiction piece

Math
- Identify similar, congruent, and symmetrical figures
- Understand perimeter as the distance around a figure
- Understand area as the number of square units needed to cover a region
- Understand volume as the number of cubic units that fit inside a figure
- Calculate time
- Measure in inches, feet, yards, and miles
- Measure in centimeters, meters, and kilometers
- Measure weights in ounces, pounds, tons, grams, and kilograms
- Measure liquids in cups, pints, quarts, and gallons
- Measure temperature in Celsius and Fahrenheit

Multi-Sensory Learning Activities

Try these fun activities for enhancing your child's learning and development during the fourth quarter of the school year. Be sure to choose activities that include speaking, listening, touching, and active movement.

 Reading and Language Arts

Give your child a passage of dialogue, omitting all punctuation. Let him or her edit the passage by adding all necessary punctuation. Reading the passage aloud may help him or her determine where it is needed.

Have your child choose a funny or memorable scene from a recorded movie, video, or TV show. Ask your child to write each line from the scene, pausing as needed to catch all the words. Remind your child to use quotation marks correctly.

Read *The Borrowers* by Mary Norton. Reread the last sentence of the book. Did the Borrowers really exist or did Mrs. May's brother make it all up? Ask your child to make a decision and write supporting arguments for his or her choice.

Write a paragraph on a piece of paper with punctuation and capitalization errors. Have your child copy the paragraph, fixing all the errors, in his or her best handwriting.

Copy paragraphs from books and textbooks. Leave out the topic sentences. Glue each paragraph on a lined index card or a sheet of writing paper, leaving space at the top for your child to write. Have your child read each paragraph and write a topic sentence on the lines provided.

2 8 4 9 6 **Math**

Ask your child to find the area of one room of your home in square feet. Then, have your child research the cost of carpet or other flooring per square foot. How much would it cost to have new flooring installed in the room?

Look at an atlas with your child. Help your child measure the mileage of your state in all directions. Determine the approximate area of your state. Compare the area of your state with the area of other states. Then, compare it with the area of other countries, such as Germany or Canada.

Fourth Quarter Introduction, cont.

Give your child a whole orange and the following tools: string, a ruler, and a balance scale. Have him or her measure the circumference of the orange using the string and ruler. Then, have your child weigh the orange before and after it is peeled. He or she should record the weight of the whole orange, just the peel, and just the fruit.

A kitchen pantry is full of items of various weights. Have your child estimate the weight of each object before weighing. Then, have your child weigh each item on the scale and record the name of the object and its weight on a piece of paper.

 **Seasonal Fun**

Make a bird feeder out of recycled materials. First, use wire cutters to cut a lightweight wire coat hanger on one side, just before it starts twisting. Leaving the handle of the hanger, straighten the rest of the wire to make one long piece. Starting at the base of the hanger hook, use needle-nose pliers to start wrapping the wire around a lemon, starting with the narrow top of the fruit. Spiral the wire loosely around the lemon until you reach the bottom of the fruit; end with a narrow curl, cutting off any remaining wire and gently removing the lemon.

Next, make your birdseed. Melt some fat in an old saucepan. Add birdseed in a ratio of two parts birdseed to one part fat, and let cool into a solid mass roughly the shape of the lemon you just used. Once cool, load the bird food into the twisty bird feeder and hang it from a nearby tree. As birds come to your feeder, invite your child to make and record observations, such as: What kinds of birds use the feeder most? Which kinds of beaks are best suited for this kind of feeding?

Week 28 Skills

Subject	Skill	Multi-Sensory Learning Activities
Reading and Language Arts	Understand and identify the main idea of a text.	• Complete Practice Pages 300–304. • Provide your child with several photos and written paragraphs. Have him or her write a topic sentence to express the main idea of each.
Math	Identify similar, congruent, and symmetrical figures.	• Complete Practice Page 305. • Ask your child to think about symmetry found in people and animals. Most creatures have two nearly identical sides. Are there any animals whose bodies are not symmetrical? Have your child do some research to find out.
	Understand perimeter as the distance around a figure.	• Complete Practice Pages 306–308. • Have your child measure the perimeter of objects around the room, recording each measurement on paper in the units used to measure each (cm, in., ft., etc.).
	Understand area as the number of square units needed to cover a region.	• Complete Practice Page 306. • Have your child imagine that he or she has a present to wrap. He or she will need a box and will need to purchase wrapping paper. Help your child measure the area of each surface on the box and add the measurements together to determine the total area. Then, have your child write a sentence telling how much wrapping paper he or she will need.

Camp Rules

Donald, Arnold and Jack are at Camp Explore-It-All this week. They think camp is a lot of fun. They have also learned from their instructors that there are some very important rules all campers must obey so that everyone has a good time.

All campers must take swimming tests to see what depth of water they can swim in safely. Donald and Jack pass the advanced test and can swim in the deep water. Arnold, however, only passes the intermediate test. He is supposed to stay in the area where the water is waist deep. When it is time to swim, Arnold decides to sneak into advanced with Donald and Jack. After all, he has been swimming in deep water for three years. No way is he going to stay in the shallow water with the babies.

Donald and Jack don't think Arnold should come into the deep water, but they can't tell him anything. So the boys jump into the water and start swimming and playing. Fifteen minutes later, Arnold is yelling, "Help!" He swims out too far and is too tired to make it back in. The lifeguard jumps in and pulls him out. Everyone stops to see what is happening. Arnold feels very foolish.

Check:
The main idea of this story is

☐ Arnold ends up feeling foolish.   ☐ Camp is fun.

☐ All campers take swimming tests.   ☐ Rules are made for good reasons.

☐ You can learn a lot from instructors.   ☐ Rules are made to be broken.

Underline:
Arnold got himself into a(n) _____ situation.

amusing   funny   dangerous   ambiguous

Circle:
Arnold thought the guys in the shallow area were (bullies/babies). However, he should have (stayed with them/gone to the advanced area).

Write:
What lesson do you think Arnold learned? _____

_____

What do you think the other campers learned? _____

_____

It's Major

Main ideas can be anywhere in a paragraph. Write the main idea for each paragraph on the blank line. Choose from the main ideas listed below.

> They had to get Fudge to the hospital.
> Peter had to sit and wait alone.
> Someone did care that he had lost Dribble.
> Fudge had eaten Dribble.
> They waited for news about Fudge.
> After spending all day in the hospital waiting room, Peter was hungry.

1. Peter walked home from school. It was a spring day, and he was thinking about Dribble. Something was wrong when he got to his room. The bowl was there but not Dribble. When he asked Fudge where he was, Fudge just smiled

   and pointed to his tummy._____

   _____

2. Peter grabbed blankets while his mother called the ambulance. Henry made

   no other elevator stops on the way down._____

   _____

   Two men in white were waiting with a stretcher and the ambulance.

3. _____
   There were no magazines or books. He watched the clock. He read all the wall signs. He found out he was in the Emergency Room.

4. _____
   Mother joined him in the hospital coffee shop for a hamburger. He didn't eat much after he found out that Fudge might need an operation if the castor oil, milk of magnesia and prune juice didn't work soon.

5. The next day was Saturday. Peter's grandmother came to stay with him.

   _____

   Every hour the telephone rang with a report about Fudge. The good news came late at night.

6. Fudge came home with many presents. He was having fun and getting lots of attention. When Mr. Hatcher arrived home from work, he gave the biggest present to Peter.

   _____

A Black Hole

Have you ever heard of a mysterious black hole? Some scientists believe that a black hole is an invisible object somewhere in space. Scientists believe that it has such a strong pull toward it, called gravity, that nothing can escape from it!

These scientists believe that a black hole is a star that has collapsed. The collapse made its pull even stronger. It seems invisible because even its own starlight cannot escape! It is believed that anything in space that comes near the black hole will be pulled into it forever. Some scientists believe there are many black holes in our galaxy.

Check:

Some scientists believe that:

☐ a black hole is an invisible object in space.

☐ a black hole is a collapsed star.

☐ a black hole will not let its own light escape.

Write:

| A – gravity |
| B – collapse |

_____ To fall or cave in

_____ A strong pull toward an object in space

Draw what you think the inside of a black hole would be like.

Case Rests

Select the correct main idea from the book for each paragraph below by circling A, B or C.

1. In "The Case of the Scattered Cards," Encyclopedia noticed that cards on the floor of the tent were dry, not wet or muddy. It had been raining for two days.

    A. Encyclopedia had brought his own dry playing cards.

    B. The tent had been put up before it started raining.

    C. Bugs had fixed all the holes to keep the floor dry.

2. In "The Case of the Civil War Sword," Encyclopedia could tell the sword was a fake by writing on the blade. Bugs knew there had been two battles at Bull Run. He claimed that this sword belonged to General Stonewall Jackson.

    A. Bugs had found a valuable war memento.

    B. The writing used the Yankee name for the battle instead of the Confederate.

    C. Bugs was as smart as Encyclopedia.

3. In "The Case of Merko's Grandson," Encyclopedia realized that Fred Gibson was the real heir. The tall woman really was a relative, too, but not Fred's grandchild. The woman insisted that the Great Merko was not Fred's grandfather.

    A. Merko died in a circus accident.

    B. The tall woman was lying.

    C. The Great Merko was a woman—Fred's grandmother.

4. In "The Case of the Bank Robber," Encyclopedia figured out why the robber and Blind Tom had rolled on the ground. When they found the robber, he did not have the money. When Encyclopedia visited Blind Tom, the lights were on and a newspaper was on the bed.

    A. Blind Tom and the robber were working together and traded yellow bags.

    B. Encyclopedia buys bread in yellow bags.

    C. Blind people can see if the lights are on.

Lucky Beth or Lucky Kim?

Kim thinks Beth is so lucky. Almost every day, Beth comes to school with something new. One day, she might be wearing a new outfit her mom bought her at the department store where her mom works. The next day, Beth may have something really unique from her father, like a watch that has the days of the week in a foreign language. He brings her gifts when he comes home from traveling on business.

Beth, however, does not think she is so lucky. Beth's mom works until 7 p.m. every night and also has to work every Saturday. Her father travels so much with his job, that Beth is lucky if she gets to see him one week a month. Beth loves her parents, but she wishes they were both home every night and every weekend like Kim's parents so they could do special things together. She also wishes she had a little brother like Kim does so she wouldn't be so lonely.

Check:
Kim thinks Beth is lucky because Beth . . .

☐ gets lots of neat gifts.

☐ doesn't have a brother or sister.

☐ has a father who travels a lot.

Circle:
Beth thinks Kim is lucky because . . .

Kim has a little brother.

Kim doesn't get a lot of new clothes.

Kim's parents are home at night and on the weekends.

Underline:
When something is unique, it is . . .

    ugly   special   small   unusual   different

Write:
Who do you think is luckier, Kim or Beth? Why? _____

_____

_____

Similar, Congruent and Symmetrical Figures

Similar figures have the same shape but have varying sizes.

Figures that are **congruent** have identical shapes but different orientations. That means they face in different directions.

Symmetrical figures can be divided equally into two identical parts.

Cross out the shape that does not belong in each group. Label the two remaining shapes as similiar, congruent, or symmetrical.

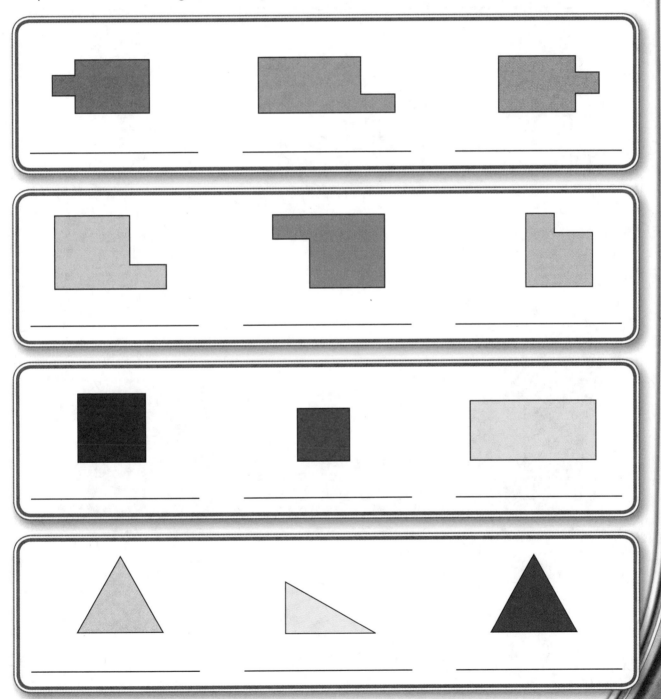

Perimeter and Area

Perimeter is the distance around a figure. It is found by adding the lengths of the sides. **Area** is the number of square units needed to cover a region. The area is found by adding the number of square units. A unit can be any unit of measure. Most often, inches, feet, or yards are used.

Find the perimeter and area for each figure. The first one is done for you.

☐ = 1 square unit

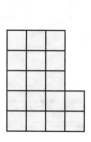

Perimeter = __18__ units

Area = __17__ sq. units

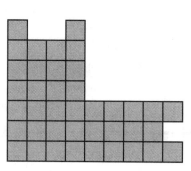

Perimeter = _____ units

Area = _____ sq. units

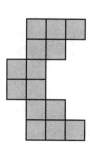

Perimeter = _____ units

Area = _____ sq. units

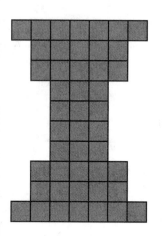

Perimeter = _____ units

Area = _____ sq. units

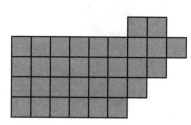

Perimeter = _____ units

Area = _____ sq. units

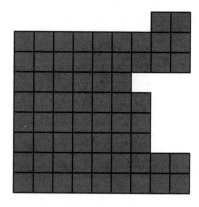

Perimeter = _____ units

Area = _____ sq. units

Perimeter

Perimeter is calculated by adding the lengths of the sides of a figure.

Examples:

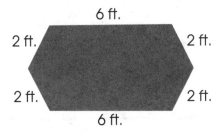

2 + 2 + 2 + 2 + 6 + 6 = 20
The perimeter of this
hexagon is 20 ft.

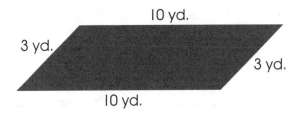

10 + 10 + 3 + 3 = 26
The perimeter of this
parallelogram is 26 yd.

Find the perimeter of the following figures.

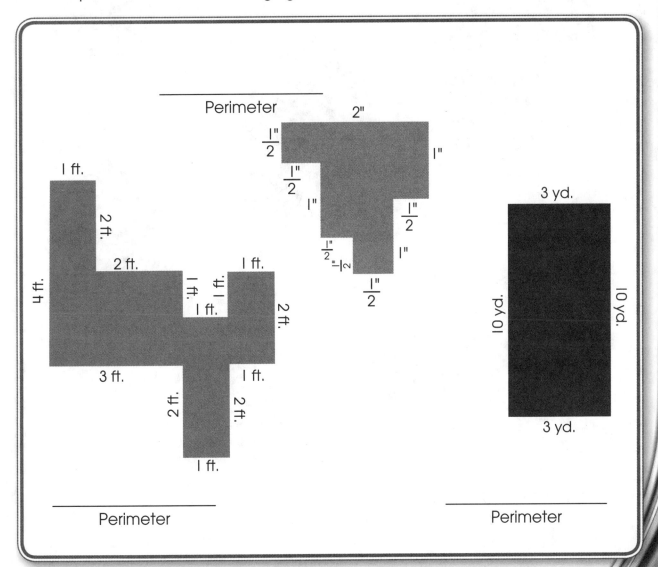

Perimeter _____

Perimeter _____   Perimeter _____

Perimeter

Calculate the perimeter of each figure.

Example: 4 + 5 + 4 + 1 + 2 + 3 + 2 = 21 meters

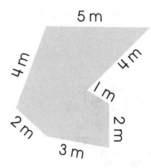

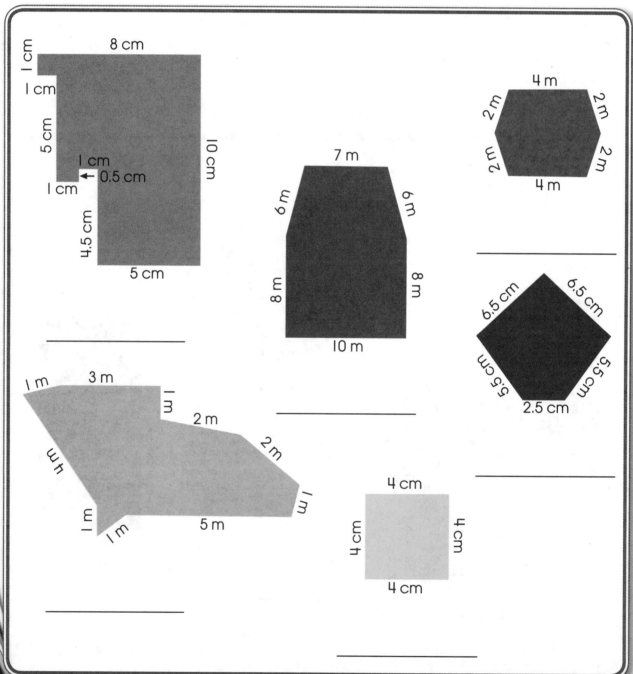

Week 29 Skills

Subject	Skill	Multi-Sensory Learning Activities
Reading and Language Arts	Review main idea.	• Complete Practice Pages 310–314. • On index cards, write the main idea for each of several books your child has read recently. Write the titles of the books on another set of cards. Have your child match each book title with the book's main idea.
Math	Review perimeter and area.	• Complete Practice Pages 315–317. • On a sheet of graph paper, use the gridlines to spell out your child's name using block letters. Then, ask your child to calculate the perimeter and area of each letter.
	Understand volume as the number of cubic units that fit inside a figure.	• Complete Practice Page 318. • Give your child a small box and many square blocks (cubes). Ask him or her to fill the box with blocks and count the total number of blocks to determine volume. • Using sugar cubes, have your child build a rectangular prism of any size. Have your child count and record the dimensions of the rectangular prism. How many sugar cubes long is it? How many sugar cubes high is it? How many sugar cubes wide is it?

Main Ideas — Location

The **main idea** of a paragraph can be located anywhere in the paragraph. Although most main ideas are stated in the first sentence, many good paragraphs contain a topic sentence in the middle or even at the end.

Draw two lines under each topic sentence. Draw one line under each support sentence.

> We had a great time at the basketball game last Friday night. My dad took four of my friends and me to the gym at seven o clock. We sat with other kids from our class. Our team was behind at the half but pulled ahead to win by eight points. After the game, we stopped for burgers before going home.
>
> The alarm rang for a full minute before Jay heard it. Even then, he put his pillow over his head, rolled over and moaned loudly. Getting up in the morning was always hard for Jay. As usual, his mom had to take the pillow off his head and make him get up for school.

On the lines below, write three paragraphs. Put the topic sentence in the correct place. Underline each topic sentence.

Paragraph 1 (Topic Sentence–Middle)

_____

_____

_____

Paragraph 2 (Topic Sentence–Beginning)

_____

_____

_____

Paragraph 3 (Topic Sentence–End)

_____

_____

_____

Dudley's Doing It Again!

Dudley is up to his old tricks again. He just finished dog school six weeks ago, and he had really been doing so well. He fetched when he was told to fetch. He heeled when Donald said, "heel." He sat when he was supposed to sit. He would even do tricks like roll over, play dead, and speak to impress Donald's friends, if Donald gave him a doggy treat. But lately, Dudley hasn't been doing any of the things he was taught.

For the past several days, Dudley has been digging in the yard. This makes Donald's dad really mad. Dudley has also been chewing up the newspapers instead of bringing them to Donald's mom. One day, he chewed up all her grocery coupons. Boy, was she angry! And, Dudley won't sit or heel when Donald tells him to. Two days ago, Dudley knocked down Donald's friend Lee. Something has to be done about Dudley!

Circle:
Dudley seems to have forgotten . . .

how to chew newspapers.

everything he learned at dog school.

everything Donald taught him.

how to learn new tricks.

Check:

	Good Dog	Bad Dog
Dudley is up to his old tricks.	☐	☐
Dudley finished dog school.	☐	☐
Lee was knocked down by Dudley.	☐	☐
Dudley did tricks for treats.	☐	☐
Dudley has been digging in the yard.	☐	☐

Write:
What has Dudley forgotten that he learned at dog school? _____

_____

_____

What do you think Donald should do about Dudley? _____

_____

Main Idea in Sentences

The **main idea** is the most important idea, or main point, in a sentence, paragraph, or story.

Circle the main idea for each sentence.

1. Emily knew she would be late if she watched the end of the TV show.

   a. Emily likes watching TV.

   b. Emily is always running late.

   c. If Emily didn't leave, she would be late.

2. The dog was too strong and pulled Jason across the park on his leash.

   a. The dog is stronger than Jason.

   b. Jason is not very strong.

   c. Jason took the dog for a walk.

3. Jennifer took the book home so she could read it over and over.

   a. Jennifer loves to read.

   b. Jennifer loves the book.

   c. Jennifer is a good reader.

4. Jerome threw the baseball so hard it broke the window.

   a. Jerome throws baseballs very hard.

   b. Jerome was mad at the window.

   c. Jerome can't throw very straight.

5. Lori came home and decided to clean the kitchen for her parents.

   a. Lori is a very nice person.

   b. Lori did a favor for her parents.

   c. Lori likes to cook.

6. It was raining so hard that it was hard to see the road through the windshield.

   a. It always rains hard in April.

   b. The rain blurred our vision.

   c. It's hard to drive in the rain.

Floating in Space

Read about life in space. Then answer the questions.

> Life in space is very different from life on Earth. There is no gravity in space. Gravity is what holds us to the ground. In space, everything floats around.
>
> Astronauts wear suction cups on their shoes to hold them to the floor of their spaceships. At night, they do not crawl into bed like you do. Instead, they climb into sleeping bags that hang on the wall and then they zip themselves in.
>
> If an astronaut is thirsty, he or she cannot simply pour a glass of water. The water would form little balls that would float around the spaceship! Instead, water has to be squirted into the astronauts' mouths from bottles or containers.
>
> When astronauts are in space, they do a lot of floating around outside their spaceship. Astronauts always have special jobs to do in space. One astronaut is the pilot of the spaceship. The other astronauts do experiments, make repairs and gather information about their trip.

1. What is the main idea?

   _____ Life in space is much different than it is on Earth.

   _____ Without gravity, people on Earth would float around.

   _____ Gravity makes life on Earth much different than life in space.

2. What does gravity do? _____

   _____

3. How do astronauts sleep? _____

   _____

4. What do astronauts do in space? _____

   _____

5. How do astronauts drink water? _____

6. Would you like to be an astronaut? Why or why not? _____

   _____

Pupping Time

Read about sea lion "pupping time." Then answer the questions.

> When sea lion cows gather on the beach to give birth, it is called "pupping time." Pupping time is never a surprise. It always occurs in June. Thousands of sea lions may gather in one spot for pupping time. It is sort of like one big birthday party.
>
> The cow stays with her pup for about a week after birth. During that time, she never leaves her baby. If she must go somewhere, she drags her pup along. She grabs the loose skin around her pup's neck with her teeth. To humans, it doesn't look comfortable, but it doesn't hurt the pup.
>
> One place the mother must go is to the water. Because of her blubber, she gets hot on land. To cool off, she takes a dip in the ocean. When she comes out, she sniffs her pup to make sure she's got the right baby. Then she drags him back again to a spot she has staked out. After a week of being dragged around, do you think the pup is ready to play?

1. Why do thousands of sea lions gather together at a certain time? _____

   _____

2. Why isn't pupping time ever a surprise? _____

   _____

3. How does a cow take her pup along when she goes for a cool dip?

   First, she grabs _____.

   Then, _____.

   After the swim, she sniffs _____.

4. What is the main idea?(Check one.)

   _____ Thousands of cows gather at pupping time to give
   birth and afterwards stay with their pups for a week.

   _____ Thousands of sea lions take cools dips and
   usually drag their pups along.

   _____ Pups are born in June.

COMPLETE YEAR GRADE 4

Perimeter and Area

Area is also calculated by multiplying the length times the width of a square or rectangular figure. Use the formula: A = l x w.

Calculate the perimeter of each figure.

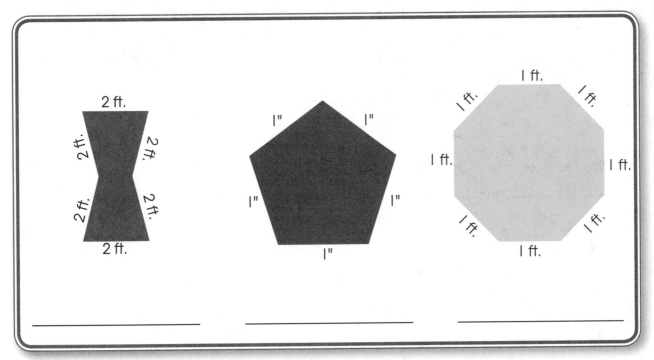

Calculate the area of each figure.

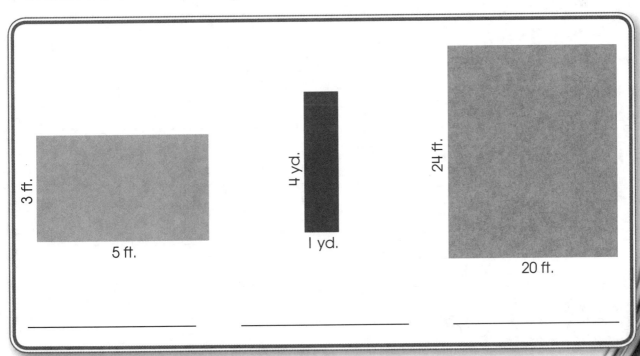

Perimeter and Area

The **perimeter (P)** of a figure is the distance around it. To find the perimeter, add the lengths of the sides.

The **area (A)** of a figure is the number of units in a figure. Find the area by multiplying the length of a figure by its width.

Example: P = 16 units
A = 16 units

Find the perimeter and area of each figure.

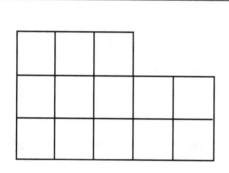

P = _____

A = _____

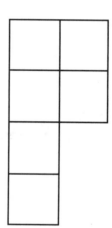

P = _____

A = _____

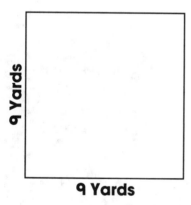

9 Yards

9 Yards

P = _____

A = _____

2 Miles

45 Miles

P = _____

A = _____

Perimeter and Area

Use the formulas for finding perimeter and area to solve these problems.

Julie's family moved to a new house. Her parents said she could have the largest bedroom. Julie knew she would need to find the area of each room to find which one was largest.

One rectangular bedroom is 7 feet wide and 12 feet long. Another is 11 feet long and 9 feet wide. The third bedroom is a square. It is 9 feet wide and 9 feet long. Which one should she select to have the largest room?

_____

The new home also has a swimming pool in the backyard. It is 32 feet long and 18 feet wide. What is the perimeter of the pool?

_____

Julie's mother wants to plant flowers on each side of the new house. She will need three plants for every foot of space. The house is 75 feet across the front and back and 37.5 feet along each side. Find the perimeter of the house.

_____

How many plants should she buy? _____

The family decided to buy new carpeting for several rooms. Complete the necessary information to determine how much carpeting to buy.

Den: 12 ft. x 14 ft. = _____ sq. ft.

Master Bedroom: 20 ft. x _____ = 360 sq. ft.

Family Room: _____ x 25 ft. = 375 sq. ft.

Total square feet of carpeting: _____

Volume

Volume is the number of cubic units that fit inside a figure.

Find the volume of each figure. The first one is done for you.

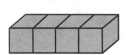

___4___ cubic units

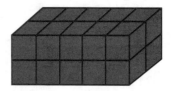

_____ cubic units

_____ cubic units

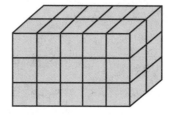

_____ cubic units

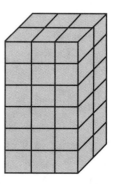

_____ cubic units

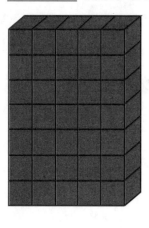

_____ cubic units

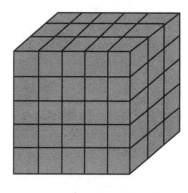

_____ cubic units

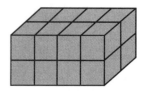

_____ cubic units

Week 30 Skills

Subject	Skill	Multi-Sensory Learning Activities
Reading and Language Arts	Follow step-by-step directions.	• Complete Practice Pages 320–324. • Allow five minutes for both you and your child to write a paragraph about how to tie a shoe or do some other simple everyday task. Read each paragraph aloud and have the listener try to follow the directions. Which set of directions was more precise?
Math	Review volume.	• Complete Practice Pages 325–328. • Have your child build three-dimensional rectangular structures with blocks. Have your child determine volume by counting the number of blocks used.
	Review area.	• Complete Practice Pages 327 and 328. • Have your child measure the area of several square and rectangular objects, such as a book, a stamp, a desktop, the floor, or a framed picture.
	Review perimeter.	• Complete Practice Page 328. • Ask your child to measure each wall of a room in your home and find the room's perimeter in feet, yards, and inches. Ask him or her if it is necessary to measure all four walls, and why.

Tennis Anyone?

Jack and Ron are playing tennis.

1. It is a very hot day. **Draw** a yellow sun in the sky above the shortest tree.

2. Use red to mark the thermometer up to **93** degrees.

3. Jack is on the right side of the net. **Color** his shirt yellow and his shorts blue with a green stripe.

4. **Color** Ron's shorts the color of Jack's stripe. **Color** his shirt the color of Jack's shorts.

5. Ron has just hit the ball. It is in the air, but it has not gone over the net yet. Use yellow to **draw** the ball.

6. Jack dropped his racket. Use brown to **draw** the racket.

7. **Count** all the balls on the ground. **Add** your age to that number. **Write** the total in the top of the tallest tree.

8. On the trunk of the middle tree, **write** the names of three other sports which use balls.

9. Between the shortest tree and the middle tree, **write** three words that you can make from the letters in the word *tennis*.

Following Directions: Maps

Follow the directions below to reach a "mystery" location on the map.

1. Begin at home.

2. Drive east on River Road.

3. Turn south on Broadway.

4. Drive to Central Street and turn west.

5. When you get to City Street, turn south.

6. Turn east on Main Street and drive one block to Park Avenue; turn north.

7. At Central Street turn east, and then turn southeast on Through Way.

8. Drive to the end of Through Way. Your "mystery" location is to the east.

You are at the _____.

Can you write an easier way to get back home? _____

_____

_____

_____

Following Directions: Recipes

Sequencing is putting items or events in logical order.
Read the recipe. Then number the steps in order for making brownies.

> Preheat the oven to 350 degrees. Grease an 8-inch square baking dish.
>
> In a mixing bowl, place two squares (2 ounces) of unsweetened chocolate and $\frac{1}{3}$ cup butter. Place the bowl in a pan of hot water and heat it to melt the chocolate and the butter.
>
> When the chocolate is melted, remove the pan from the heat. Add 1 cup sugar and two eggs to the melted chocolate and beat it. Next, stir in $\frac{3}{4}$ cup sifted flour, $\frac{1}{2}$ teaspoon baking powder, and $\frac{1}{2}$ teaspoon salt. Finally, mix in $\frac{1}{2}$ cup chopped nuts.
>
> Spread the mixture in the greased baking dish. Bake for 30 to 35 minutes. The brownies are done when a toothpick stuck in the center comes out clean. Let the brownies cool. Cut them into squares.

_____ Stick a toothpick in the center of the brownies to make sure they are done.

_____ Mix in chopped nuts.

_____ Melt chocolate and butter in a mixing bowl over a pan of hot water.

_____ Cool brownies and cut into squares.

_____ Beat in sugar and eggs.

_____ Spread mixture in a baking dish.

_____ Stir in flour, baking powder, and salt.

_____ Bake for 30 to 35 minutes.

_____ Turn oven to 350 degrees and grease pan.

Following Directions: Salt Into Pepper

Read how to do a magic trick that will amaze your friends. Then number the steps in order to do the trick.

> Imagine doing this trick for your friends. Pick up a salt shaker that everyone can see is full of salt. Pour some into your hand. Tell your audience that you will change the salt into pepper. Say a few magic words, such as "Fibbiddy, dibbiddy, milkshake and malt. What will be pepper once was salt!" Then open your hand and pour out pepper!
>
> How is it done? First you need a clear salt shaker with a screw-on top. You also need a paper napkin and a small amount of pepper.
>
> Take off the top of the salt shaker. Lay the napkin over the opening and push it down a little to make a small pocket. Fill the pocket with pepper. Put the top back on the salt shaker and tear off the extra napkin. Now you are ready for the trick.
>
> Hold up the salt shaker so your audience can see that it is full of salt. Shake some "salt" into your hand. Close your fist so no one can see that it is really pepper. Say the magic words and open your hand.

_____ Say some magic words.

_____ Find a clear salt shaker with a screw-on top.

_____ Open your hand and pour out the pepper.

_____ Take off the top of the salt shaker.

_____ Show the audience the shaker full of salt.

_____ Place the napkin over the opening of the salt shaker.

_____ Get a paper napkin and some pepper.

_____ Put the pepper in the napkin pocket.

_____ Shake some "salt" into your hand and close your fist.

_____ Put the top back on the salt shaker and tear off the extra napkin.

Following Directions: Recipes

Follow these steps for making a peanut butter and jelly sandwich.

1. Get a jar of peanut butter, a jar of jelly, two slices of bread and a knife.

2. Open the jar lids.

3. Using the knife, spread peanut butter on one slice of bread.

4. Spread jelly on the other slice of bread.

5. Put the two slices of bread together to make a sandwich.

Write the steps for a recipe of your own. Be very specific. When you are done, give the recipe to a friend to make. You will know right away if any steps are missing!

Recipe for: _____

1. _____

2. _____

3. _____

4. _____

5. _____

6. _____

Volume

The volume of a figure can also be calculated by multiplying the length times the width times the height. Use the formula: V= l x w x h.

Example: 3 x 5 x 2 = 30 cubic feet

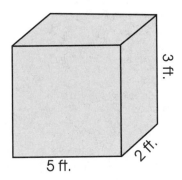

Find the volume of the following figures. Label your answers in cubic feet, inches or yards. The first one is done for you.

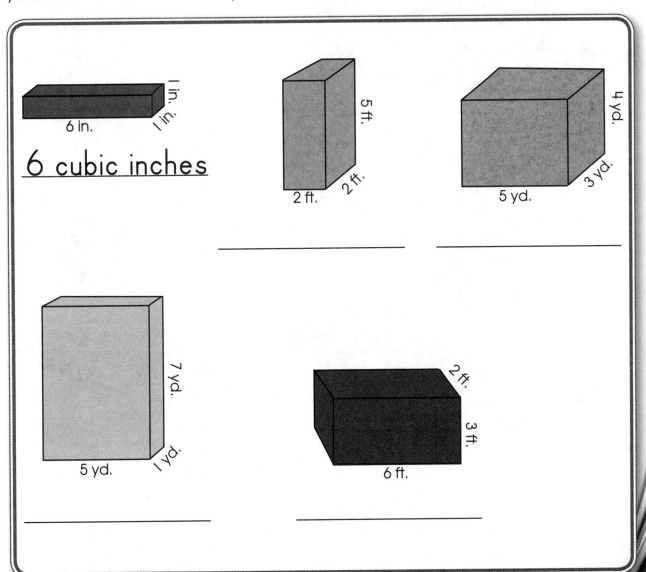

<u>6 cubic inches</u>

Volume

The formula for finding the volume of a box is length times width times height **(L x W x H)**. The answer is given in cubic units.

Solve the problems.

Example: Height 8 ft.

Length 8 ft.

Width   8 ft. **L** x **W** x **H** = **volume**
8' x 8' x 8' = 512 cubic ft.
or 512 ft³

Height 8 ft.

Width 8 ft.

Length 8 ft.

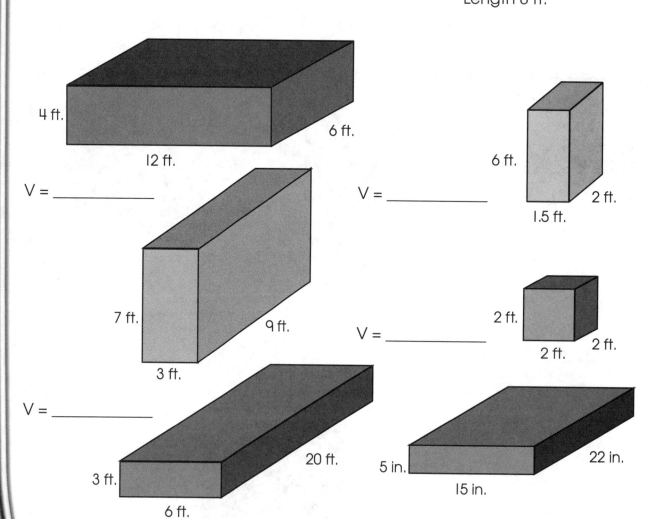

4 ft.

6 ft.

12 ft.

V = _____

6 ft.

2 ft.

1.5 ft.

V = _____

7 ft.

9 ft.

3 ft.

V = _____

2 ft.

2 ft.

2 ft.

V = _____

3 ft.

20 ft.

6 ft.

V = _____

5 in.

22 in.

15 in.

V = _____ in.³   V = _____ ft.³

Area and Volume

Calculate the area of each figure. Use the formula: A = l x w.

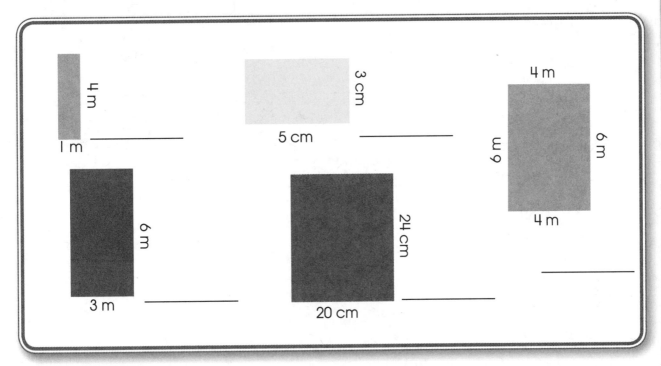

Calculate the volume of each figure. Use the formula: V = l x w x h.

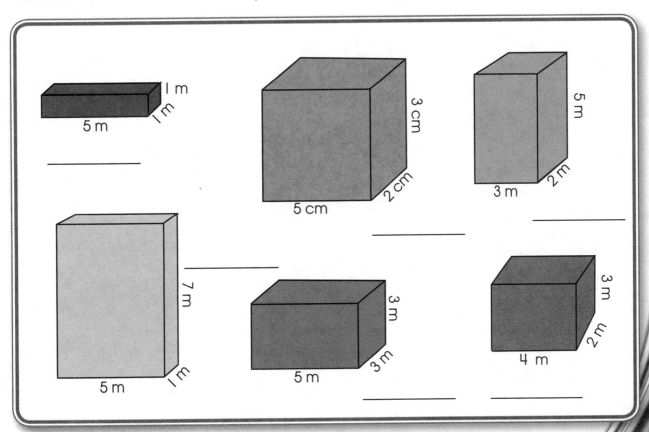

Perimeter, Area and Volume

Find the perimeter and area.

1. Length = 8 ft.

   Width = 11 ft.

   P = _____   A = _____

2. Length = 12 ft.

   Width = 10 ft.

   P = _____   A = _____

3. Length = 121 ft.

   Width = 16 ft.

   P = _____   A = _____

4. Length = 72 in.

   Width = 5 ft.

   P = _____   A = _____

Find the perimeter, area, and volume.

5. Length = 7 ft.

   Width = 12 ft.

   Height = 10 ft.

   P = _____

   A = _____

   V = _____

6. Length = 48 in.

   Width = 7 ft.

   Height = 12 in.

   P = _____

   A = _____

   V = _____

7. Length = 12 in.

   Width = 15 in.

   Height = 20 in.

   P = _____

   A = _____

   V = _____

8. Length = 22 ft.

   Width = 40 ft.

   Height = 10 ft.

   P = _____

   A = _____

   V = _____

Week 31 Skills

Subject	Skill	Multi-Sensory Learning Activities
Reading and Language Arts	Understand and identify cause and effect situations.	• Complete Practice Pages 330–334. • Read *Encyclopedia Brown, Boy Detective* by Donald J. Sobol with your child. As you are reading, ask questions about the story, such as "What caused…?" or "What was the effect of…?"
Basic Skills	Calculate time.	• Complete Practice Page 335. • Think of some "events" that your child experiences often. Make a list of these events and have your child guess how long each one lasts. Then, have him or her time the events the next time they occur.
	Measure in inches.	• Complete Practice Pages 337 and 338. • Gather some friends together for a seed-spitting contest. Provide the children with some watermelon or pumpkin seeds. Go outside, if weather permits, and have each person stand in a line and spit one seed as far as he or she can. Then, give your child a ruler and ask him or her to measure the distance in inches that each seed flew. Play the game again and see who can win round two.

If...Then

Match the sentence parts that go together best. Write the number of the first sentence part on the line in front of the last sentence part for each one.

1. If you baby-sit for me Saturday night

2. If you are nice

3. If we leave work by 4:30

4. If you leave a note on your door

5. If you don't have enough money for the movie

6. If my father isn't too tired

7. If the wind keeps up

8. If you want to get a seat at the concert

9. If our neighbor cuts the grass early Sunday morning

10. If the plant doesn't feel damp

11. If my house were painted white

12. If everyone talked at the same time

13. If you don't get a haircut

14. If the tea kettle whistles

15. If no one answers the door

16. If the little boy crosses the street

17. If the horse is tired

18. If you have a long stick

19. If you don't want any dessert

20. If a king comes into a room

21. If it snows a lot tomorrow

_____ the delivery man will leave the package.

_____ it needs to be watered.

_____ you could roast marshmallows.

_____ probably no one is at home.

_____ everyone will rise.

_____ I'll pay you double.

_____ the water is boiling.

_____ tomorrow will be a great kite-flying day.

_____ let him rest.

_____ no one could hear directions.

_____ we will avoid rush hour.

_____ say "No, thank you."

_____ the noise will wake me up.

_____ we can build an igloo.

_____ he said he would show me how to shoot baskets.

_____ it would look like a miniature White House.

_____ I'll loan you the rest.

_____ he must hold onto his mother's hand.

_____ you will have many friends.

_____ you will have to be at the auditorium early.

_____ you will have long hair.

If...

then...

Cause and Effect Sentences

A **cause and effect sentence** has two parts: a **cause**, which tells why, and an **effect**, which tells what happened. It can be written two ways.

Example: <u>Today is Saturday</u>, so <u>I don't have to go to school.</u>
          cause   **effect**

          <u>I don't have to go to school</u> because <u>today is Saturday.</u>
                 effect   **cause**

Combine the two sentences into a cause and effect sentence. Write the sentence two ways: **A. cause-effect**, **B. effect-cause**

1. I could not eat my dessert. I was full from dinner.

    A. _____

    B. _____

2. I forgot to take my umbrella. I got wet in the rain.

    A. _____

    B. _____

3. The astronomer could not see clearly. The night was cloudy.

    A. _____

    B. _____

4. I love animals. I want to be a veterinarian someday.

    A. _____

    B. _____

Write two sets of cause and effect sentences about any subject.

    A. _____

    B. _____

    A. _____

    B. _____

Elf on an Elephant

Use the words to fill in the blanks.
Look for a cause/effect relationship in each situation.

1. **cause:** cutting in _____

   effect: sharing a candy bar

2. **cause:** having a _____

   effect: covering your mouth

3. **cause:** hearing the _____

   effect: answering "hello"

4. **cause:** reading about an _____

   effect: enjoying a fairy tale

5. **cause:** telling a joke

   effect: hearing _____

6. **cause:** having a _____

   effect: blowing your nose

coffee
cough
different
elephant
elf
enough
graph
half
laughter
oneself
photo
rough
sniffle
telephone
tough

Complete these statements by filling in the blanks.

1. An antonym for "alike" is _____.

2. An antonym for "fragile" is _____.

3. An antonym for "smooth" is _____.

4. A kind of beverage is _____.

5. The word that is a pronoun is _____.

Four words have not been used. Use two of them in one sentence and the other two in a separate sentence. Underline the words.

_____

_____

_____

_____

COMPLETE YEAR GRADE 4

Twice the Fun

airport
barefoot
birthday
cardboard
downstairs
earthquake
farewell
flyswatter
afternoon
iceberg
landlord
northwest
scarecrow
teakettle
throughout

Fill in the blanks.

Look for a cause/effect relationship in each situation.

1. **cause:** a _____

    effect: receiving gifts

2. **cause:** using a _____

    effect: dead insects

3. **cause:** an _____

    effect: a shipwreck

4. **cause:** an _____

    effect: toppled buildings

5. **cause:** going _____

    effect: cutting a toe

6. **cause:** have a _____

    effect: a good harvest

7. **cause:** using a _____

    effect: boiled water

Complete these statements by filling in the blanks.

1. Which word names a part of the day? _____

2. A synonym for "goodbye" is _____.

3. Boxes are often made of _____.

4. As the plane took off from the _____,

    it flew in a _____ direction.

5. The _____ who owns the duplex lives upstairs, and my

    family lives _____.

6. Which word is a preposition? _____

What Made It Happen?

Each set of sentences includes a cause and an effect. Remember: The cause is what makes something happen, and the effect is the result. Write the cause on the line and circle the effect.

1. The snow came down harder than anyone could ever remember. For days the people of the village were housebound.

   _____

2. Many of the soldiers decided to learn to ski. The children called one soldier "Lieutenant Sit-Down," because he fell down more than he stood.

   _____

3. The Commandant kept kicking the snowman covering the gold. Peter threw a snowball to distract the Commandant from discovering the gold.

   _____

4. Per Garson was skiing in crazy patterns around and around the Lundstrom's house. Uncle Victor had been there earlier on his skis.

   _____

5. Peter was sailing down the slope at high speed. In his path, he could see approaching soldiers. Peter was going so fast he could not stop his sled. The soldiers scattered to let Peter through.

   _____

6. Mrs. Holms seemed very excited to see the Lundstroms coming to her home. She acted as though she could not wait to speak. Earlier in the day a German soldier had been in the Holms's barn.

   _____

Minute Monsters

The Minute Monsters have their pairs of shoes mixed-up. Cut out the shoes. Glue the matching pairs onto another paper.

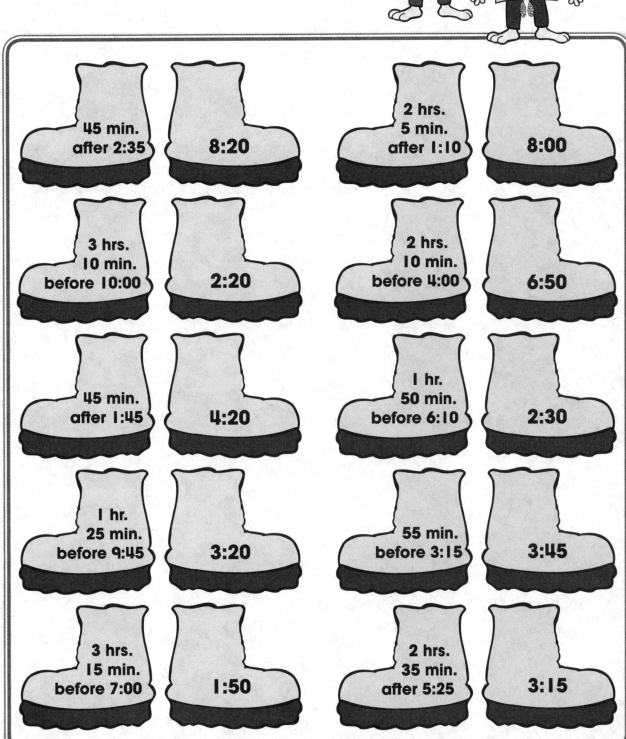

45 min. after 2:35

8:20

2 hrs. 5 min. after 1:10

8:00

3 hrs. 10 min. before 10:00

2:20

2 hrs. 10 min. before 4:00

6:50

45 min. after 1:45

4:20

1 hr. 50 min. before 6:10

2:30

1 hr. 25 min. before 9:45

3:20

55 min. before 3:15

3:45

3 hrs. 15 min. before 7:00

1:50

2 hrs. 35 min. after 5:25

3:15

How Far Is It?

Use your ruler to measure each distance on the map. Then, use the letters on the tires and your answers to solve the message at the bottom of the page.

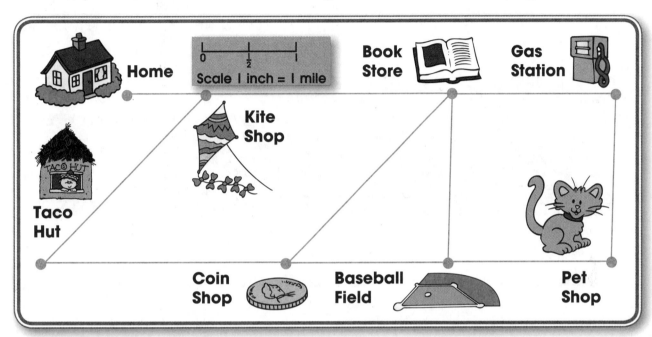

How far is it from . . .

1. home to the Kite Shop? _____ **s**

2. home to the Book Store to the Gas Station? _____ **e**

3. home to the Kite Shop to the Taco Hut? _____ **p**

4. the Taco Hut to the Coin Shop to the Book Store to the Gas Station? _____ **a**

5. the Taco Hut to the Coin Shop? _____ **u**

6. the Baseball Field to the Book Store to the Kite Shop? _____ **d**

7. the Pet Shop to the Gas Station? _____ **r**

8. the Gas Station to the Pet Shop to the Baseball Field to the Coin Shop to the Taco Hut? _____ **m**

You ___ ___ ___ ___ ___ ___ ___ ___ ___ ___!
    9   6   8   1   3   2   6   5   3   4

Inches

An **inch** is a unit of length in the standard system equal to $\frac{1}{12}$ of a foot. A ruler is used to measure inches.

This illustration shows a ruler measuring a 4-inch pencil, which can be written as 4" or 4 in.

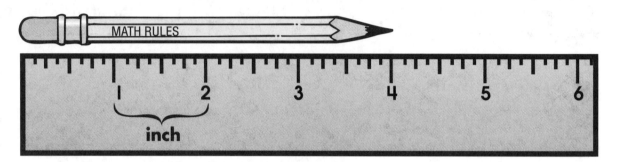

Use a ruler to measure each object to the nearest inch.

1. The length of your foot   _____

2. The width of your hand   _____

3. The length of this page   _____

4. The width of this page   _____

5. The length of a large paper clip _____

6. The length of your toothbrush _____

7. The length of a comb   _____

8. The height of a juice glass   _____

9. The length of your shoe   _____

10. The length of a fork   _____

Week 32 Skills

Subject	Skill	Multi-Sensory Learning Activities
Reading and Language Arts	Use context clues to interpret meaning.	• Complete Practice Pages 340–344. • Encourage your child to read a newspaper or nonfiction article with challenging vocabulary. Have your child choose one unfamiliar word in the piece. Together, look for context clues that help define the word.
Math	Review measurement in inches and fractions of an inch.	• Complete Practice Pages 345–347. • Give your child a straight-sided, clear container that will hold water. Tape a ruler to the outside with zero at the base. Face the ruler out so your child can read the numbers. Place the rain gauge outside in an open area. Ask your child to measure the water to the nearest fraction of an inch every day for two weeks and create a chart to show his or her findings.
	Measure in feet, yards, and miles.	• Complete Practice Page 348. • Have your child measure different distances by pacing. You can measure the length of a pace by walking along a yardstick or by measuring the length between footprints. Place the end of the stick at the back of one heel. Take a normal step and note the measurement from the heel to the tip of the front foot.

Context Clues

When you read, you may confuse words that look alike. You can tell when you read a word incorrectly because it doesn't make sense. You can tell from the **context** (the other words in the sentence or the sentences before or after) what the word should be. These **context clues** can help you figure out the meaning of a word by relating it to other words in the sentence.

Circle the correct word for each sentence below. Use the context to help you.

1. We knew we were in trouble as soon as we heard the crash. The baseball had gone (through, thought) the picture window!

2. She was not able to answer my question because her (month, mouth) was full of pizza.

3. Asia is the largest continent in the (world, word).

4. I'm not sure I heard the teacher correctly. Did he say what I (through, thought) he said?

5. I was not with them on vacation so I don't know a (think, thing) about what happened.

6. My favorite (month, mouth) of the year is July because I love fireworks and parades!

7. You will do better on your book report if you (think, thing) about what you are going to say.

Context Clues

Read each sentence carefully and circle the word that makes sense.

1. We didn't (except, expect) you to arrive so early.

2. "I can't hear a (word, world) you are saying. Wait until I turn down the stereo," said Val.

3. I couldn't sleep last night because of the (noise, nose) from the apartment below us.

4. Did Peggy say (weather, whether) or not we needed our binoculars for the game?

5. He broke his (noise, nose) when he fell off the bicycle.

6. All the students (except, expect) the four in the front row are excused to leave.

7. The teacher said we should have good (whether, weather) for our field trip.

Choose a word pair from the sentences above to write two sentences of your own.

1. _____

   _____

2. _____

   _____

Context Clues

Use context clues to help you choose the correct word for each sentence below.

> designs   studying   collection

Our fourth-grade class will be _____ castles for the next four weeks. Mrs. Oswalt will be helping with our study. She plans to share her _____ of castle models with the class. We are all looking forward to our morning in the sand at the school's volleyball court. We all get to try our own _____ to see how they work.

> breath   excited   quietly

Michelle was very _____ the other day when she came into the classroom. We all noticed that she had trouble sitting _____ in her seat until it was her turn to share with us. When her turn finally came, she took a deep _____ and told us that her mom was going to have a baby!

> responsibility   chooses   messages

Each week, our teacher _____ classroom helpers. They get to be part of the Job Squad. Some helpers have the _____ of watering the plants. Everyone's favorite job is when they get to take _____ to the office or to another teacher's room.

Context Clues

Read the story. Match each bold word with its definition below.

Where the northern shores of North America meet the Arctic Ocean, the winters are very long and cold. No plants or crops will grow there. This is the land of the **Eskimo**.

Eskimos have figured out ways to live in the snow and ice. They sometimes live in **igloos**, which are made of snow. It is really very comfortable inside! An oil lamp provides light and warmth.

Often, you will find a big, furry **husky** sleeping in the long tunnel that leads to the igloo. Huskies are very important to Eskimos because they pull their sleds and help with hunting. Eskimos are excellent hunters. Many, many years ago they learned to make **harpoons** and spears to help them hunt their food.

Eskimos get much of their food from the sea, especially fish, seals, and whales. Often, an Eskimo will go out in a **kayak** to fish. Only one Eskimo fits inside, and he drives it with a paddle. The waves may turn the kayak upside down, but the Eskimo does not fall out. He is so skillful with a paddle that he quickly is right side up again.

A _____ is a large, strong dog.

An _____ is a member of the race of people who live on the Arctic coasts of North America and in parts of Greenland.

_____ are houses made of packed snow.

A _____ is a one-person canoe made of animal skins.

_____ are spears with a long rope attached. They are used for spearing whales and other large sea animals.

Context Clues

In each sentence below, circle the correct meaning for the nonsense word.

1. Be careful when you put that plate back on the shelf—it is **quibbable**.

   flexible   colorful   breakable

2. What is your favorite kind of **tonn**, pears or bananas?

   fruit   salad   purple

3. The **dinlay** outside this morning was very chilly; I needed my sweater.

   tree   vegetable   temperature

4. The whole class enjoyed the **weat**. They wanted to see it again next Friday.

   colorful   plant   video

5. Ashley's mother brought in a **zundy** she made by hand.

   temperature   quilt   plant

6. "Why don't you sit over here, Ronnie? That **sloey** is not very comfortable," said Mr. Gross.

   chair   car   cat

Inches

Use a ruler to measure the width of each foot to the nearest inch.

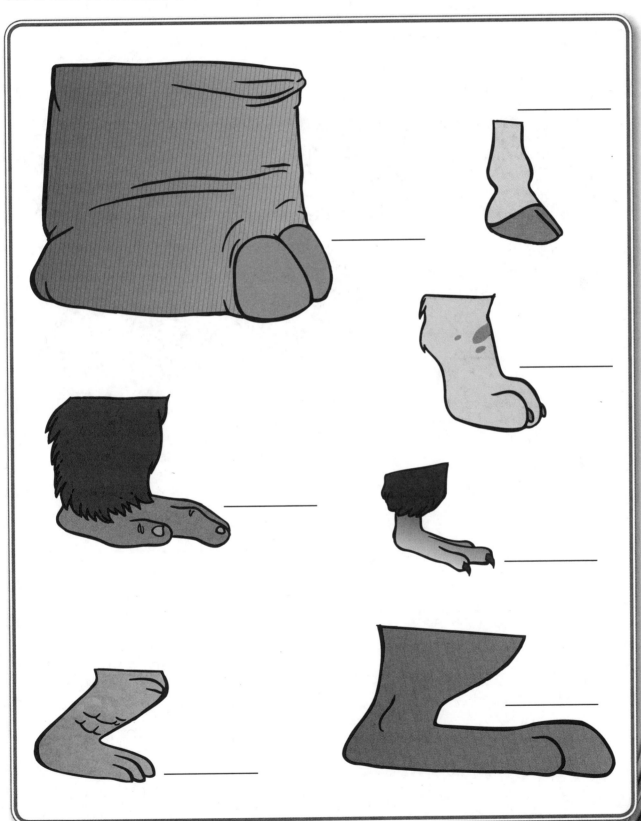

Fractions of an Inch

An inch is divided into smaller units, or fractions of an inch.

Example: This stick of gum is $2\frac{3}{4}$ inches long.

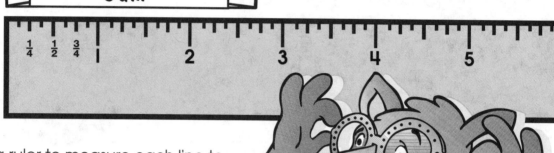

Use a ruler to measure each line to the nearest quarter of an inch. The first one is done for you.

1. $\frac{3}{4}$ inch _____

2. _____ _____

3. _____ _____

4. _____ _____

5. _____ _____

6. _____ _____

7. _____ _____

Fractions of an Inch

Use a ruler to measure to the nearest quarter of an inch.

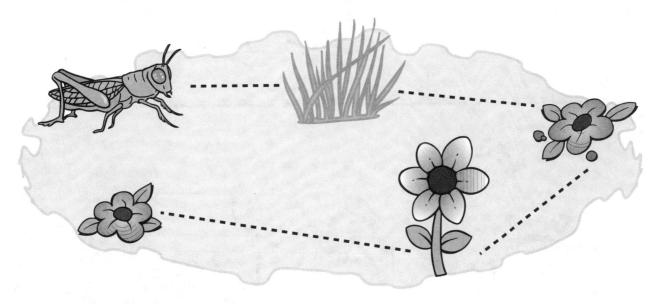

How far did the grasshopper jump?

_____ + _____ + _____ + _____ = _____

What is the total length of the paintbrushes?

_____ + _____ + _____ + _____ + _____ = _____

Foot, Yard, Mile

Choose the measure of distance you would use for each object.

I foot = 12 inches
I yard = 3 feet
I mile = 1,760 yards or 5,280 feet

inches

Week 33 Skills

Subject	Skill	Multi-Sensory Learning Activities
Reading and Language Arts	Draw conclusions from a reading passage.	• Complete Practice Pages 350 and 351. • Re-read chapter 18 of *The Whipping Boy*. Have your child imagine what will happen to Jemmy in the future. Then, have him or her write a paragraph describing Jemmy's life five years in the future. • Briefly describe a situation. For example, say, "Matt just turned 4. He has chocolate all over his face and he looks sheepish." Have your child draw a conclusion about what must have happened. Repeat with other situations.
	Use quotation marks around song titles, poems, and dialogue.	• Complete Practice Pages 352–354. • Practice reading dialogue with your child. Choose a conversational dialogue from a book. Let your child pick a role and you take the other. Read the dialogue as actual conversation, reading only the words within quotation marks.
Math	Measure in centimeters, meters, and kilometers.	• Complete Practice Pages 355–358. • List several objects for your child, such as the length of the room, the height of the door, the width of his or her desk, the length of his or her pencil, or the distance to a friend's house. Then, ask him or her whether it would be most appropriate to measure in centimeters, meters, or kilometers.

Star Light, Star Bright

Lie on your back. Gaze up into the night sky. Which star is the brightest? On a clear night you can see hundreds of stars, some are bright and others are dim. Why are some stars brighter than others? Let's try to find out by looking at the picture on this page.

1. Look at the two streetlights in the picture. Which streetlight appears brighter?

   _____

   Why?_____

   _____

2. Look at the bicycle and the truck. Which headlights appear brighter?

   _____

   Why?_____

3. Some stars appear brighter than other stars for the same reasons as those stated above. What are the two reasons?

   a. _____

   b. _____

Color Me Hot

Stars differ not only in brightness but also in color. As a star gets hotter, its color changes. Color these stars. Use the chart to find the correct color.

Star Colors

36,000°F Blue	18,000°F White
9,000°F Yellow	5,400°F Red

Spica 36,000°F   Sirius 18,000°F   Sun 9,000°F   Betelgeuse 5,400°F

A Picture Is Worth ...

Look at the first picture. Put a check in the box by each sentence which seems sensible. Look at the second picture. Write six sentences that tell your conclusions about the picture.

☐ It is a very hot day.

☐ The beach is a popular place to go.

☐ The beach is a quiet place to study.

☐ Some people picnic at the beach.

☐ A lifeguard helps protect swimmers.

☐ It is hard to nap at a noisy beach.

☐ Sailing is just for kids.

☐ Sailing and swimming are fun water sports.

☐ Every town has a beach.

Write your own conclusions.

1. _____

2. _____

3. _____

4. _____

5. _____

6. _____

Quotation Marks

Use quotation marks around the titles of songs and poems.

Examples: Have you heard "Still Cruising" by the Beach Boys?

"Ode To a Nightingale" is a famous poem.

Write **C** if the sentence is punctuated correctly. Draw an **X** if the sentence is not punctuated correctly. The first one has been done for you.

_C_ 1. Do you know "My Bonnie Lies Over the Ocean"?

_____ 2. We sang The Stars and Stripes Forever" at school.

_____ 3. Her favorite song is "The Eensy Weensy Spider."

_____ 4. Turn the music up when "A Hard Day's "Night comes on!

_____ 5. "Yesterday" was one of Paul McCartney's most famous songs.

_____ 6. "Mary Had a Little Lamb" is a very silly poem!

_____ 7. A song everyone knows is "Happy Birthday."

_____ 8. "Swing Low, Sweet Chariot" was first sung by slaves.

_____ 9. Do you know the words to Home on "the Range"?

_____ 10. "Hiawatha" is a poem many older people had to memorize.

_____ 11. "Happy Days Are Here Again! is an upbeat tune.

_____ 12. Frankie Valli and the Four Seasons sang "Sherry."

_____ 13. The words to "Rain, Rain" Go Away are easy to learn.

_____ 14. A slow song I know is called "Summertime."

_____ 15. Little children like to hear "The Night Before Christmas."

Quotation Marks

Use quotation marks (" ") before and after the exact words of a speaker.

Examples: I asked Aunt Martha, "How do you feel?"

"I feel awful," Aunt Martha replied.

Do not put quotation marks around words that report what the speaker said.

Examples: Aunt Martha said she felt awful.

I asked Aunt Martha how she felt.

Write **C** if the sentence is punctuated correctly. Draw an **X** if the sentence is not punctuated correctly. The first one has been done for you.

___C___ 1. "I want it right now!" she demanded angrily.

_____ 2. "Do you want it now? I asked."

_____ 3. She said "she felt better" now.

_____ 4. Her exact words were, "I feel much better now!"

_____ 5. "I am so thrilled to be here!" he shouted.

_____ 6. "Yes, I will attend," she replied.

_____ 7. Elizabeth said "she was unhappy."

_____ 8. "I'm unhappy," Elizabeth reported.

_____ 9. "Did you know her mother?" I asked.

_____ 10. I asked "whether you knew her mother."

_____ 11. I wondered, "What will dessert be?"

_____ 12. "Which will it be, salt or pepper?" the waiter asked.

_____ 13. "No, I don't know the answer!" he snapped.

_____ 14. He said "yes he'd take her on the trip.

_____ 15. Be patient, he said. "it will soon be over."

Direct Quotations

Use **quotation marks** to enclose the exact words of the speaker. The speaker's first word must begin with a capital letter. Also follow these rules:

1. When the speaker is named **before** the direct quotation, separate the speaker from the quotation with a comma.

2. When the speaker is named **after** the direct quotation, use a comma or the proper end mark inside the last quotation.

Examples: 1. *Mother said, "You must clean your room."*

2. *"Sara is cleaning her room," said Mother.*

3. *"Have you found your shoes?" asked Tina.*

4. *"Hurry up!" yelled John.*

Punctuate these sentences correctly.

1. Father asked John, Will you be home for dinner

2. No, I will be at football practice said John

3. When will you have time to eat asked Dad

4. I'll have to eat after practice grumbled John

5. Hurry up yelled Pete

6. Pete commented We'll be late for practice if you don't move faster

Rewrite these sentences. Punctuate and capitalize them correctly.

1. will you take out the garbage asked Mother

_____

2. Mary answered I don't have time now

_____

3. is it alright if I do it later she added

_____

4. please do that job as soon as you get home Mother said

_____

It Suits Me to a Tee!

How many inches and centimeters from the tee to the flag?

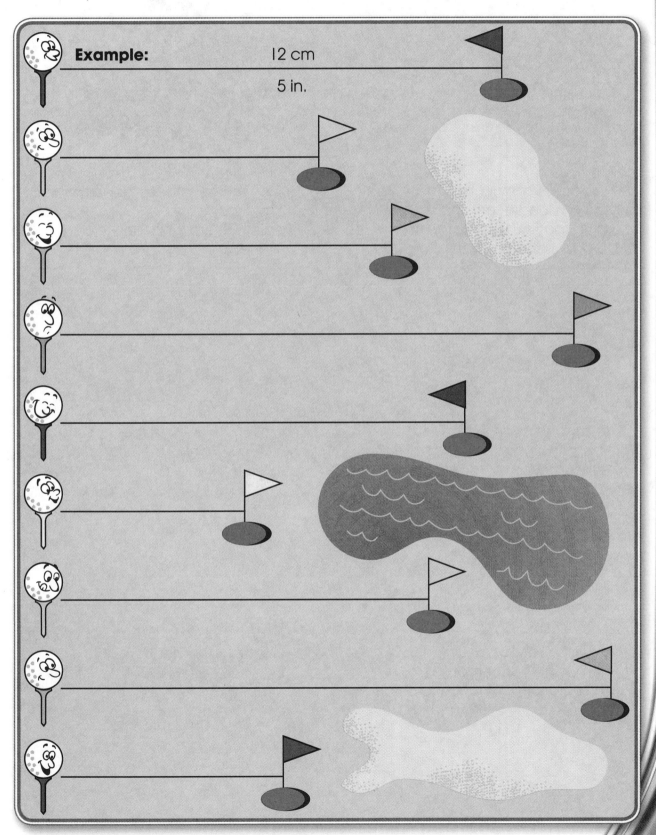

Example: 12 cm

5 in.

Animal Trivia

1. An earthworm is 14.9 cm long. A grasshopper is 8.7 cm long. What is the difference?

2. A pocket gopher has a hind foot 3.5 cm long. A ground squirrel's hind foot is 6.4 cm long. How much longer is the ground squirrel's hind foot?

5. A cottontail rabbit has ears which are 6.8 cm long. A jackrabbit has ears 12.9 cm long. How much shorter is the cottontail's ear?

6. The hind foot of a river otter is 14.6 cm long. The hind foot of a hog-nosed skunk is 9.0 cm long. What is the difference?

3. A porcupine has a tail 30.0 cm long. An opossum has a tail 53.5 cm long. How much longer is the opossum's tail?

7. A rock mouse is 26.1 cm long. His tail adds another 14.4 cm. What is his total length from his nose to the tip of his tail?

4. A wood rat has a tail which is 23.6 cm long. A deer mouse has a tail 12.2 cm long. What is the difference between the two?

Centimeter

Use a centimeter ruler to measure the width of each foot to the nearest centimeter.

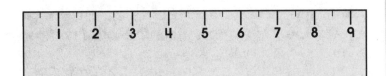

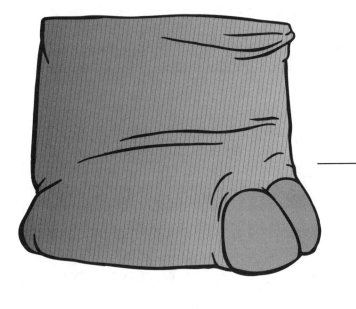 _____

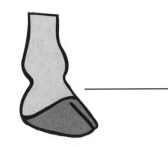 _____

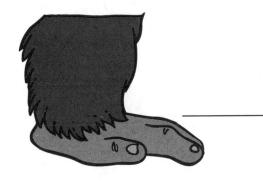 _____

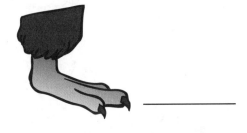 _____

 _____

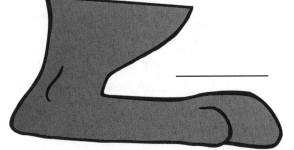 _____

Centimeter, Meter, Kilometer

In the metric system, there are three units of linear measurement: centimeter (cm), meter (m) and kilometer (km).

Centimeters (cm) are used to measure the lengths of small to medium-sized objects. **Meters (m)** measure the lengths of longer objects, such as the width of a swimming pool or height of a tree (100 cm = 1 meter). **Kilometers (km)** measure long distances, such as the distance from Cleveland to Cincinnati or the width of the Atlantic Ocean (1,000 m = 1 km).

Write whether you would use cm, m, or km to measure each object.

Week 34 Skills

Subject	Skill	Multi-Sensory Learning Activities
Reading and Language Arts	Use correct capitalization and punctuation.	• Complete Practice Pages 360–364. • Read *Shiloh* by Phyllis Reynolds Naylor. On a piece of paper, copy a paragraph from the book, leaving off all punctuation. Have your child replace the missing punctuation.
Math	Review metric measurement.	• Complete Practice Page 365. • Have your child draw a simple maze using straight paths. Then, have him or her write specific directions for solving the maze. For example, your child may write, "Start at the garage and go 5 cm west. Turn and go 2 cm south," etc.
	Measure weights in ounces, pounds, tons, grams, and kilograms.	• Complete Practice Pages 366 and 367. • Have your child compare a bag of flour and a bag of potato chips that are about the same size, noting that the flour is much heavier. Then, give your child other pairs of similar-sized objects and compare their weights, such as a bowling ball and a beach ball, a cement block and a wooden block, and a pillow and a folded blanket.
	Measure liquids in cups, pints, quarts, and gallons.	• Complete Practice Page 368. • Look through cupboards for containers of liquids. Read their measurements. Have your child line up the bottles in order of volume from smallest to largest capacity.

Paragraph Form

A **paragraph** is a group of sentences about one main idea.

When writing a paragraph:
1. Indent the first line.
2. Capitalize the first word of each sentence.
3. Punctuate each sentence.

Example: There are many reasons to write a paragraph. A paragraph can describe something or tell a story. It can tell how something is made or give an opinion. Do you know other reasons to write a paragraph?

Read the paragraphs below. They contain errors. Rewrite the paragraphs correctly on the lines by following three basic rules:
1. Indent
2. Capitalize
3. Punctuate

1. the number of teeth you have depends on your age a baby has no teeth at all gradually, milk teeth, or baby teeth, begin to grow later, these teeth fall out and permanent teeth appear by the age of twenty-five, you should have thirty-two permanent teeth

_____

_____

_____

_____

_____

2. my family is going to Disneyland tomorrow we plan to arrive early my dad will take my little sister to Fantasyland first meanwhile, my brother and I will visit Frontierland and Adventureland after lunch we will all meet to go to Tomorrowland

_____

_____

_____

_____

_____

Proofreading

It is important to be able to proofread things that you write to correct any errors.

Read each paragraph. Proofread for these errors:
- indentation
- punctuation
- capitalization
- sentences which do not belong (mark out)
- spelling
- run-on sentences (rewrite as two sentences)

Rewrite each paragraph correctly on the lines.

1. my brother will graduate from high school this week everyone is so excited for him Many of our relatives are coming from out of town for his graduation our town has a university. mom and Dad have planed a big surprise party

_____

_____

_____

_____

2. riding in a hot air balloon is an incredible experience first, everyone climbs into the basket the pilot then starts the fuel which produces the hot air that makes the ballone rise. The road leads to an open field to lower the balloon, the pilot gradually releases air

_____

_____

_____

_____

3. a caterpiller is a young butterfly the caterpillar originally hatches from an egg and later, it develops a hard case around its body inside the case, the caterpillow becomes a butterfly after a short time, the case opens and a beautiful butterfly flies out the tree has hndreds of blossoms

Rewrite this paragraph on another sheet of paper.

Capital Letters and Periods

The first letter of a person'ts first, last, and middle name is always capitalized.

Example: **E**lizabeth **J**ane **M**arks is my best friend.

the first letter of a person's title is always capitalized.
If the title is abbreviated, the title is followed by a period.

Examples: Her mother is **Dr**. Susan Jones Marks.
Ms. Jessica Joseph was a visitor.

Write **C** if the sentence is punctuated and capitalized correctly.
Daw an **X** if the sentence is not punctuated and capitalized correctly. The first one has been done for you.

_____X_____ 1. I asked Elizabeth if I should call her mother Mrs. marks or dr. Marks.

_____ 2. Mr. and Mrs. Francesco were friends of the DeVuonos.

_____ 3. Dr. Daniel Long and Dr Holly Barrows both spoke with the patient.

_____ 4. Did you get Mr. MacMillan for English next year?

_____ 5. Mr. Sweet and Ms. Ellison were both at the concert.

_____ 6. When did the doctor. tell you about this illness?

_____ 7. Dr. Donovan is the doctor that Mr. Winham trusted.

_____ 8. Why don't you ask Doctor. Williams her opinion?

_____ 9. All three of the doctors diagnosed Ms. Twelp.

_____ 10. Will Ms. Davis and Ms Simpson be at school today?

_____ 11. Did Dr Samuels see your father last week?

_____ 12. Is Judy a medical doctor or another kind of specialist?

_____ 13. We are pleased to introduce Ms King and Mr. Graham.

Commas

Use a comma to separate the number of the day of a month and the year. Do not use a comma to separate the month and year if no day is given.

Examples: June 14, 1999
June 1999

Use a comma after **yes** or **no** when it is the first word in a sentence.

Examples: Yes, I will do it right now.
No, I don't want any.

Write **C** if the sentence is punctuated correctly. Draw an **X** if the sentence is not punctuated correctly. The first one has been done for you.

C _____ 1. No, I don't plan to attend.

_____ 2. I told them, oh yes, I would go.

_____ 3. Her birthday is March 13, 1995.

_____ 4. He was born in May, 1997.

_____ 5. Yes, of course I like you!

_____ 6. No I will not be there.

_____ 7. They left for vacation on February, 14.

_____ 8. No, today is Monday.

_____ 9. The program was first shown on August 12, 1991.

_____ 10. In September, 2007 how old will you be?

_____ 11. He turned 12 years old on November, 13.

_____ 12. I said no, I will not come no matter what!

_____ 13. Yes, she is a friend of mine.

_____ 14. His birthday is June 12, 1992, and mine is June 12, 1993.

_____ 15. No I would not like more dessert.

Commas

Use a comma to separate words in a series. A comma is used after each word in a series but is not needed before the last word. Both ways are correct. In your own writing, be consistent about which style you use.

Examples: We ate apples, oranges, and pears.
We ate apples, oranges and pears.

Always use a comma between the name of a city and a state.

Example: She lives in Fresno, California.
He lives in Wilmington, Delaware.

Write **C** if the sentence is punctuated correctly. Draw an **X** if the sentence is not punctuated correctly. The first one has been done for you.

__X__ 1. She ordered shoes, dresses and shirts to be sent to her home in Oakland California.

_____ 2. No one knew her pets' names were Fido, Spot and Tiger.

_____ 3. He likes green beans lima beans, and corn on the cob.

_____ 4. Typing paper, pens and pencils are all needed for school.

_____ 5. Send your letters to her in College Park, Maryland.

_____ 6. Orlando Florida is the home of Disney World.

_____ 7. Mickey, Minnie, Goofy and Daisy are all favorites of mine.

_____ 8. Send your letter to her in Reno, Nevada.

_____ 9. Before he lived in New York, City he lived in San Diego, California.

_____ 10. She mailed postcards, and letters to him in Lexington, Kentucky.

_____ 11. Teacups, saucers, napkins, and silverware were piled high.

_____ 12. Can someone give me a ride to Indianapolis, Indiana?

_____ 13. He took a train a car, then a boat to visit his old friend.

_____ 14. Why can't I go to Disney World to see Mickey, and Minnie?

Meter and Kilometer

A meter is a little longer than a yard—39.37 inches (a yard is 36 inches). A kilometer is equal to about $\frac{5}{8}$ of a mile.

Choose the measure of distance you would use for the following.

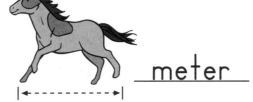

meter

Ounce, Pound, Ton

The **ounce**, **pound**, and **ton** are units in the standard system for measuring weight.

Choose the measure of weight you would use for each object.

16 ounces = 1 pound
2,000 pounds = 1 ton

ounce

pound

ton

Example: ounces

Gram and Kilogram

Grams and **kilograms** are measurements of weight in the metric system. A gram (g) weighs about $\frac{1}{28}$ of an ounce. A grape or paper clip weighs about one gram. There are 1,000 grams in a kilogram. A kilogram (kg) weighs about 2.2 pounds. A brick weighs about 1 kilogram.

Choose grams or kilograms to measure the following.

Example: grams

_____

_____

_____

_____

_____

_____

_____

_____

_____

Liquid

The **cup**, **pint**, **quart**, and **gallon** are units in the standard system for measuring liquids.

Gather the following materials: 2 dish tubs, one filled with water, sand, or rice; measuring cups; pint container; quart container; gallon container. Then, answer the questions and complete the chart.

1. Use the cup measure to pour water, sand, or rice into the pint container. How many cups did it take?

   _____ cups = 1 pint

2. Use the cup measure to find out how many cups are in a quart and a gallon.

   _____ cups = 1 quart

   _____ cups = 1 gallon

3. Use the pint container to pour water, sand, or rice into the quart container. How many pints are in a quart?

   _____ pints = 1 quart

4. How many pints does it take to fill a gallon?

   _____ pints = 1 gallon

5. Use the quart measure to find out how many quarts are in a gallon.

   _____ quarts = 1 gallon

Measurement Chart

_____ cups = 1 pint   _____ pints = 1 quart

_____ cups = 1 quart   _____ pints = 1 gallon

_____ cups = 1 gallon   _____ quarts = 1 gallon

Week 35 Skills

Subject	Skill	Multi-Sensory Learning Activities
Reading and Language Arts	Identify and write topic sentences and supporting sentences.	• Complete Practice Pages 370–374. • Have your child recall a recent dream. Discuss the content of the dream and help your child fill in the missing parts. Help him or her start writing about the dream by creating a topic sentence. Then, follow up with at least three supporting sentences. • Give your child a topic and ask him or her to write a topic sentence about it. Possible topics include bicycling, wolves, my bedroom, or favorite books.
Math	Review measurement.	• Complete Practice Pages 375–378. • Provide your child with measuring tools and objects to measure. Measuring tools may include a ruler, meter stick, or yardstick. Objects may include tables, desks, books, toys, small drawn shapes, or appliances. • Conduct an experiment with your child. You will need several bowls, a milliliter measuring cup, and a variety of liquids, such as tap water, different juices, vinegar, boiling water, or cooking oil. Have your child measure the same amount of each liquid and pour into the bowls. Leave the liquids on a sunny windowsill for several days. Have your child take a measurement each day for several days and graph the data.

Topic Sentences — Paragraphs

Read each topic listed below. Write a topic sentence for each topic.

Example: Topic: Seasons
Topic Sentence Examples:
There are four seasons in every year.
Of all the seasons, my favorite is summer.

1. Topic: Winter
   Topic Sentence: _____

2. Topic: Skateboards
   Topic Sentence: _____

3. Topic: America
   Topic Sentence: _____

4. Topic: Horses
   Topic Sentence: _____

5. Topic: Books
   Topic Sentence: _____

Choose two of your best topic sentences from above. Write each as the beginning sentence for the two paragraphs below. Write at least four support sentences to go with each topic sentence to make two complete paragraphs.

_____

_____

_____

_____

_____

_____

_____

_____

_____

Topic Sentences

A **paragraph** is a group of sentences that tells about one main idea. A topic sentence tells the main idea of a paragraph.

Many topic sentences come first in the paragraph. The topic sentence in the paragraph below is underlined. Do you see how it tells the reader what the whole paragraph is about?

 Friendships can make you happy or make you sad. You feel happy to do things and go places with your friends. You get to know each other so well that you can almost read each others' minds. But friendships can be sad when your friend moves away—or decides to be best friends with someone else.

Underline the topic sentence in the paragraph below.

 We have two rules about using the phone at our house. Our whole family agreed on them. The first rule is not to talk longer than 10 minutes. The second rule is to take good messages if you answer the phone for someone else.

After you read the paragraph below, write a topic sentence for it.

_____

_____

_____

_____

 For one thing, you could ask your neighbors if they need any help. They might be willing to pay you for walking their dog or mowing their grass or weeding their garden. Maybe your older brothers or sisters would pay you to do some of their chores. You also could ask your parents if there's an extra job you could do around the house to make money.

Write a topic sentence for a paragraph on each of these subjects.

Homework:_____

_____

Television: _____

_____

Support Sentences

The **topic sentence** gives the main idea of a paragraph. The support sentences give the details about the main idea. Each sentence must relate to the main idea.

Read the paragraph below. Underline the topic sentence. Cross out the sentence that is not a support sentence. On the line, write a support sentence to go in its place.

   Giving a surprise birthday party can be exciting but tricky. The honored person must not hear a word about the party! On the day of the party, everyone should arrive early. A snack may ruin your appetite.

_____

Write three support sentences to go with each topic sentence.

Giving a dog a bath can be a real challenge!

1. _____

2. _____

3. _____

I can still remember how embarrassed I was that day!

1. _____

2. _____

3. _____

Sometimes I like to imagine what our prehistoric world was like.

1. _____

2. _____

3. _____

A daily newspaper features many kinds of news.

1. _____

2. _____

3. _____

Supporting Sentences

Supporting sentences provide details about the topic sentence of a paragraph.

In the paragraph below, underline the topic sentence. Then cross out the supporting sentence that does not belong in the paragraph.

    One spring it started to rain and didn't stop for 2 weeks. All the rivers flooded. Some people living near the rivers had to leave their homes. Farmers couldn't plant their crops because the fields were so wet. Plants need water to grow. The sky was dark and gloomy all the time.

Write three supporting sentences to go with each topic sentence below. Make sure each supporting sentence stays on the same subject as the topic sentence.

Not everyone should have a pet.

_____

_____

_____

I like to go on field trips with my class.

_____

_____

_____

I've been thinking about what I want to be when I get older.

_____

_____

_____

Topic Sentences and Supporting Details

For each topic below, write a topic sentence and four supporting details.

Example: Playing with friends:
        (topic sentence) <u>Playing with my friends can be lots of fun.</u>

   (details)
 1. We like to ride our bikes together.

 2. We play fun games like "dress up" and "animal hospital."

 3. Sometimes, we swing on the swings or slide down the slides on our swingsets.

 4. We like to pretend we are having tea with our stuffed animals.

Recess at school: _____

_____

_____

_____

_____

Summer vacation: _____

_____

_____

_____

_____

Brothers or sisters: _____

_____

_____

_____

_____

Cup, Pint, Quart, Gallon

Circle the number of objects to the right that equal the objects on the left. The first one is done for you.

2 cups = 1 pint

2 pints = 1 quart

4 quarts = 1 gallon

 = 1 cup   = 1 pint    = 1 quart    = 1 gallon

Milliliter and Liter

Liters and **milliliters** are measurements of liquid in the metric system. A milliliter (mL) equals 0.001 liter or 0.03 fluid ounces. A drop of water equals about 1 milliliter. Liters (L) measure large amounts of liquid. There are 1,000 milliliters in a liter. One liter measures 1.06 quarts. Soft drinks are often sold in 2-liter bottles.

Choose milliliters or liters to measure these liquids.

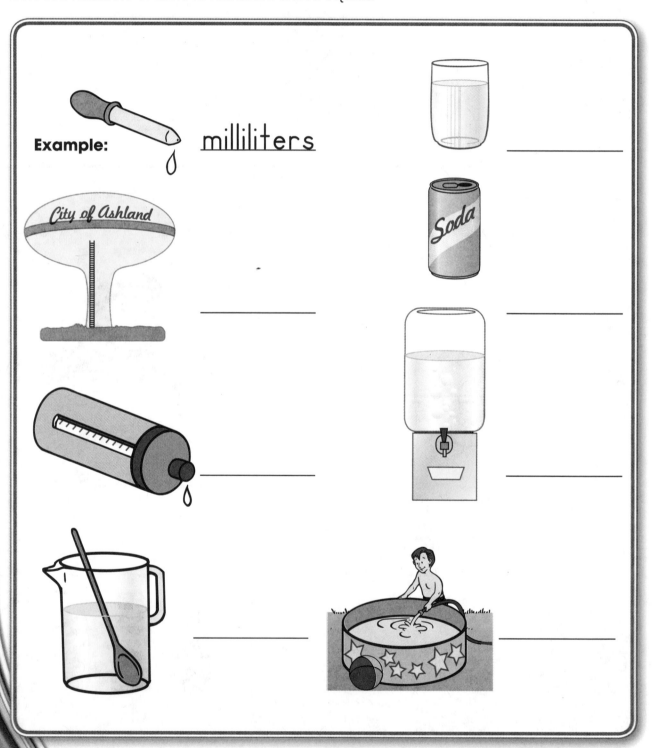

Example: milliliters

Weight and Liquid

Choose grams (g) or kilograms (kg) to weigh the following objects. The first one is done for you.

rhinoceros	kg	person	_____
dime	_____	airplane	_____
bucket of wet sand	_____	spider	_____
eyeglasses	_____	pair of scissors	_____
toy train engine	_____	horse	_____

Choose milliliters (mL) or liters (L) to measure the liquids in the following containers. The first one is done for you.

swimming pool	L	baby bottle	_____
small juice glass	_____	teapot	_____
gasoline tank	_____	outdoor fountain	_____
test tube	_____	ink pen	_____
washing machine	_____	Lake Erie	_____

Review

Find the perimeter and area of each figure.

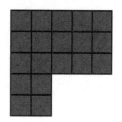 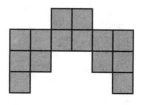

☐ = I square unit

Perimeter = _____ units

Perimeter = _____ units

Area = _____ sq. units

Area = _____ sq. units

How much does it equal?

 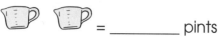 = _____ pints

 = _____ quarts

Write whether you would use ounce, pound or ton to weigh the following.

_____

_____

_____

Write whether you would use an inch, foot, yard, or mile to measure the following.

  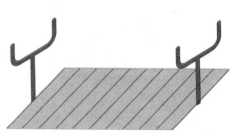

_____ _____

_____

Week 36 Skills

Subject	Skill	Multi-Sensory Learning Activities
Reading and Language Arts	Determine purpose and point of view.	• Complete Practice Pages 380 and 381. • Read *Tales of a Fourth Grade Nothing* by Judy Blume. Discuss the purposes of different types of print (books, newspapers, magazines, ads). Introduce the concepts of persuasion, entertainment, and information as they relate to print.
	Write a friendly letter, outline ideas, and write a fiction piece.	• Complete Practice Pages 382–384. • Teach your child the format for writing a business letter. Use the block style and compare the style to that of a personal letter. Then, show your child how to address the envelope. Have your child write a letter to a local tourist office requesting materials (maps, brochures, etc.) of your area.
Math	Measure temperature in Celsius and Fahrenheit.	• Complete Practice Pages 385–388. • Have your child measure the temperature of different liquids using both Celsius and Fahrenheit scales. Fill cups with different liquids, such as tap water, rain water, boiling water, milk from the refrigerator, fresh-squeezed orange juice, and water with ice cubes. Have your child measure and record the temperature of each.

What's the Point?

Write the correct purpose of each sentence on the line provided.

 **Persuade**    **Entertain**    **Inform**

1. Exercise and maintain a good diet and you won't become over-weight.

_____

2. Dad yelled at Timmy, "Don't ride that Toddle-Bike in the street!"

_____

3. "You ate the broccoli and left all the cookies," cried Mother.

_____

4. The advertiser uses cute kindergarteners in his ads to sell products.

_____

5. The Toddle-Bike was just voted the best new toy vehicle for 1999.

_____

6. "I saw the new Julie on TV and I just had to have it," said Katy.

_____

7. Keep current on homework assignments and you'll be less frustrated at school.

_____

8. "My fingers are numb after only four hours of video games," complained Brad.

_____

9. Toddle-Bikes are so fun your children will be entertained for hours.

_____

10. Fast food and video game advertisers target their ads toward the Saturday morning television audience.

_____

11. There are many more vitamins in vegetables than there are in hamburgers.

_____

12. "Toddle-Bikes will change your life," promised the television announcer.

_____

13. Eat more fruits and vegetables for a healthier, stronger body.

_____

14. Two out of every three teenagers eat fast food more than twice a week.

_____

15. Avoid a steady routine of TV-watching and video games to stay alert.

_____

From Whose Point of View?

Read each sentence below. Decide if it is the first or third person's point of view. If it is a first person's point of view, rewrite the sentence to make it a third person's point of view. If it is a third person's point of view, rewrite it to make it a first person's point of view.

1. I wanted to tell Anh and Thant the secret of our leaving, but I had given my word.

   _____

2. The grandmother did not want to go aboard the boat.

   _____

3. The people on shore were pushing to get on the deck of the boat.

   _____

4. Though I had worked many days in the rice paddies watching planes fly over, I never thought I'd be on one.

   _____

5. Loi made a net from pieces of string and caught a turtle with his new device.

   _____

6. I know of a place where we can wash our clothes.

   _____

7. The officer looked at them with great interest.

   _____

8. When I looked into the harbor, I could see the shape of the sampan boats.

   _____

9. This is my duck and I choose to share it with everyone for the celebration of Tet.

   _____

Friendly Letter

A friendly letter is a casual letter between family or friends. A friendly letter can express your own personality. It can be written for a special reason or just for fun.

Write a friendly letter to a "friend" in another city. Invite the friend to visit you sometime during the summer. Follow these guidelines:

A. Write your address and the date.
B. Write a greeting (**Example:** Dear _____,).
C. Write three paragraphs.
   First: pleasant greeting and invitation
   Second: details about the visit
   Third: summarize your excitement about the visit
D. Closing (**Example:** Your friend,).
E. Your signature

What's the Story?

Create a story just for fun! Choose the kind of story you want to write. Now, brainstorm for ideas. Write your ideas on the correct lines below.

_____

Kind of Story (mystery, adventure, etc.)

I. Setting (where and when the story takes place)

　　A. Where _____ Description_____

　　_____

　　B. When _____

II. Plot (events of the story)

　　List main events in order

　　A. _____

　　B. _____

　　C. _____

　　D. _____

III. Characters (people in the story)

　　A. Name _____ Description _____

　　B. Name _____ Description _____

　　C. Name _____ Description _____

　　D. Name _____ Description _____

Use your ideas to write a story. Remember to tell the story in the correct time order. Organize the events into a **beginning**, **middle**, and **ending** section of the story.

_____

_____

_____

_____

_____

Finish your story on another sheet of paper

Review

Write a police report about an event in which someone your age was a hero or heroine. Follow these steps:

1. Write all your ideas in any order on another sheet of paper. What happened? Who saw it? Who or what do you think caused it? Why were the police called?

2. Now, write in complete sentences to tell what happened. Combine some short sentences using **and**, **but**, **or**, **after**, or **when**. Make sure all your sentences end with a period or question mark.

3. Read your sentences aloud. Did you leave out any important facts? Will your "commanding officer" know what happened?

4. Make any necessary changes and write your report below.

5. Read your report to someone.

OFFICIAL POLICE REPORT

Reporting officer: _____

Date of accident: _____ Time of accident: _____

_____

_____

_____

_____

_____

_____

_____

_____

_____

Temperature: Fahrenheit

28° F

Fahrenheit is used to measure temperature in the standard system. °**F** stands for degrees Fahrenheit.

72° F

Use the thermometer to answer these questions.

At what temperature does water boil?

_____

At what temperature does water freeze?

_____

What is normal body temperature?

_____

Is a 100°F day warm, hot or cold?

_____

Is a 0°F day warm, hot or cold?

_____

Which temperature best describes room temperature?
58°F   70°F   80°F

_____

Which temperature best describes a cold winter day?
22°F   38°F   32°F

_____

°**F**

water boils
212° F →

body temperature
98.6° F →

water freezes
32° F →

220
210
200
190
180
170
160
150
140
130
120
110
100
90
80
70
60
50
40
30
20
10
0
-10
-20

Temperature: Fahrenheit

Degrees Fahrenheit (°F) is a unit for measuring temperature.

Write the temperature in degrees Fahrenheit (°F).

Example:

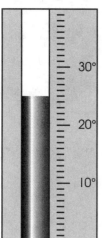

25° F

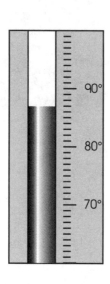

_____

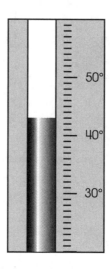

_____

_____

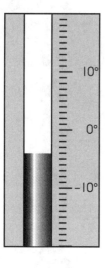

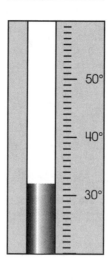

_____

Temperature: Celsius

Celsius is used to measure temperature in the metric system. **°C** stands for degrees Celsius.

Use the thermometer to answer these questions.

At what temperature does
water boil?   _____

At what temperature does
water freeze?   _____

What is normal body
temperature?   _____

Is it a hot or cold day when
the temperature is 30°C?   _____

Is it a hot or cold day when
the temperature is 5°C?   _____

Which temperature best
describes a hot summer day?
5°C   40°C   20°C   _____

Which temperature best
describes an icy winter day?
0°C   15°C   10°C   _____

Temperature: Celsius

Degrees Celsius (°C) is a unit for measuring temperature in the metric system.

Write the temperature in degrees Celsius (°C).

Example:

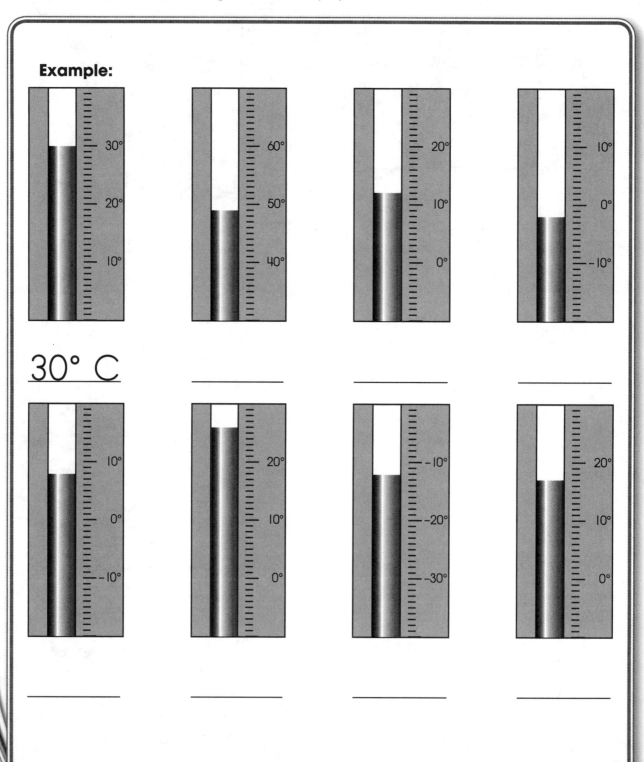

30° C

_____   _____   _____

_____   _____   _____   _____

Fourth Quarter Check-Up

Reading and Language Arts

❑ I understand and can identify the main idea of a text.

❑ I can follow step-by-step directions.

❑ I understand and can identify cause and effect situations.

❑ I can use context clues to interpret meaning.

❑ I can draw conclusions from a reading passage.

❑ I know to use quotation marks around song titles, poems, and dialogue.

❑ I can use correct capitalization and punctuation.

❑ I can identify and write topic sentences and supporting sentences.

❑ I can determine purpose and point of view.

❑ I can write a friendly letter, outline ideas, and write a fiction piece.

Math

❑ I can identify similar, congruent, and symmetrical figures.

❑ I understand perimeter as the distance around a figure.

❑ I understand area as the number of square units needed to cover a region.

❑ I understand volume as the number of cubic units that fit inside a figure.

❑ I can calculate time.

❑ I can measure in inches, feet, yards, and miles.

❑ I can measure in centimeters, meters, and kilometers.

❑ I can measure weights in ounces, pounds, tons, grams, and kilograms.

❑ I can measure liquids in cups, pints, quarts, and gallons.

❑ I can measure temperature in Celsius and Fahrenheit.

Final Project

Choose a play to read aloud with a friend or family member. Use lots of expression and omit the words that tell who is speaking. Then, find other children in the neighborhood who would like to perform the play. Be sure to practice the play and create simple costumes and sets. Invite guests to a performance. After the performance, measure the set to find its area and perimeter.

Student Reference

Numbers 1-100

1	2	3	4	5	6	7	8	9	10
11	12	13	14	15	16	17	18	19	20
21	22	23	24	25	26	27	28	29	30
31	32	33	34	35	36	37	38	39	40
41	42	43	44	45	46	47	48	49	50
51	52	53	54	55	56	57	58	59	60
61	62	63	64	65	66	67	68	69	70
71	72	73	74	75	76	77	78	79	80
81	82	83	84	85	86	87	88	89	90
91	92	93	94	95	96	97	98	99	100

Multiplication Chart

x	1	2	3	4	5	6	7	8	9	10
1	1	2	3	4	5	6	7	8	9	10
2	2	4	6	8	10	12	14	16	18	20
3	3	6	9	12	15	18	21	24	27	30
4	4	8	12	16	20	24	28	32	36	40
5	5	10	15	20	25	30	35	40	45	50
6	6	12	18	24	30	36	42	48	54	60
7	7	14	21	28	35	42	49	56	63	70
8	8	16	24	32	40	48	56	64	72	80
9	9	18	27	36	45	54	63	72	81	90
10	10	20	30	40	50	60	70	80	90	100

Equivalent Fractions

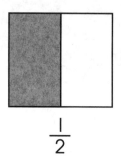

$\frac{1}{2}$

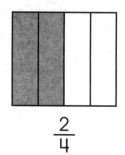

$\frac{2}{4}$

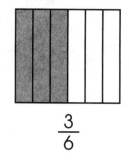

$\frac{3}{6}$

Fractions to Decimals

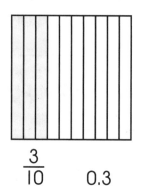

$\frac{3}{10}$ 0.3

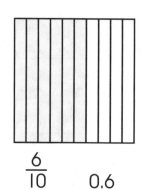

$\frac{6}{10}$ 0.6

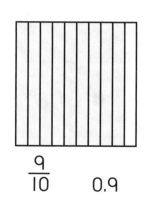

$\frac{9}{10}$ 0.9

Polygons

triangle
3 sides

square
4 equal
sides

rectangle
4 sides

pentagon
5 sides

hexagon
6 sides

octagon
8 sides

Geometry

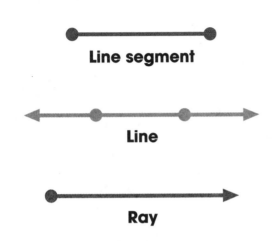

Line segment

Line

Ray

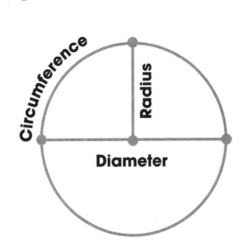

Circumference

Radius

Diameter

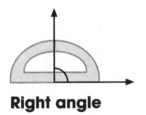

Right angle

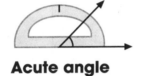

Acute angle

Obtuse angle

Three-Dimensional Shapes

rectangular prism

cone

cube

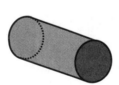

cylinder

sphere

pyramid

Frequently Confused Words

Good	You're	Can	This
Well	Your	May	These
There	Its	Sit	Than
Their	It's	Set	Then
They're			

Recommended Read-Alouds for Grade 4

- ☐ *Beezus and Ramona* by Beverly Cleary
- ☐ *No Talking* by Andrew Clements
- ☐ *The School Story* by Andrew Clements
- ☐ *Sahara Special* by Esme Codell
- ☐ *Waiting for Normal* by Leslie Connor
- ☐ *The Misadventures of Maude March* by Audrey Couloumbis
- ☐ *James and the Giant Peach* by Roald Dahl
- ☐ *The Miraculous Journey of Edward Tulane* by Kate DiCamillo
- ☐ *Jim Ugly* by Sid Fleischman
- ☐ *The Contest: Everest #1* by Gordon Korman
- ☐ *Day of Tears : A Novel in Dialogue* by Julius Lester
- ☐ *Snow Treasure* by Marie McSwigan
- ☐ *Edgar & Ellen Under Town* by Charles Ogden
- ☐ *Keeping Score* by Linda Sue Park
- ☐ *Fooled You! Fakes and Hoaxes Through the Years* by Elaine Pascoe
- ☐ *Brian's Winter* by Gary Paulsen
- ☐ *Sideways Stories from Wayside School* by Louis Sachar
- ☐ *The Trouble With Wishes* by Diane Stanley
- ☐ *On Board the Titanic: What It Was Like When the Great Liner Sank* by Shelley Tanaka
- ☐ *Jumanji* by Chris Van Allsburg
- ☐ *Gaia Girls: Enter the Earth* by Lee Welles
- ☐ *2030: A Day in the Life of Tomorrow's Kids* by Amy Zuckerman and Jim Daly

Answer Key

Page 18 — A Is for Apple

Week 1 Practice

Word box: ache, admit, animal, April, bacon, bathroom, camera, flap, grateful, happiness, manage, navy, plane, radish, waste

Write the words that contain a **short a** that sounds like the **a** in **apple**.
admit, flap, animal, happiness, bathroom, manage, camera, radish

List all the words that contain a **long a** that sounds like the **a** in **cake**.
ache, navy, April, plane, bacon, waste, grateful

Use the words to complete the word search. The words are written vertically, horizontally, and diagonally.

18

Page 19 — As Are Back

Week 1 Practice

Word box: afraid, aide, bay, break, chain, delay, failure, great, maize, payment, prey, refrain, remain, stain, waist

Write the words in which the letters **ai** have a **long a** sound.
afraid, chain, refrain, aide, failure, remain, waist, maize, stain

Write the words in which the letters **ea** have a **long a** sound.
great, break

Write the words in which the letters **ay** have a **long a** sound.
bay, delay, payment

Which word is left? prey
Which two letters make the **long a** sound? ey

Homophones are words that sound like another word but are spelled differently and have different meanings.
The words contain six homophones. List each below with its missing sound-alike. The first pair is given.

1. break / brake
2. aide / aid
3. prey / pray
4. waist / waste
5. great / grate
6. maize / maze

19

Page 20 — Easy Does It

Week 1 Practice

Word box: bedtime, being, beverage, cedar, decoy, elegant, female, jelly, lemon, medicine, meteor, rectangle, recycle, secret, skeleton

Use words containing the **short e** sound to fill in the blanks.
1. A lemon is sour.
2. The new living room carpet was stained by grape jelly and a spilled beverage.
3. For your sore throat, you can take medicine before bedtime.
4. The body's bony frame is called a skeleton.
5. A queen would probably be elegant.
6. A rectangle has four sides.

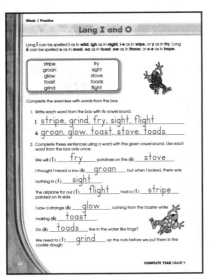

Use words containing a **long e** sound to fill in the blanks.
1. In the night sky, a meteor could be seen near the Big Dipper.
2. It is no secret that the female star of the movie is quite ill.
3. Our neighbor is being thoughtful of the environment because he tries to recycle things like newspaper, aluminum cans and plastic milk jugs.
4. For his birthday, Dad received a decoy to use when he goes duck hunting.
5. The storm damaged a large cedar tree in our yard.

20

Page 21 — Still Easy

Week 1 Practice

Put a check to the left of the words in which the letters **ea** make the **long e** sound.
Put a star to the right of the words in which the letters **ee** make the **long e** sound.
Which word uses the letters **eo** for the **long e** sound? people

agree ★, easel ✓, preach ✓, between ★, greenery ★, season ✓, breathe ✓, greetings ★, wheat ✓, disease ✓, meek ★, wheel ★, eagle ✓, people, yeast ✓

Fill in the blanks.
1. During the holiday season, our family sends lots of greetings.
2. The Reverend Smith will agree to preach a shorter time because of extra musical selections.
3. In earlier times, wheat was ground into flour with a large stone wheel.
4. The soaring eagle is a proud creature, not meek or timid.
5. In the park surrounded by greenery stood the artist painting at his easel.
6. The swimming coach taught the swimmers to breathe evenly between strokes.
7. Two topics or terms studied in life science are disease and people.

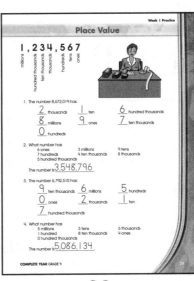

21

Page 22 — Long I and O

Week 1 Practice

Long ī can be spelled i as in **wild**, **igh** as in **night**, **i-e** as in **wipe**, or y as in **try**. Long ō can be spelled o as in **most**, **oa** as in **toast**, **ow** as in **throw**, or **o-e** as in **hope**.

Word box: stripe, groan, glow, toast, grind, fry, sight, stove, toads, flight

Complete the exercises with words from the box.

1. Write each word from the box with its vowel sound.
ī stripe, grind, fry, sight, flight
ō groan, glow, toast, stove, toads

2. Complete these sentences using a word with the given vowel sound. Use each word from the box only once.
We will (ī) fry potatoes on the (ō) stove.
I thought I heard a low (ō) groan, but when I looked, there was nothing in (ī) sight.
The airplane for our (ī) flight had a (ī) stripe painted on its side.
I saw a strange (ō) glow coming from the toaster while making (ō) toast.
Do (ō) toads live in the water like frogs?
We need to (ī) grind up the nuts before we put them in the cookie dough.

22

Page 23 — Place Value

Week 1 Practice

1,234,567
millions, hundred thousands, ten thousands, thousands, hundreds, tens, ones

1. The number 8,672,019 has:
2 thousands, 1 ten, 6 hundred thousands, 8 millions, 9 ones, 7 ten thousands, 0 hundreds

2. What number has
6 ones, 3 millions, 9 tens, 7 hundreds, 4 ten thousands, 8 thousands, 5 hundred thousands
The number is 3,548,796

3. The number 6,792,510 has:
9 ten thousands, 6 millions, 5 hundreds, 0 ones, 2 thousands, 1 ten, 7 hundred thousands

4. What number has
5 millions, 3 tens, 6 thousands, 1 hundred, 8 ten thousands, 4 ones, 0 hundred thousands
The number is 5,086,134

23

395

Answer Key

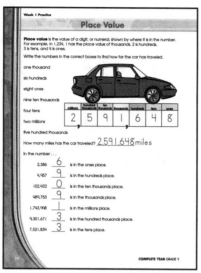

24

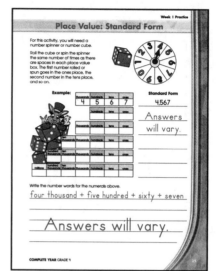

25

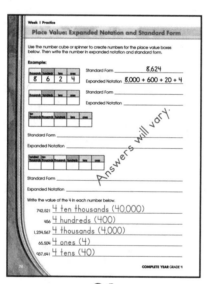

26

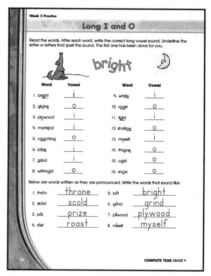

28

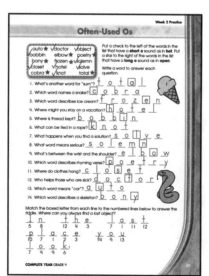

29

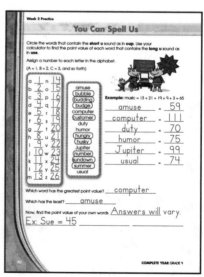

30

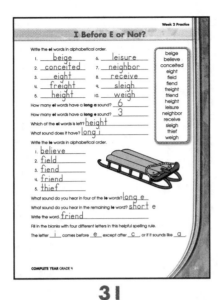

Week 2 Practice

I Before E or Not?

Write the **ei** words in alphabetical order.

1. beige
2. conceited
3. eight
4. freight
5. height
6. leisure
7. neighbor
8. receive
9. sleigh
10. weigh

Word box: beige, believe, conceited, eight, field, fiend, freight, friend, height, leisure, neighbor, receive, sleigh, thief, weigh

How many **ei** words have a **long a** sound? 6
How many **ei** words have a **long e** sound? 3
Which of the **ei** words is left? height
What sound does it have? long i

Write the **ie** words in alphabetical order.

1. believe
2. field
3. fiend
4. friend
5. thief

What sound do you hear in four of the **ie** words? long e
What sound do you hear in the remaining **ie** word? short e
Write the word. friend

Fill in the blanks with four different letters in this helpful spelling rule.
The letter i comes before e except after c, or if it sounds like a.

COMPLETE YEAR GRADE 4

31

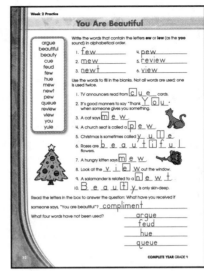

Week 2 Practice

You Are Beautiful

Word box: argue, beautiful, beauty, cue, feud, hue, mew, newt, pew, queue, review, view, you, yule

Write the words that contain the letters **ew** or **iew** (as the **yoo** sound) in alphabetical order.

1. few
2. mew
3. newt
4. pew
5. review
6. view

Use the words to fill in the blanks. Not all words are used; one is used twice.

1. TV announcers read from c u e cards.
2. It's good manners to say "Thank Y o u." when someone gives you something.
3. A cat says m e w.
4. A church seat is called a p e w.
5. Christmas is sometimes called y u l e.
6. Roses are b e a u t i f u l flowers.
7. A hungry kitten says m e w.
8. Look at the v i e w out the window.
9. A salamander is related to a n e w t.
10. B e a u t y is only skin-deep.

Read the letters in the box to answer the question: What have you received if someone says, "You are beautiful"? compliment

What four words have not been used?
argue
feud
hue
queue

COMPLETE YEAR GRADE 4

32

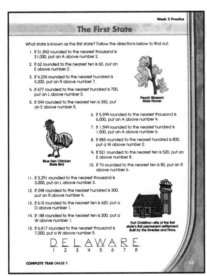

Week 2 Practice

The First State

What state is known as the first state? Follow the directions below to find out.

1. If 31,842 rounded to the nearest thousand is 31,000, put an A above number 2.
2. If 62 rounded to the nearest ten is 60, put an E above number 2.
3. If 4,234 rounded to the nearest hundred is 4,200, put an R above number 7.
4. If 677 rounded to the nearest hundred is 700, put an L above number 3.
5. If 344 rounded to the nearest ten is 350, put an E above number 5.
6. If 5,599 rounded to the nearest thousand is 6,000, put an A above number 4.
7. If 1,599 rounded to the nearest hundred is 1,500, put an A above number 6.
8. If 885 rounded to the nearest hundred is 800, put an W above number 2.
9. If 521 rounded to the nearest ten is 520, put an E above number 8.
10. If 74 rounded to the nearest ten is 80, put an R above number 6.
11. If 3,291 rounded to the nearest thousand is 3,000, put an L above number 3.
12. If 248 rounded to the nearest hundred is 300, put an R above number 4.
13. If 615 rounded to the nearest ten is 620, put a D above number 1.
14. If 188 rounded to the nearest ten is 200, put a W above number 1.
15. If 6,817 rounded to the nearest thousand is 7,000, put a W above number 5.

Peach Blossom State Flower
Blue Hen Chicken State Bird
Fort Christina—site of the first state's first permanent settlement. Built by the Swedes and Finns.

D E L A W A R E
1 2 3 4 5 6 7 8

COMPLETE YEAR GRADE 4

33

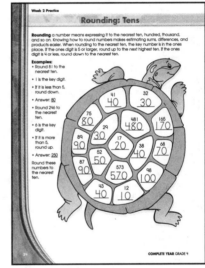

Week 2 Practice

Rounding: Tens

Rounding a number means expressing it to the nearest ten, hundred, thousand, and so on. Knowing how to round numbers makes estimating sums, differences, and products easier. When rounding to the nearest ten, the key number is in the ones place. If the ones digit is 5 or larger, round up to the next highest ten. If the ones digit is 4 or less, round down to the nearest ten.

Examples:
- Round 81 to the nearest ten.
- 1 is the key digit.
- If it is less than 5, round down.
- Answer: 80
- Round 246 to the nearest ten.
- 6 is the key digit.
- If it is more than 5, round up.
- Answer: 250

Round these numbers to the nearest ten.

41 → 40   32 → 30
75 → 80   29   481 → 480   165 → 170
89 → 90   30   17 → 20   38 → 40   68 → 70
    52 → 50
87 → 90   573 → 570   98 → 100
43 → 40   12 → 10

COMPLETE YEAR GRADE 4

34

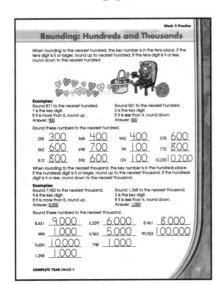

Week 2 Practice

Rounding: Hundreds and Thousands

When rounding to the nearest hundred, the key number is in the tens place. If the tens digit is 5 or larger, round up to nearest hundred. If the tens digit is 4 or less, round down to the nearest hundred.

Examples:
Round 871 to the nearest hundred.
7 is the key digit.
If it is more than 5, round up.
Answer: 900

Round 421 to the nearest hundred.
2 is the key digit.
If it is less than 4, round down.
Answer: 400

Round these numbers to the nearest hundred.

255 → 300   368 → 400   443 → 400   578 → 600
562 → 600   698 → 700   99 → 100   775 → 800
812 → 800   592 → 600   124 → 100   10,235 → 10,200

When rounding to the nearest thousand, the key number is in the hundreds place. If the hundreds digit is 5 or larger, round up to the nearest thousand. If the hundreds digit is 4 or less, round down to the nearest thousand.

Examples:
Round 7,932 to the nearest thousand.
9 is the key digit.
If it is more than 5, round up.
Answer: 8,000

Round 1,368 to the nearest thousand.
3 is the key digit.
If it is less than 4, round down.
Answer: 1,000

Round these numbers to the nearest thousand.

8,631 → 9,000   6,229 → 6,000   8,461 → 8,000
999 → 1,000   4,963 → 5,000   99,923 → 100,000
9,654 → 10,000   798 → 1,000
1,248 → 1,000

COMPLETE YEAR GRADE 4

35

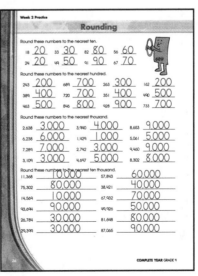

Week 2 Practice

Rounding

Round these numbers to the nearest ten.

18 → 20   33 → 30   82 → 80   56 → 60
24 → 20   49 → 50   91 → 90   67 → 70

Round these numbers to the nearest hundred.

243 → 200   689 → 700   263 → 300   162 → 200
389 → 400   720 → 700   351 → 400   490 → 500
463 → 500   846 → 800   733 → 700

Round these numbers to the nearest thousand.

2,638 → 3,000   3,940 → 4,000   8,653 → 9,000
6,238 → 6,000   1,429 → 1,000   5,061 → 5,000
7,289 → 7,000   2,742 → 3,000   9,460 → 9,000
3,109 → 3,000   4,647 → 5,000   8,302 → 8,000

Round these numbers to the nearest ten thousand.

11,368 → 10,000   57,843 → 60,000
75,302 → 80,000   38,421 → 40,000
14,569 → 10,000   67,932 → 70,000
93,694 → 90,000   49,926 → 50,000
26,784 → 30,000   81,648 → 80,000
29,399 → 30,000   87,065 → 90,000

COMPLETE YEAR GRADE 4

36

Answer Key

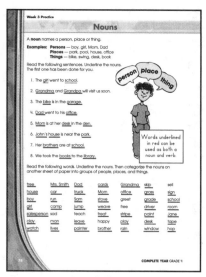

Page 38 — Week 3 Practice — Nouns

A **noun** names a person, place or thing.

Examples: Persons — boy, girl, Mom, Dad
Places — park, pool, house, office
Things — bike, swing, desk, book

Read the following sentences. Underline the nouns. The first one has been done for you.

1. The girl went to school.
2. Grandma and Grandpa will visit us soon.
3. The bike is in the garage.
4. Dad went to his office.
5. Mom is at her desk in the den.
6. John's house is near the park.
7. Her brothers are at school.
8. We took the books to the library.

Words underlined in red can be used as both a noun and verb.

Read the following words. Underline the nouns. Then categorize the nouns on another sheet of paper into groups of people, places, and things.

tree	Mrs. Smith	Dad	cards	Grandma	skip	sell
house	car	truck	Mom	office	grass	sign
boy	run	Sam	stove	greet	grade	school
girl	camp	jump	weave	free	driver	room
salesperson	sad	teach	treat	stripe	paint	Jane
clay	man	leave	happy	play	desk	tape
watch	lives	painter	brother	rain	window	hop

COMPLETE YEAR GRADE 4

Page 39 — Week 3 Practice — Nouns

Write nouns that name persons.

1. Could you please give this report to my _____?
2. The _____ works many long hours to plant crops.
3. I had to help my little _____ when he wrecked his bike yesterday.

Write nouns that name places.

4. I always keep my library books on top of the _____ so I can find them.
5. We enjoyed watching the kites fly in the _____.
6. Dad built a nice fire in the _____ barn.

Write nouns that name things.

7. The little _____ purred softly as I held it.
8. Wouldn't you _____ would get tired of carrying its house all day?
9. The _____ scurried into its hole with the piece of cheese.
10. I _____ by the writing that this _____ is mine.
11. Look at the _____ I made in art.
12. His _____ blew away because of the strong wind.

Answers will vary.

COMPLETE YEAR GRADE 4

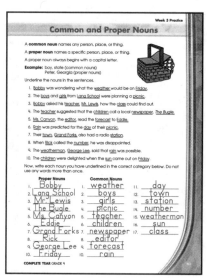

Page 40 — Week 3 Practice — Common and Proper Nouns

Common nouns name general people, places, and things.

Examples: boy, girl, cat, dog, park, city, building

Proper nouns name specific persons, places, and things.

Examples: John, Mary, Fluffy, Rover, Central Park, Chicago, Empire State Building
Proper nouns begin with capital letters.

Read the following nouns. On the blanks, indicate whether the nouns are common or proper. The first two have been done for you.

1. New York City — proper
2. house — common
3. car — common
4. Ohio — proper
5. river — common
6. Rocky Mountains — proper
7. Mrs. Jones — proper
8. nurse — common
9. Dr. DiCarlo — proper
10. man — common
11. Rock River — proper
12. building — common
13. lawyer — common
14. Grand Canyon — proper
15. city — common
16. state — common

On another sheet of paper, write proper nouns for the above common nouns.

Read the following sentences. Underline the common nouns. Circle the proper nouns.

1. Mary's birthday is Friday, October 7.
2. She likes having her birthday in a fall month.
3. Her friends will meet her at the Video Arcade for a party.
4. Ms. McCarthy and Mr. Landry will help with the birthday party games.
5. Mary's friends will play video games all afternoon.
6. Amy and John will bring refreshments and games to the party.

COMPLETE YEAR GRADE 4

Page 41 — Week 3 Practice — Common and Proper Nouns

A **common noun** names any person, place, or thing.
A **proper noun** names a specific person, place, or thing.
A proper noun always begins with a capital letter.

Example: boy, state (common nouns)
Peter, Georgia (proper nouns)

Underline the nouns in the sentences.

1. Bobby was wondering what the weather would be on Friday.
2. The boys and girls from Lang School were planning a picnic.
3. Bobby asked his teacher, Mr. Lewis, how the class could find out.
4. The teacher suggested that the children call a local newspaper, The Bugle.
5. Ms. Canyon, the editor, read the forecast to Eddie.
6. Rain was predicted for the day of their picnic.
7. Their town, Grand Forks, also had a radio station.
8. When Rick called the number, he was disappointed.
9. The weatherman, George Lee, said that rain was possible.
10. The children were delighted when the sun came out on Friday.

Now, write each noun you have underlined in the correct category below. Do not use any words more than once.

Proper Nouns
1. Bobby
2. Lang School
3. Mr. Lewis
4. The Bugle
5. Ms. Canyon
6. Eddie
7. Grand Forks
8. Rick
9. George Lee
10. Friday

Common Nouns
1. weather
2. boys
3. girls
4. picnic
5. teacher
6. children
7. newspaper
8. editor
9. forecast
10. rain
11. day
12. town
13. station
14. number
15. weatherman
16. sun
17. class

COMPLETE YEAR GRADE 4

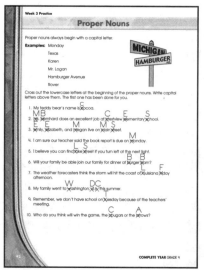

Page 42 — Week 3 Practice — Proper Nouns

Proper nouns always begin with a capital letter.

Examples: Monday
Texas
Karen
Mr. Logan
Hamburger Avenue
Rover

Cross out the lowercase letters at the beginning of the proper nouns. Write capital letters above them. The first one has been done for you.

1. My teddy bear's name is Cocoa.
2. Mr. Bernhard does an excellent job at Crestview Elementary School.
3. Emily, Elizabeth, and Megan live on Main Street.
4. I am sure our teacher said the book report is due on Monday.
5. I believe you can find Lake Street if you turn left at the next light.
6. Will your family be able join our family for dinner at Burger Barn?
7. The weather forecasters think the storm will hit the coast of Louisiana Friday afternoon.
8. My family went to Washington, DC this summer.
9. Remember, we don't have school on Tuesday because of the teachers' meeting.
10. Who do you think will win the game, the Cougars or the Arrows?

COMPLETE YEAR GRADE 4

Page 43 — Week 3 Practice — Add 'Em Up!

Addition is "putting together" or adding two or more numbers to find the sum.

Add the following problems as quickly and as accurately as you can.

3 + 2 = 5	6 + 4 = 10	5 + 4 = 9	2 + 9 = 11
6 + 2 = 8	4 + 1 = 5	9 + 6 = 15	7 + 6 = 13	8 + 7 = 15	8 + 9 = 17
4 + 9 = 13	1 + 8 = 9	4 + 7 = 11	7 + 4 = 11	5 + 3 = 8
		6 + 6 = 12	8 + 8 = 16	7 + 7 = 14	4 + 4 = 8
		2 + 8 = 10	5 + 2 = 7	3 + 6 = 9	8 + 5 = 13

How quickly did you complete this page? _Answers will vary._

COMPLETE YEAR GRADE 4

Answer Key

44

45

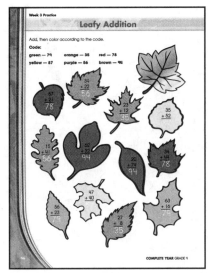

46

48

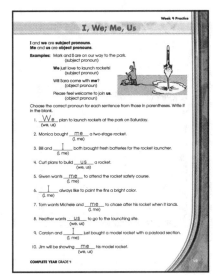

49

50

Answer Key

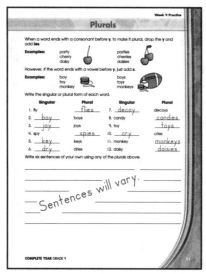

51

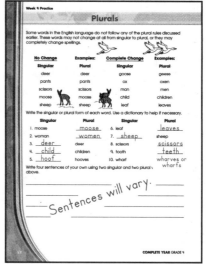

52

53

54

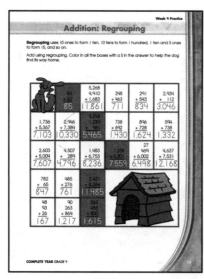

55

56

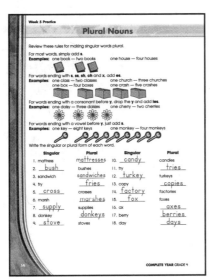

58

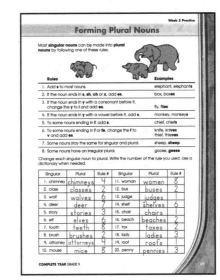

59

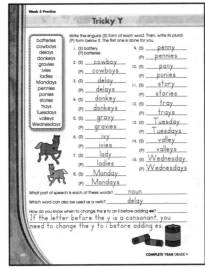

60

Plurals With F (page 61)

Categories may vary.

1. colts, ~~kittens~~, hogs — calves / calf
2. pine cones, ~~tulips~~, twigs — leaves / leaf
3. canyons, ~~mountains~~ gorges — cliffs / cliff
4. ~~lawyer~~, aunts, husbands — wives / wife
5. ~~totals~~, fourths, thirds — halves / half
6. collars, ~~shoes~~ sleeves — cuffs / cuff
7. neckties, beads, ~~belts~~ — scarves / scarf
8. pixies, ~~giants~~ fairies — elves / elf
9. ~~followers~~ leaders, directors — chiefs / chief
10. hatchets, swords, ~~pencils~~ — knives / knife

Five words have not been used. Write both the singular (S) and plural (P) forms.

1. (S) belief   4. (S) roofs
   (P) beliefs   (P) roof
2. (S) life   5. (S) shelf
   (P) lives   (P) shelves
3. (S) loaf
   (P) loaves

61

Subtracting Larger Numbers (page 62)

Solve these subtraction problems.

29 − 26 = 3
99 − 58 = 41
359 − 55 = 304
735 − 734 = 1
849 − 726 = 123
7,678 − 4,321 = 3,357
865 − 731 = 134
55 − 25 = 30
9,876 − 1,234 = 8,642

62

Subtraction: Regrouping (page 63)

81 − 53 = 28
76 − 49 = 27
94 − 38 = 56
156 − 77 = 79
341 − 83 = 258
726 − 29 = 697

568 − 173 = 395
806 − 738 = 68
743 − 550 = 193
903 − 336 = 567
647 − 289 = 358
254 − 69 = 185

730 − 518 = 212
961 − 846 = 115
573 − 76 = 497
604 − 55 = 549
265 − 19 = 246
372 − 59 = 313

111 − 82 = 29
358 − 99 = 259
147 − 49 = 98

180 − 106 = 74
325 − 68 = 257
873 − 35 = 838

63

64

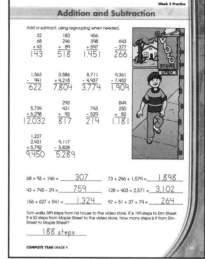

65

66

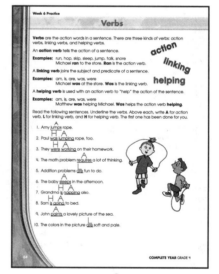

68

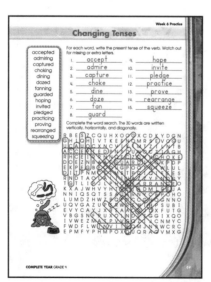

69

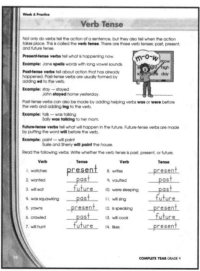

70

Answer Key

71

Week 6 Practice
Present, Past, and Future Tense

Read the following sentences. Write **PRES** if the sentence is in present tense. Write **PAST** if the sentence is in past tense. Write **FUT** if the sentence is in future tense. The first one has been done for you.

FUT 1. I will be thrilled to accept the award.
FUT 2. Will you go with me to the dentist?
PAST 3. I thought he looked familiar!
PAST 4. They ate every single slice of pizza.
PRES 5. I run myself ragged sometimes.
PRES 6. Do you think this project is worthwhile?
PAST 7. No one has been able to repair the broken plate.
PRES 8. Thoughtful gifts are always appreciated.
PAST 9. I liked the way he sang!
FUT 10. With a voice like that, he will go a long way.
PRES 11. It's my fondest hope that they visit soon.
PAST 12. I wanted that coat very much.
FUT 13. She'll be happy to take your place.
PRES 14. Everyone thinks the test is easy.
PRES 15. Collecting stamps is her favorite hobby.

COMPLETE YEAR GRADE 4

72

Week 6 Practice
Using ing Verbs

Remember, use **is** and **are** when describing something happening right now. Use **was** and **were** when describing something that already happened.

Use the verb in bold to complete each sentence. Add **ing** to the verb and use **is, are, was** or **were**.

Examples: When it started to rain, we __were raking__ the leaves.
rake

When the soldiers marched up that hill, Captain Stevens __was commanding__ them.
command

1. Now, the police __are accusing__ them of stealing the money.
accuse
2. Look! The eggs __are hatching__.
hatch
3. A minute ago, the sky __was glowing__.
glow
4. My dad says he __is treating__ us to ice cream!
treat
5. She __was sneezing__ the whole time we were at the mall.
sneeze
6. While we were playing outside at recess, he __was grading__ our tests.
grade
7. I hear something. Who __was groaning__?
groan
8. As I watched, the workers __were grinding__ the wood into little chips.
grind

COMPLETE YEAR GRADE 4

73

Week 6 Practice
Skip-Counting

Skip-counting is a quick way to count by skipping numbers. For example, when you skip-count by 2s, you count 2, 4, 6, 8, and so on. You can skip-count by many different numbers such as 2s, 4s, 5s, 10s, and 100s.

The illustration below shows skip-counting by 2s to 14.

Use the number line to help you skip-count by 2s from 0 to 20.
a. 2 4 6 8. 10 12 14 16 18 20

Skip-count by 3s by filling in the rocks across the pond.

COMPLETE YEAR GRADE 4

74

Week 6 Practice
Multiples

A **multiple** is the product of a specific number and any other number. For example, the multiples of 2 are 2 (2 x 1), 4 (2 x 2), 6, 8, 10, 12, and so on.

Write the missing multiples.

Example: Count by 5s.
5, 10, 15, 20, 25, 30, 35. These are multiples of 5.

COMPLETE YEAR GRADE 4

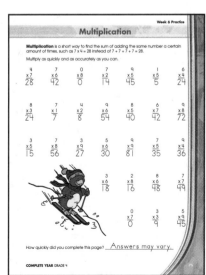

75

Week 6 Practice
Multiplication

Multiplication is a short way to find the sum of adding the same number a certain amount of times, such as 7 x 4 = 28 instead of 7 + 7 + 7 + 7 = 28.

Multiply as quickly and as accurately as you can.

4 ×7 = 28	7 ×6 = 42	0 ×8 = 0	7 ×2 = 14	9 ×5 = 45	1 ×5 = 5	6 ×4 = 24
8 ×3 = 24	7 ×1 = 7	4 ×2 = 8	9 ×6 = 54	8 ×5 = 40	6 ×7 = 42	9 ×8 = 72
3 ×5 = 15	7 ×8 = 56	3 ×9 = 27	5 ×6 = 30	9 ×9 = 81	7 ×5 = 35	9 ×4 = 36
			3 ×6 = 18	2 ×8 = 16	8 ×6 = 48	7 ×7 = 49
				0 ×7 =	3 ×3 =	9 ×9 = 45

How quickly did you complete this page? __Answers may vary.__

COMPLETE YEAR GRADE 4

76

Week 6 Practice
Multiplication

Multiply.

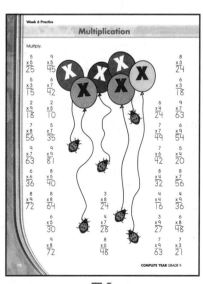

COMPLETE YEAR GRADE 4

Answer Key

Week 7 Practice

Present-Tense Verbs

Write two sentences for each verb below. Tell about something that is happening now and write the verb as both simple present tense and present tense with a helping verb.

Example: run

Mia runs to the store. Mia is running to the store.

1. hatch

2. check

3. spell

4. blend

Answers will vary.

5. lick

6. cry

7. write

8. dream

COMPLETE YEAR GRADE 4

78

Week 7 Practice

Verb Tense

Read the following sentences. Underline the verbs. Above each verb, write whether it is past, present, or future tense.

past
1. The crowd was booing the referee.
future
2. Sally will compete on the balance beam.
present
3. Matt marches with the band.
present
4. Nick is marching, too.
past
5. The geese swooped down to the pond.
future
6. Dad will fly home tomorrow.
past
7. They were looking for a new book.
present
8. Presently, they are going to the garden.
future
9. The children will pick the ripe vegetables.
past
10. Grandmother canned the green beans.

Write six sentences of your own using the correct verb tense.

Past tense:

Present tense:

Sentences will vary.

Fut...

COMPLETE YEAR GRADE 4

79

Week 7 Practice

Past-Tense Verbs

To write about something that already happened, you can add **ed** to the verb.

Example: Yesterday, we **talked.**

You can also use **was** and **were** and add **ing** to the verb.

Example: Yesterday, we were talking.

When a verb ends with **e**, you usually drop the **e** before adding **ing**.

Examples: grade — was grading weave — were weaving
tape — was taping sneeze — were sneezing

Write two sentences for each verb below. Tell about something that has already happened and write the verb both ways. (Watch the spelling of the verbs that end with **e**.)

Example: stream

The rain streamed down the window.
The rain was streaming down the window.

1. grade

2. tape

Sentences will vary.

3. weave

4. snee...

COMPLETE YEAR GRADE 4

80

Week 7 Practice

Review

Write **PRES** for present tense, **PAST** for past tense, or **FUT** for future tense.

FUT 1. She will help him study.
PAST 2. She helped him study.
PRES 3. She helps him study.
PAST 4. She promised to help him study.

Write the past tense form of these verbs.

5. cry ___cried___
6. sigh ___sighed___
7. hurry ___hurried___
8. pop ___popped___

Write the past tense of these irregular verbs with helpers.

9. (go) have ___have gone___
10. (sleep) have ___have slept___
11. (sing) have ___have sung___
12. (see) have ___have seen___

Write the correct form of **be.**

13. They ___are/were___ my closest neighbors.
14. I ___am/was___ very happy for you today.
15. He ___was___ there on time yesterday.
16. She ___is/was___ still the nicest girl I know.

Circle the correct verb.

17. He (went) gone to my locker.
18. I (went) gone to the beach many times.
19. Have you went (gone) to this show before?
20. We (went) gone all the way to the top!

COMPLETE YEAR GRADE 4

81

Week 7 Practice

Verb Tenses

A **present-tense** verb shows action that is happening now. A **past-tense** verb shows action that happened earlier. A **future-tense** verb shows action that will take place in the future.

Examples: The clockmaker **repairs** the clock. (present)
The clockmaker **repaired** the clock. (past)
The clockmaker **will repair** the clock. (future)

Write these verbs using the tenses shown in parentheses.

	try	**walk**	**work**
(present)	Tom __tries__	Karen __walks__	They __work__
(past)	Tom __tried__	Karen __walked__	They __worked__
(future)	Tom __will try__	Karen __will walk__	They __will work__

Write the correct verb in each blank below.

1. time (future) 4. use (past) 7. dine (present) 10. invent (past)
2. chart (present) 5. tell (present) 8. move (future)
3. trickle (past) 6. reset (future) 9. help (past)

1. John __will time__ the runners in the race.
2. A calendar __charts__ the days of each month.
3. Sand __trickled__ through the hourglass.
4. People __used__ the hourglass before clocks were invented.
5. A pendulum __tells__ time by Earth's rotation.
6. John __will reset__ his watch when changing time zones.
7. He __dines__ at 8:00 every evening during the week.
8. Martha __will move__ the hands of the clock.
9. In the distant past, the Sun and the Moon __helped__ man tell time.
10. The Egyptians __invented__ the solar calendar.

COMPLETE YEAR GRADE 4

82

Week 7 Practice

Multiplying 2 to 12

Multiplication is simply a quick way to add!

Example: 3 x 6

1. The first factor tells how many groups there are. There are 3 groups.
2. The second factor tells how many are in each group. There are 6 in each group.

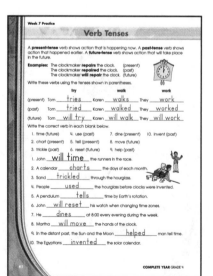

6 + 6 + 6 = 18

3 groups of 6 equal 18.
3 x 6 = 18

Some helpful hints to remember when multiplying:

- When you multiply by 0, the product is always 0. **Example:** 0 x 7 = 0
- When you multiply by 1, the product is always the factor being multiplied. **Example:** 1 x 12 = 12
- When multiplying by 2, double the factor other than 2. **Example:** 2 x 4 = 8
- The order doesn't matter when multiplying. **Example:** 5 x 3 = 15, 3 x 5 = 15
- When you multiply by 9, the digits in the product add up to 9 (until 9 x 11). **Example:** 7 x 9 = 63, 6 + 3 = 9
- When you multiply by 10, multiply by 1 and add 0 to the product. **Example:** 10 x 3 = 30
- When you multiply by 11, double the factor you're multiplying by (until 10). **Example:** 11 x 8 = 88

Multiply:

2	3	4	2	5	5	7	8
x9	x8	x9	x11	x9	x10	x6	x8
18	24	36	22	45	50	42	64

11	8	8 x 5 = 40	4 x 8 = 32	10 x 10 = 100
x12	x7			
132	63			

5
x5
40

5 x 5 = 25 6 x 6 = 36 7 x 8 = 56

COMPLETE YEAR GRADE 4

83

Answer Key

Week 7 Practice

Multiplication

Follow the steps for multiplying a one-digit number by a two-digit number using regrouping.

Example: Step 1: Multiply the ones. Regroup.
$$\begin{array}{r} 54 \\ \times\ 7 \\ \hline 8 \end{array}$$

Step 2: Multiply the tens. Add two tens.
$$\begin{array}{r} 54 \\ \times\ 7 \\ \hline 378 \end{array}$$

Multiply.

27 ×3 = 81	63 ×4 = 252	52 ×5 = 260	91 ×9 = 819	45 ×7 = 315	75 ×2 = 150
64 ×5 = 320	76 ×3 = 228	93 ×6 = 558	87 ×4 = 348	66 ×7 = 462	38 ×2 = 76
47 ×8 = 376	64 ×9 = 576	51 ×8 = 408	99 ×3 = 297	13 ×7 = 91	32 ×4 = 128
25 ×8 = 200	15 ×7 = 105				

The chickens on the Smith farm produce 48 dozen eggs each day. How many dozen eggs do they produce in 7 days? **336**

COMPLETE YEAR GRADE 4

84

Week 7 Practice

Multiplication

Multiply. "Come on, this is easy!"

1. 32 ×3 = 96
2. 21 ×4 = 84
3. 43 ×3 = 129
4. 20 ×3 = 60
5. 11 ×3 = 33
6. 34 ×3 = 102
7. 21 ×3 = 63
8. 33 ×3 = 99
9. 24 ×2 = 48
10. 22 ×4 = 88
11. 40 ×2 = 80
12. 32 ×2 = 64
13. 13 ×3 = 39
14. 22 ×2 = 44
15. 20 ×4 = 80
16. 23 ×2 = 46
17. 11 ×3 = 33
18. 41 ×2 = 82
19. 31 ×3 = 93
20. 44 ×2 = 88
21. 23 ×3 = 69
22. 24 ×2 = 48
23. 33 ×2 = 66
24. 30 ×3 = 90
25. 21 ×2 = 42
26. 13 ×2 = 26
27. 42 ×2 = 84
28. 12 ×3 = 36
29. 14 ×2 = 28
30. 22 ×3 = 66

COMPLETE YEAR GRADE 4

85

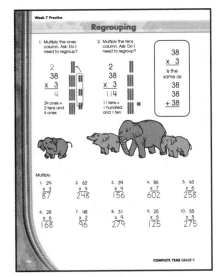

Week 7 Practice

Regrouping

1. Multiply the ones column. Ask: Do I need to regroup?
2. Multiply the tens column. Ask: Do I need to regroup?

$$\begin{array}{r} 2 \\ 38 \\ \times\ 3 \\ \hline 4 \end{array}$$
24 ones = 2 tens and 4 ones

$$\begin{array}{r} 2 \\ 38 \\ \times\ 3 \\ \hline 114 \end{array}$$
11 tens = 1 hundred and 1 ten

$$\begin{array}{r} 38 \\ \times\ 3 \end{array}$$ is the same as
$$\begin{array}{r} 38 \\ 38 \\ +\ 38 \end{array}$$

Multiply.

1. 29 ×3 = 87
2. 62 ×4 = 248
3. 39 ×4 = 156
4. 86 ×7 = 602
5. 43 ×6 = 258
6. 28 ×6 = 168
7. 48 ×2 = 96
8. 31 ×9 = 279
9. 25 ×5 = 125
10. 55 ×5 = 275

COMPLETE YEAR GRADE 4

86

Week 8 Practice

Irregular Verbs

Verbs that do not add **ed** to form the past tense are called **irregular verbs**. The spelling of these verbs changes.

Examples:
present	past	present	past
begin, begins	began	do, does	did
break, breaks	broke	eat, eats	ate

Write the past tense of each irregular verb below.

1. Samuel almost **fell** (fall) when he kicked a rock in the path.
2. Diana made sure she **took** (take) a canteen on her hike.
3. David **ran** (run) over to a shady tree for a quick break.
4. Jimmy **broke** (break) off a long piece of grass to put in his mouth while he was walking.
5. Eva **knew** (know) the path along the river very well.
6. The clouds **began** (begin) to sprinkle raindrops on the hikers.
7. Kathy **threw** (throw) a small piece of bread to the birds.
8. Everyone **ate** (eat) a very nutritious meal after a long adventure.
9. We all **slept** (sleep) very well that night.

Many irregular verbs have a different past-tense ending when the helping verbs **have** and **has** are used.

Examples: Steven **has worn** special hiking shoes today.
Marlene and I **have known** about this trail for years.

Circle the correct irregular verb below.

1. Peter has (flew, **flown**) down to join us for the adventure.
2. Mark has (saw, **seen**) a lot of animals on the hike today.
3. Andy and Mike have (went, **gone**) on this trail before.
4. Bill has (took, **taken**) extra precautions to make sure no cacti prick his legs.
5. Heather has (ate, **eaten**) all the snacks her mom packed for her.

COMPLETE YEAR GRADE 4

88

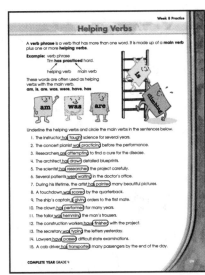

Week 8 Practice

Helping Verbs

A **verb phrase** is a verb that has more than one word. It is made up of a **main verb** plus one or more **helping verbs**.

Example: verb phrase
Tim **has practiced** hard.
helping verb / main verb

These words are often used as helping verbs with the main verb.
am, is, are, was, were, have, has

Underline the helping verbs and circle the main verbs in the sentences below.

1. The instructor has (taught) science for several years.
2. The concert pianist was (practicing) before the performance.
3. Researchers are (attempting) to find a cure for the disease.
4. The architect has (drawn) detailed blueprints.
5. The scientist has (researched) the project carefully.
6. Several patients were (waiting) in the doctor's office.
7. During his lifetime, the artist has (painted) many beautiful pictures.
8. A touchdown was (scored) by the quarterback.
9. The ship's captain is (giving) orders to the first mate.
10. The clown has (performed) for many years.
11. The tailor was (hemming) the man's trousers.
12. The construction workers have (finished) with the project.
13. The secretary was (typing) the letters yesterday.
14. Lawyers have (passed) difficult state examinations.
15. A cab driver has (transported) many passengers by the end of the day.

COMPLETE YEAR GRADE 4

89

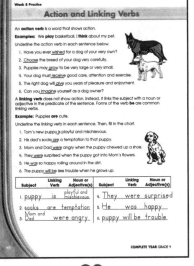

Week 8 Practice

Action and Linking Verbs

An **action verb** is a word that shows action.

Examples: We **play** basketball. I **think** about my pet.

Underline the action verb in each sentence below.

1. Have you ever **wished** for a dog of your very own?
2. **Choose** the breed of your dog very carefully.
3. Puppies may **grow** to be very large or very small.
4. Your dog must **receive** good care, attention and exercise.
5. The right dog will **give** you years of pleasure and enjoyment.
6. Can you **imagine** yourself as a dog owner?

A **linking verb** does not show action. Instead, it links the subject with a noun or adjective in the predicate of the sentence. Forms of the verb **be** are common linking verbs.

Example: Puppies **are** cute.

Underline the linking verb in each sentence. Then, fill in the chart.

1. Tom's new puppy **is** playful and mischievous.
2. His dad's socks **are** a temptation to that puppy.
3. Mom and Dad **were** angry when the puppy chewed up a shoe.
4. They **were** surprised when the puppy got into Mom's flowers.
5. He **was** so happy rolling around in the dirt.
6. The puppy **will be** trouble when he grows up.

Subject	Linking Verb	Noun or Adjective(s)	Subject	Linking Verb	Noun or Adjective(s)
1. puppy	is	playful and mischievous	4. They	were	surprised
2. socks	are	temptation	5. He	was	happy
3. Mom and Dad	were	angry	6. puppy	will be	trouble

COMPLETE YEAR GRADE 4

90

91

Week 8 Practice

Subject/Verb Agreement

The **subject** and **verb** in a sentence must agree. If the subject is **singular**, add **s** to the verb. If the subject is **plural**, do not add an ending to the verb.

Examples: Lava only **flows** when it is very hot. (singular)
Cinders **shoot** out of an active volcano. (plural)

Complete each sentence below using a form of the verb in parentheses.

1. Some volcanoes _____erupt_____ quietly. (erupt)
2. The ground _____swells_____ around a volcano just before an eruption. (swell)
3. Volcanoes _____explode_____ with great fury. (explode)
4. Tremors _____increase_____ as magma works its way to the surface. (increase)
5. Magma _____escapes_____ to the Earth's surface. (escape)
6. A volcano _____erupts_____ so violently that the mountain can be blown apart. (erupt)
7. Obsidian _____forms_____ when flying volcanic debris cools quickly in the air. (form)
8. Volcanoes _____spew_____ hot lava high into the air. (spew)
9. The sky _____darkens_____ from the ash and dust that explode out of a volcano. (darken)
10. Ash _____covers_____ the ground for many miles around a volcanic explosion. (cover)
11. Molten lava _____glows_____ bright red and yellow as it escapes from underneath the Earth's surface. (glow)
12. Steam _____forms_____ when molten lava comes in contact with water. (form)

COMPLETE YEAR GRADE 4

92

Week 8 Practice

Pronoun/Verb Agreement

The **subject pronoun** and the **verb** in a sentence must agree. If the subject pronoun is **singular**, add **s** to the verb. If the subject pronoun is **plural**, do not add an ending to the verb.

Examples: He **wears** a helmet every time he rides his bike. (singular)
They **wear** helmets whenever they go roller-blading. (plural)

Circle the verb in parentheses that agrees with the subject pronoun.

1. She (ride, rides) her bike to band practice on Tuesdays.
2. They (zoom, zooms) down the hill to help them get up the steep incline on the other side.
3. He (glide, glides) nicely on his skateboard when he's going around the corners on the skating path.
4. We (travel, travels) as a family every Saturday to the park on our bikes.
5. It (rain, rains) sometimes while we're riding our bikes to school.
6. He (love, loves) to climb the hills on bikes with his mom and dad.
7. She (wear, wears) a helmet and kneepads whenever she goes roller-blading with her friends.

Write the subject pronoun that agrees with the verb.

1. __He__ (They, We, He) tries very hard to skate backwards at the skating rink.
2. __She__ (I, She, You) tells everyone about all the fun things there are to do at the park.
3. __He__ (We, You, He) invites a friend every time he goes to the bicycle acrobatic demonstrations.
4. __They__ (She, They, He) look both ways very carefully before crossing the street on their roller-blades.
5. __We__ (It, We, He) send invitations to all our friends whenever there is a safety seminar at our school.

COMPLETE YEAR GRADE 4

93

Week 8 Practice

Fact Factory

Factors are the numbers multiplied together in a multiplication problem. The **product** is the answer.

Write the missing factors or products.

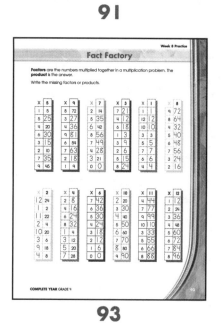

COMPLETE YEAR GRADE 4

94

Week 8 Practice

Space Math

Blast off into multiplication.

406 × 3 = 1,218	326 × 5 = 1,630	281 × 4 = 1,124	923 × 2 = 1,846	817 × 6 = 4,902
231 × 6 = 1,386	214 × 2 = 428	262 × 7 = 1,834	218 × 5 = 1,090	126 × 9 = 1,134
241 × 8 = 1,928	329 × 6 = 1,974	310 × 5 = 1,550	204 × 8 = 1,632	431 × 3 = 1,293
231 × 4 = 924	624 × 7 = 4,368			421 × 6 = 2,526
896 × 1 = 896				742 × 8 = 5,936
606 × 7 = 4,242				525 × 4 = 2,100
				814 × 9 = 7,326

COMPLETE YEAR GRADE 4

95

Week 8 Practice

Amazing Arms

What will happen to a starfish that loses an arm? To find out, solve the following problems and write the corresponding letter above the answer at the bottom of the page.

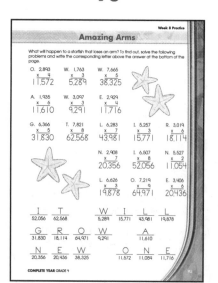

O. 2,893 × 4 = 11,572   W. 1,763 × 3 = 5,289   W. 7,665 × 5 = 38,325

A. 1,935 × 6 = 11,610   W. 3,097 × 3 = 9,291   E. 2,929 × 4 = 11,716

G. 6,366 × 5 = 31,830   T. 7,821 × 8 = 62,568   L. 6,283 × 7 = 43,981   I. 5,257 × 3 = 15,771   R. 3,019 × 6 = 18,114

N. 2,908 × 7 = 20,356   I. 6,507 × 8 = 52,056   N. 5,527 × 2 = 11,054

L. 6,626 × 3 = 19,878   O. 7,219 × 9 = 64,971   E. 3,406 × 6 = 20,436

```
  I      T              W      I      L      L
52,056 62,568         5,289 15,771 43,981 19,878

  G      R      O      W              A
31,830 18,114 64,971 9,291         11,610

  N      E      W                    O      N      E
20,356 20,436 38,325              11,572 11,054 11,716
```

COMPLETE YEAR GRADE 4

96

Week 8 Practice

Multiplication

Follow the steps for multiplying a two-digit number by a two-digit number using regrouping.

Example:

Step 1: Multiply the ones. Regroup.

```
   63        63
  ×68       ×68
           504
```

Step 2: Multiply the tens. Regroup. Add.

```
   63        63
  ×68       ×68
  504       504
3,780     +3,780
           4,284
```

Multiply.

12 × 55 = 660	27 × 15 = 405	65 × 27 = 1,755	19 × 39 = 741	99 × 13 = 1,287	35 × 14 = 490
43 × 26 = 1,118	38 × 17 = 646	53 × 86 = 4,558	47 × 72 = 3,384	57 × 62 = 3,534	48 × 33 = 1,584
	27 × 54 = 1,458	93 × 45 = 4,185	64 × 16 = 1,024	53 × 23 = 1,219	

The Jones farm has 24 cows that each produce 52 quarts of milk a day. How many quarts are produced each day altogether?

_____1,248 quarts_____

COMPLETE YEAR GRADE 4

Answer Key

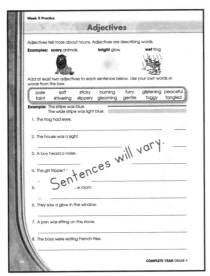

Page 98

Week 9 Practice

Adjectives

Adjectives tell more about nouns. Adjectives are describing words.

Examples: **scary** animals   **bright** glow   **wet** frog

Add at least two adjectives to each sentence below. Use your own words or words from the box.

| pale | soft | sticky | burning | furry | glistening | peaceful |
| faint | shivering | slippery | gleaming | gentle | foggy | tangled |

Example: The stripe was blue.
The wide stripe was light blue.

1. The frog had eyes.

2. The house was a sight.

3. A boy heard a noise.

4. The girl tripped.

5. ...e room.

6. They saw a glow in the window.

7. A pan was sitting on the stove.

8. The boys were eating French fries.

Sentences will vary.

COMPLETE YEAR GRADE 4

98

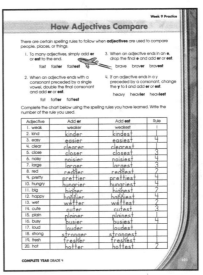

Page 99

Week 9 Practice

Adjectives

Adjectives tell a noun's size, color, shape, texture, brightness, darkness, personality, sound, taste, and so on.

Examples: **color** — red, yellow, green, black
size — small, large, huge, tiny
shape — round, square, rectangular, oval
texture — rough, smooth, soft, scaly
brightness — glistening, shimmering, dull, pale
personality — gentle, grumpy, happy, sad

Follow the instructions below.

1. Get an apple, orange or other piece of fruit. Look at it very carefully and write adjectives that describe its size, color, shape, and texture.

Answers will vary.

2. Take a bite of your fruit. Write adjectives that describe its taste, texture, smell, and so on.

Answers will vary.

3. Using all the adjectives from above, write a cinquain about your fruit. A **cinquain** is a five-line poem. See the form and sample poem below.

Form: Line 1 — noun   **Example:** Apple
Line 2 — two adjectives   red, smooth
Line 3 — three sounds   cracking, smacking, slurping
Line 4 — four-word phrase   drippy, sticky, sour juice
Line 5 — noun   Apple

Poems will vary

COMPLETE YEAR GRADE 4

99

Page 100

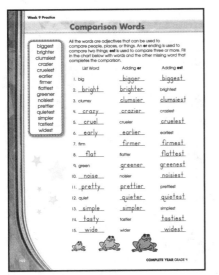

Week 9 Practice

Descriptive Sentences

Turn a good sentence into a great sentence by using more descriptive words.

Example: The dog chased the boy.
The big brown dog playfully chased the little boy.

Add descriptive words to make each sentence a great sentence. Write the improved sentence on each line.

1. The man climbed the mountain.
Example: The old man climbed slowly up the steep mountain.

2. The group found a buried tomb.
Example: The archaeological group found an ancient buried tomb.

3. The girls painted a sign.

4. The sunlight came through the window.

5. Ice cream _Answers will vary._

6. The snake moved down the tree.

7. The storm rocked the boat.

COMPLETE YEAR GRADE 4

100

Page 101

Week 9 Practice

How Adjectives Compare

There are certain spelling rules to follow when **adjectives** are used to compare people, places, or things.

1. To many adjectives, simply add **er** or **est** to the end.
fast   faster   fastest

2. When an adjective ends with a consonant preceded by a single vowel, double the final consonant and add **er** or **est**.
fat   fatter   fattest

3. When an adjective ends in an **e**, drop the final **e** and add **er** or **est**.
brave   braver   bravest

4. If an adjective ends in a y preceded by a consonant, change the y to i and add **er** or **est**.
heavy   heavier   heaviest

Complete the chart below using the spelling rules you have learned. Write the number of the rule you used.

	Adjective	Add **er**	Add **est**	Rule
1.	weak	weaker	weakest	1
2.	kind	kinder	kindest	1
3.	easy	easier	easiest	4
4.	clear	clearer	clearest	1
5.	close	closer	closest	3
6.	noisy	noisier	noisiest	4
7.	large	larger	largest	3
8.	red	redder	reddest	2
9.	pretty	prettier	prettiest	4
10.	hungry	hungrier	hungriest	4
11.	big	bigger	biggest	2
12.	happy	happier	happiest	4
13.	wet	wetter	wettest	2
14.	cute	cuter	cutest	3
15.	plain	plainer	plainest	1
16.	busy	busier	busiest	4
17.	loud	louder	loudest	1
18.	strong	stronger	strongest	1
19.	fresh	fresher	freshest	1
20.	hot	hotter	hottest	2

COMPLETE YEAR GRADE 4

101

Page 102

Week 9 Practice

Comparison Words

All the words are adjectives that can be used to compare people, places, or things. An **er** ending is used to compare two things; **est** is used to compare three or more. Fill in the chart below with words and the other missing word that completes the comparison.

| biggest | brighter | clumsiest | crazier | cruelest | earlier | firmer | flattest | greener | noisiest | prettier | quietest | simpler | tastiest | widest |

	List Word	Adding **er**	Adding **est**
1.	big	bigger	biggest
2.	bright	brighter	brightest
3.	clumsy	clumsier	clumsiest
4.	crazy	crazier	craziest
5.	cruel	crueler	cruelest
6.	early	earlier	earliest
7.	firm	firmer	firmest
8.	flat	flatter	flattest
9.	green	greener	greenest
10.	noise	noisier	noisiest
11.	pretty	prettier	prettiest
12.	quiet	quieter	quietest
13.	simple	simpler	simplest
14.	tasty	tastier	tastiest
15.	wide	wider	widest

COMPLETE YEAR GRADE 4

102

Page 103

Week 9 Practice

Elephant Escapades

Multiply:

56 × 43 = 2,408	13 × 24 = 312	24 × 56 = 1,344	20 × 93 = 1,860
23 × 54 = 1,242	28 × 43 = 1,204	13 × 82 = 1,066	21 × 64 = 1,344
25 × 34 = 850	13 × 64 = 832	34 × 21 = 714	32 × 55 = 1,760
42 × 23 = 966	62 × 31 = 1,922	51 × 43 = 2,193	21 × 64 = 1,344
10 × 84 = 840	35 × 24 = 840	24 × 30 = 720	
24 × 53 = 1,272	81 × 46 = 3,726	32 × 27 = 864	

COMPLETE YEAR GRADE 4

103

Answer Key

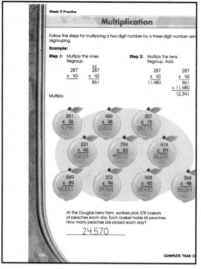

104

105

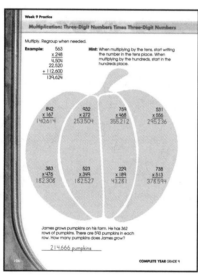

106

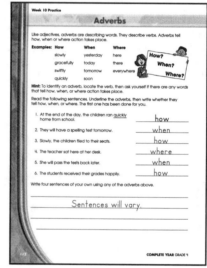

112

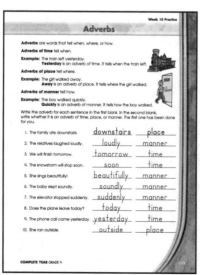

113

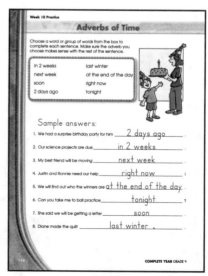

114

115

Week 10 Practice

Adverbs of Place

Choose one word from the box to complete each sentence. Make sure the adverb you choose makes sense with the rest of the sentence.

| inside | upstairs | below | everywhere |
| home | somewhere | outside | there |

Sample answers:

1. Each child took a new library book __home__.
2. We looked __everywhere__ for his jacket.
3. We will have recess __inside__ because it is raining.
4. From the top of the mountain we could see the village far __below__.
5. My sister and I share a bedroom __upstairs__.
6. The teacher warned the children, "You must play with the ball __outside__."
7. Mother said, "I know that recipe is __somewhere__ in this file box!"
8. You can put the chair __there__.

COMPLETE YEAR GRADE 4

116

Week 10 Practice

Adverbs of Manner

Choose a word from the box to complete each sentence. Make sure the adverb you choose makes sense with the rest of the sentence. One word will be used twice.

| quickly | carefully | loudly | easily | carelessly | slowly |

Sample answers:

1. The scouts crossed the old bridge __carefully__.
2. We watched the turtle move __slowly__ across the yard.
3. Everyone completed the math test __quickly__.
4. The quarterback scampered __easily__ down the sideline.
5. The mother __carefully__ cleaned the child's sore knee.
6. The fire was caused by someone __carelessly__ tossing a match.
7. The alarm rang __loudly__ while we were eating.

COMPLETE YEAR GRADE 4

117

Week 10 Practice

Multiplication Drill

Multiply.

134 × 22 = 2,948	48 × 66 = 3,168	876 × 13 = 11,388	432 × 64 = 27,648
68 × 11 = 748	5,478 × 8 = 43,824	248 × 61 = 15,128	6,897 × 6 = 41,382
82 × 4 = 328	6,798 × 5 = 33,990	79 × 86 = 6,794	694 × 38 = 26,372

Color the picture by matching each number with its paintbrush.

COMPLETE YEAR GRADE 4

118

Week 10 Practice

Wheels of Wonder

Solve the following problems by multiplying each number by the power of 10 in the center.

COMPLETE YEAR GRADE 4

119

Week 10 Practice

Multiplication: Tens, Hundreds, Thousands

When multiplying a number by 10, the answer is the number with a 0. It is like counting by tens.

Examples:

| 10 × 1 = 10 | 10 × 2 = 20 | 10 × 3 = 30 | 10 × 4 = 40 | 10 × 5 = 50 | 10 × 6 = 60 |

When multiplying a number by 100, the answer is the number with two 0's. When multiplying by 1,000, the answer is the number with three 0's.

Examples:

| 100 × 1 = 100 | 100 × 2 = 200 | 100 × 3 = 300 | 1,000 × 1 = 1,000 | 1,000 × 2 = 2,000 | 1,000 × 3 = 3,000 |
| 4 × 2 = 8 | 400 × 2 = 800 | 8 × 3 = 24 | 800 × 3 = 2,400 | 7 × 5 = 35 | 700 × 5 = 3,500 |

Multiply.

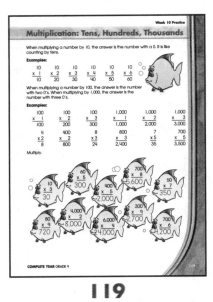

COMPLETE YEAR GRADE 4

120

Week 10 Practice

Puzzling Numbers

Fill in the tables with the missing factors and products.

factor	factor	product
45	4	180
16	8	128
55	5	275
4	26	104

factor	factor	product
3	41	123
2	5	10
6	53	318
47	3	141

factor	factor	product
5	25	125
44	7	308
30	3	90
42	20	840

factor	factor	product
114	2	228
6	33	198
3	40	120
2	66	132

Shade in your answers below to reveal a picture.

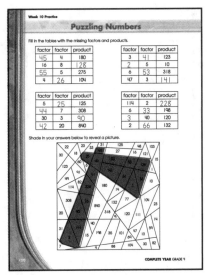

COMPLETE YEAR GRADE 4

Answer Key

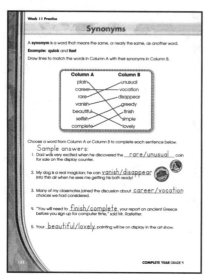

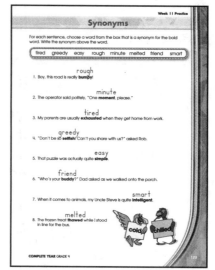

122

123

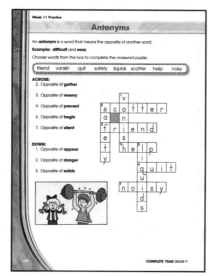

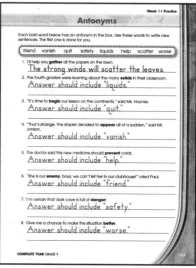

124

125

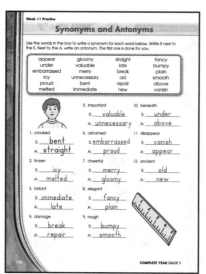

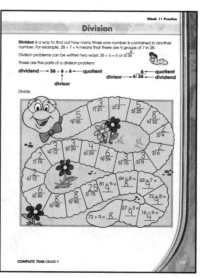

126

127

Answer Key

128

Division

Divide.

(worksheet with division problems)

129

Snowball Bash

Help Pete climb down this mound of giant snowballs.

130

Division With Remainders

Sometimes groups of objects or numbers cannot be divided into equal groups. The **remainder** is the number left over in the quotient of a division problem. The remainder must be smaller than the divisor.

Example:

Divide 18 butterflies into groups of 5.
You have 3 equal groups,
with 3 butterflies left over.

$18 \div 5 = 3\ r3$

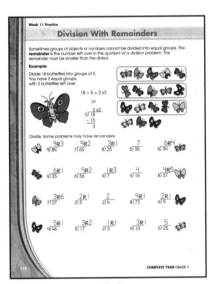

Divide. Some problems may have remainders.

132

Same Spelling But ...

bass
bowl
close
cobbler
does
flie
flounder
grave
hawk
list
minute
object
paddle
present
sow

Homophones are words that have the same spelling but are different in meaning and sometimes pronunciation. Use the spelling words to fill in the blanks. Indicate the part of speech in the parentheses. The same word is used twice in each sentence.

1. The secretary wanted to __file__ (v.) her fingernails before she put all the papers in the __file__ (n.).
2. Before my dad goes to __bowl__ (v.), he eats a big __bowl__ (n.) of cereal.
3. Our __paddle__ (n.) broke, the boat overturned and we had to __paddle__ (v.) quite a distance.
4. The __bass__ (n.) singer enjoys fishing for __bass__ (n.).
5. The ship's captain was reading the __list__ (n.) of passengers when he suddenly felt the ship __list__ (v.).
6. After the __cobbler__ (n.) has repaired shoes all day, he enjoys eating a fruit __cobbler__ (n.).
7. The __flounder__ (n.) was hooked tightly, but I couldn't reel it in, so it began to __flounder__ (v.) in the shallow water.
8. As the peddler was getting ready to __hawk__ (v.) his vegetables, a hungry __hawk__ (n.) was perched on a nearby tree branch.
9. The company hired to dig the __grave__ (n.) realized the cemetery needed __grave__ (a.) attention.

Circle the correct pronunciation and write the word on the line.

1. The president was so __close__ I could shake his hand. klōz (klōs)
2. Three __does__ were nibbling grass by the road. (dŭz) dūz
3. After doing our research, we had to __present__ a report. (prē′ ənt) prĭ zĕnt′
4. The gardener will __sow__ grass seed for a new lawn. (sō) sou

133

Bizarre Bazaar!

board
bored
coarse
council
counsel
course
creak
creek
knot
lead
led
not
ring
who's
whose
wring

Three pairs of homophones are not next to each other in the spelling list because of alphabetical order. Write those three pairs.

a. __coarse__   a. __knot__   a. __ring__
b. __course__   b. __not__   b. __wring__

Fill in the blanks with spelling words. Not all words are used.

1. The pipe was made out of l e a [d].
2. She broke the b o [a] r d with a karate chop.
3. In scouting, he learned to tie a k n o [t].
4. Students will elect class members to the student c o u n c i [l].
5. The umpire shouted, "[W] h o s e bat is this?"
6. Grandpa gave me good c o u n s e [l] whenever I had important decisions to make.
7. With nothing to do, I am b [o] r e d.
8. It is n [o] t nice to hit anyone.
9. The c o a r s [e] material made my arms itch.
10. The hikers followed a c o u r s [e] to the north.
11. The thief stole a diamond r i n [g].
12. We sailed paper boats in the c r e e [k].
13. The old floor started to c r e a [k] when I walked across it.

Match the boxed letter from each sentence to the numbered lines below to answer the riddle: Why was the man happy to get a job at the bakery?

B e c a u s e   h e
9 13 2 4 1 5   6

k n e a d e d   t h e
12 6 3 8 11 10   7

d o u g h
1 7 5

134

Homophones

Homophones are two words that sound the same, have different meanings, and are usually spelled differently.

Example: write and right

Write the correct homophone in each sentence below.

weight — how heavy something is
wait — to be patient

threw — tossed
through — passing between

steal — to take something that doesn't belong to you
steel — a heavy metal

1. The bands marched __through__ the streets lined with many cheering people.
2. __Wait__ for me by the flagpole.
3. One of our strict rules at school is: Never __steal__ from another person.
4. Could you estimate the __weight__ of this bowling ball?
5. The bleachers have __steel__ rods on both ends and in the middle.
6. He walked in the door and __threw__ his jacket down.

Answer Key

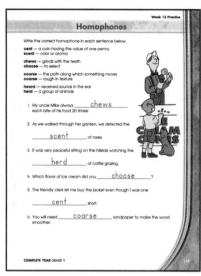

135

136

137

138

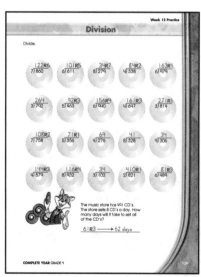

139

140

Answer Key

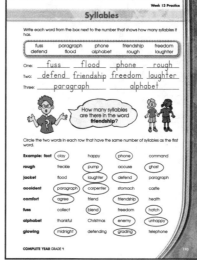

142 — Homophone Hype

Week 13 Practice

Homophone Hype

Word search grid:
```
G S B R I D L E W O J M
E H R O M N S L R G V A
G N I L A X H E A R W N
D R O W I O R N F A S E
R M A N N B G I O Z K R
V G L V W N F S C E N T
N D I M S T L L H N S
R U U O N P M E I I G N D
D E W S P C H D L I V E Y
O F A I S L E I U B R L
R L Y O M S Y E R G T A
```

For each word given below, list the homophones in the spaces provided. Find and circle the homophone in the word sea. glw

Sentences will vary.

1. Here — Example: hear
   Sentence: I did not hear her say, "Come here!"
2. Bridle — bridal
   Sentence: _____
3. I'll — aisle / isle
   Sentence: _____
4. Graze (Hint: plural forms of a color) — greys / grays
   Sentence: _____
5. Main — mane / Maine
   Sentence: _____
6. Whey — way / weigh
   Sentence: _____
7. Dew — do / due
   Sentence: _____
8. Scent — sent / cent
   Sentence: _____

COMPLETE YEAR GRADE 4

143 — Is the Bear Bare?

Week 13 Practice

Is the Bear Bare?

Word box: bare, bear, berry, bury, groan, grown, hall, haul, pain, pane, raise, rays, stair, stare, wait, weight

Use each pair of homophones correctly in the sentences. Indicate the part of speech in the parentheses.

1. When my brother moved into the dormitory, he had to __haul__ (v) all his belongings down the __hall__ (n).
2. The camper was __bare__ (a) when he swam in the lake, but only a __bear__ (n) saw him.
3. I decided to __raise__ (v) the blinds to let in the sun's __rays__ (n).
4. My dad let out a __groan__ (n) when he discovered he had __grown__ (v) too large for his pants.
5. I felt a small __pain__ (n) when I cut my hand on the __pane__ (n) of glass.
6. It's not polite to __stare__ (v) when someone stumbles on a __stair__ (n).
7. When our pet canary died, we decided to __bury__ (v) it near the bush with the one red __berry__ (n) on it.

COMPLETE YEAR GRADE 4

144 — Syllables

Week 13 Practice

Syllables

A **syllable** is a word—or part of a word—with only one vowel sound. Some words have just one syllable, such as **cat, dog,** and **house**. Some words have two syllables, such as **in-sist** and **be-fore**. Some words have three syllables, such as **re-mem-ber**; four syllables, such as **un-der-stand-ing**; or more. Often words are easier to spell if you know how many syllables they have.

syl-la-bles

Write the number of syllables in each word below.

Word	Syllables		Word	Syllables
1. amphibian	4		11. want	1
2. liter	2		12. communication	5
3. guild	1		13. pedestrian	4
4. chill	1		14. kilo	2
5. vegetarian	5		15. autumn	2
6. comedian	4		16. dinosaur	3
7. warm	1		17. grammar	2
8. piano	3		18. dry	1
9. barbarian	4		19. solar	2
10. chef	1		20. wild	1

Next to each number, write words with the same number of syllables.

1. _____
2. _____
3. _____ **Answers will vary.**
4. _____
5. _____

COMPLETE YEAR GRADE 4

145 — Syllables

Week 13 Practice

Syllables

Write each word from the box next to the number that shows how many syllables it has.

Word box: fuss, paragraph, phone, friendship, freedom, defend, flood, alphabet, rough, laughter

One: fuss / flood / phone / rough
Two: defend / friendship / freedom / laughter
Three: paragraph / alphabet

How many syllables are there in the word **friendship**?

Circle the two words in each row that have the same number of syllables as the first word.

Example: fact	(clay)	happy	(phone)	command
rough	freckle	(pump)	accuse	(ghost)
jacket	flood	(laughter)	(defend)	paragraph
accident	(paragraph)	(carpenter)	stomach	castle
comfort	(agree)	friend	(friendship)	health
fuss	collect	(blend)	freedom	(hatch)
alphabet	thankful	Christmas	(enemy)	(unhappy)
glowing	(midnight)	defending	(grading)	telephone

COMPLETE YEAR GRADE 4

146 — Grouping Letters

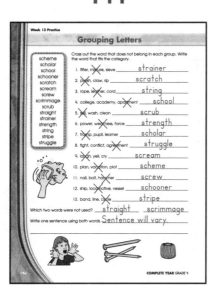

Week 13 Practice

Grouping Letters

Word box: scheme, scholar, school, schooner, scratch, scream, screw, scrimmage, scrub, straight, strainer, strength, string, stripe, struggle

Cross out the word that does not belong in each group. Write the word that fits the category.

1. filter, ~~mixture~~, sieve — strainer
2. ~~pinch~~, claw, rip — scratch
3. rope, ~~leather~~, cord — string
4. college, academy, ~~apartment~~ — school
5. ~~dust~~, wash, clean — scrub
6. power, ~~weakness~~, force — strength
7. tramp, pupil, learner — scholar
8. fight, conflict, ~~agreement~~ — struggle
9. ~~laugh~~, yell, cry — scream
10. plan, ~~vacation~~, plot — scheme
11. nail, bolt, ~~hammer~~ — screw
12. ship, ~~locomotive~~, vessel — schooner
13. band, line, ~~circle~~ — stripe

Which two words were not used? straight / scrimmage

Write one sentence using both words. **Sentence will vary.**

COMPLETE YEAR GRADE 4

147 — Yum-Yum!

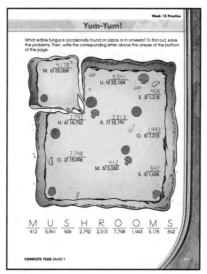

Week 13 Practice

Yum-Yum!

What edible fungus is occasionally found on pizzas or in omelets? To find out, solve the problems. Then, write the corresponding letter above the answer at the bottom of the page.

M. 6)25,068 — 4,178
U. 4)22,164 — 5,541
S. 3)1,218 — 406
H. 6)16,752 — 2,792
R. 7)16,191 — 2,313
O. 5)7,215 — 1,443
O. 2)15,496 — 7,748
M. 5)2,060 — 412
S. 3)1,626 — 542

M U S H R O O M S
412 5,541 406 2,792 2,313 7,748 1,443 4,178 542

COMPLETE YEAR GRADE 4

413

Answer Key

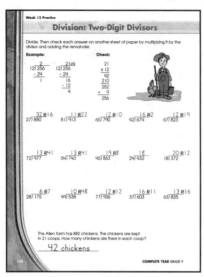

Page 148

Week 13 Practice

Division: Two-Digit Divisors

Divide. Then check each answer on another sheet of paper by multiplying it by the divisor and adding the remainder.

Example:

$$12\overline{)256} \quad \frac{2}{}$$

Check:

```
   21
 x 12
   42
  210
  252
 +  4
  256
```

32 R16   11 R22   12 R10   16 R2   12 R19

13 R41   13 R41   19 R8   18   20 R12

6 R7   10 R48   12 R12   16 R11   13 R16

The Allen farm has 882 chickens. The chickens are kept in 21 coops. How many chickens are there in each coop?

42 chickens

COMPLETE YEAR GRADE 4

Page 149

Week 13 Practice

China's Dragon Kite

Solve the problems in this incredible dragon kite!

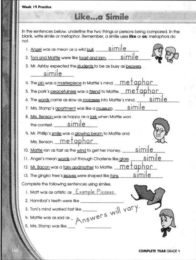

7 R4   3 R5   7 R1
6 R20   4 R2   3 R3
2 R10   3 R3   3 R2
6 R3   5 R6   5 R5   3 R2   3 R2
5 R10   3 R3

COMPLETE YEAR GRADE 4

Page 150

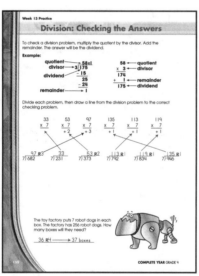

Week 13 Practice

Division: Checking the Answers

To check a division problem, multiply the quotient by the divisor. Add the remainder. The answer will be the dividend.

Example:

```
quotient ──▶  58 R1
divisor ──▶ 3)175        58  ◀── quotient
            -15         x  3  ◀── divisor
dividend ──▶ 25         174
            -24        +  1  ◀── remainder
remainder ──▶ 1        175  ◀── dividend
```

Divide each problem, then draw a line from the division problem to the correct checking problem.

The toy factory puts 7 robot dogs in each box. The factory has 256 robot dogs. How many boxes will they need?

36 R4 ──▶ 37 boxes

COMPLETE YEAR GRADE 4

Page 152

Week 14 Practice

Like...a Simile

In the sentences below, underline the two things or persons being compared. In the blank, write simile or metaphor. Remember, a simile uses like or as; metaphors do not.

1. Angel was as mean as a wild bull. **simile**
2. Toni and Mattie were like toast and jam. **simile**
3. Mr. Ashby expected the students to be as busy as beavers. **simile**
4. The pin was a masterpiece in Mattie's mind. **metaphor**
5. The park's peacefulness was a friend to Mattie. **metaphor**
6. The words came as slow as molasses into Mattie's mind. **simile**
7. Mrs. Stamp's apartment was like a museum. **simile**
8. Mrs. Benson was as happy as a lark when Mattie won the contest. **simile**
9. Mr. Phillip's smile was a glowing beam to Mattie and Mrs. Benson. **metaphor**
10. Mattie ran as fast as the wind to get her money. **simile**
11. Angel's mean words cut through Charlene like glass. **simile**
12. Mr. Bacon was a fairy godmother to Mattie. **metaphor**
13. The gingko tree's leaves were shaped like fans. **simile**

Complete the following sentences using similes.

1. Matt was as artistic as **Example: Picasso**.
2. Hannibal's teeth were like _____
3. Toni's mind worked fast like _____ *Answers will vary.*
4. Mattie was as sad as _____
5. Mrs. Stamp was like _____

COMPLETE YEAR GRADE 4

Page 153

Week 14 Practice

Similes

A **simile** uses the words **like** or **as** to compare two things.

Examples: The snow glittered **like** diamonds.
He was **as** slow **as** a turtle.

Circle the two objects being compared in each sentence.

1. The kittens were like gymnasts performing tricks.
2. My old computer is as slow as molasses.
3. When the lights went out in the basement it was as dark as night.
4. The sun was like a fire heating up the earth.
5. The young girl was as graceful as a ballerina.
6. The puppy cried like a baby all night.
7. He flies that airplane like a daredevil.
8. The girl was as pretty as a picture.
9. The snow on the mountain tops was like whipped cream.
10. The tiger's eyes were like emeralds.

Complete the simile in each sentence.

11. My cat is as _____ as _____
12. He was as _____ as _____
13. Melissa's eyes shone like _____
14. The paints were like _____ *Answers will vary.*
15. The opera singer's voice was as _____ as _____
16. My friend is as _____ as _____

COMPLETE YEAR GRADE 4

Page 154

Week 14 Practice

Metaphors

A **metaphor** is a direct comparison between two things. The words **like** or **as** are not used in a metaphor.

Example: The **sun** is a **yellow ball** in the sky.

Underline the metaphor in each sentence. Write the two objects being compared on the line.

1. As it bounded toward me, the dog was a quivering furball of excitement.
   dog/furball of excitement
2. The snow we skied on was mashed potatoes.
   snow/mashed potatoes
3. John is a mountain goat when it comes to rock climbing.
   John/mountain goat
4. The light is a beacon shining into the dark basement.
   light/beacon
5. The famished child was a wolf, eating for the first time in days.
   famished child/wolf
6. The man's arm was a tireless lever as he fought to win the wrestling contest.
   man's arm/tireless lever
7. The flowers were colorful circles against the green of the yard.
   flowers/colorful circles

COMPLETE YEAR GRADE 4

148 **149** **150** **152** **153** **154**

Answer Key

155

Idioms

An **idiom** is a phrase that says one thing but actually means something quite different.

Example: A **horse of a different color** means something quite unusual.

Write the letter of the correct meaning for each bold phrase. The first one has been done for you.

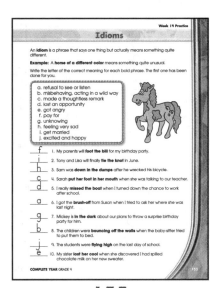

a. refusal to see or listen
b. misbehaving, acting in a wild way
c. made a thoughtless remark
d. lost an opportunity
e. got angry
f. pay for
g. unknowing
h. feeling very sad
i. get married
j. excited and happy

f 1. My parents will **foot the bill** for my birthday party.
i 2. Tony and Lisa will finally **tie the knot** in June.
h 3. Sam was **down in the dumps** after he wrecked his bicycle.
c 4. Sarah **put her foot in her mouth** when she was talking to our teacher.
d 5. I really **missed the boat** when I turned down the chance to work after school.
a 6. I got the **brush-off** from Susan when I tried to ask her where she was last night.
g 7. Mickey is **in the dark** about our plans to throw a surprise birthday party for him.
b 8. The children were **bouncing off the walls** when the baby-sitter tried to put them to bed.
j 9. The students were **flying high** on the last day of school.
e 10. My sister **lost her cool** when she discovered I had spilled chocolate milk on her new sweater.

COMPLETE YEAR GRADE 4

156

Idioms

An **idiom** is a figure of speech that has a meaning different from the literal one.

Example: Dad is **in the doghouse** because he was late for dinner.

Meaning: Dad is in trouble because he was late for dinner.

Write the meanings of the idioms in bold.

1. He was a **bundle of nerves** waiting for his test scores.
very nervous

2. It was **raining cats and dogs**.
raining very hard

3. My friend and I decided to **bury the hatchet** after our argument.
make peace

4. He gave me **the cold shoulder** when I spoke to him.
ignored

5. My mom **blew up** when she saw my poor report card.
got very upset

6. I was **on pins and needles** before my skating performance.
nervous and anxious

7. When the student didn't answer, the teacher asked, "**Did the cat get your tongue?**"
Why are you not speaking?

8. The city **rolled out the red carpet for** the returning Olympic champion.
welcomed

9. They hired a clown for the young boy's birthday party to help **break the ice**.
put everyone at ease

COMPLETE YEAR GRADE 4

157

Identifying Operations

Fill in the correct sign for each problem.

$5 \div 5 = 10$ $14 + 59 = 73$ $21 + 9 = 30$ $36 + 63 = 99$
$9 \times 9 = 81$ $56 + 17 = 73$ $64 \div 8 = 8$ $6 \times 9 = 54$
$56 - 8 = 48$ $40 \div 5 = 8$ $7 \times 8 = 56$ $33 + 57 = 90$
$91 - 16 = 75$ $9 \times 3 = 27$ $76 - 19 = 57$ $27 \div 3 = 9$
$54 \div 6 = 9$ $29 + 37 = 66$ $43 + 7 = 50$ $63 - 9 = 54$
$28 - 17 = 11$ $6 \times 5 = 30$ $9 \times 4 = 36$ $8 + 38 = 46$
$25 + 5 = 5$ $36 \div 5 = 31$ $48 + 2 = 6$ $2 \times 9 = 18$
$72 - 9 = 63$ $56 + 8 = 7$ $9 \times 1 = 9$ $55 + 37 = 92$
$64 \div 8 = 56$ $7 \times 1 = 7$ $45 + 5 = 9$ $81 + 9 = 9$
$36 \div 4 = 9$ $57 - 9 = 48$ $36 + 27 = 63$ $80 - 17 = 63$
$45 \div 5 = 40$ $7 \times 6 = 42$ $48 - 6 = 42$ $32 + 4 = 8$
$82 + 9 = 91$ $8 \times 8 = 64$ $9 \times 8 = 72$ $71 + 15 = 86$
$17 + 77 = 94$ $40 - 6 = 34$ $47 - 38 = 9$ $56 - 9 = 47$
$36 - 6 = 30$ $15 + 38 = 53$ $3 \times 6 = 18$ $9 + 5 = 14$
$72 \div 8 = 9$ $43 + 48 = 91$ $27 + 18 = 45$ $6 \times 6 = 36$
$49 \div 7 = 7$ $7 \times 7 = 49$ $8 \times 3 = 24$ $16 + 16 = 32$

COMPLETE YEAR GRADE 4

158

A Visit to Space Camp

Circle the correct problem and write the answer on the line.

1. Five astronauts had flown a total of 637 hours so far that year. How many hours did each astronaut fly?
$637 + 637$ (circled: $637 \div 5$) 5×5 637×5 — 127 hours R2 (or 24 minutes)

2. Terri's class ate 3 meals in the cafeteria at space camp. The cafeteria served 420 meals in all that day. How many people ate at each meal (breakfast, lunch and dinner) in the cafeteria the day Terri was there?
420×2 $3 + 420$ (circled: $420 \div 3$) $3 + 3$ — 140 people

3. Eight children can ride the moon gravitation simulator at a time. Ninety-seven children rode the simulator that day. How many groups of 8 rode the simulator?
8×9 (circled: $97 \div 8$) 8×8 $97 + 9$ — 12 groups (R1)

4. At the souvenir shop, 9 children bought t-shirts. The total price was $106. They split the cost evenly. How much did each of the children spend on a space camp t-shirt?
$106 \div 9$ 9×106 (circled: $106 \div 9$) 9×9 — $11.78

5. They drove 193 miles round trip. How many miles is it from the space camp to their hometown?
(circled: $193 \div 2$) $2 + 193$ 2×57 $193 \div 193$ — 96.5 miles or $96\frac{1}{2}$ miles

6. Terri was in a small group of 8 children who, in one day, spent an accumulated total of 82 hours in the museum. How many hours was that per child?
8×82 (circled: $82 \div 8$) $8 - 8$ 8×82 — 10.25 hrs. (10 hrs. 15 minutes)

7. The children stayed overnight in the dorms with their counselors. There were 124 girls and 8 counselors in the girls' dorm. How many girls was each counselor in charge of?
(circled: $124 \div 8$) 8×124 $8 + 8$ $124 + 124$ — 15 girls (R4)

Use your calculator.
The Moon is 238,866 miles from Earth. It took 3 days for the rocket to get there. How many miles did the rocket go each day? — 79,622 miles

COMPLETE YEAR GRADE 4

159

Number Puzzles

Solve the puzzles.

Answers will vary.

1
Write your age. — 10
Multiply it by 3. — 30
Add 18. — 48
Multiply by 2. — 96
Subtract 36. — 60
Divide by 6 (your age). — 10

2
Write any number. — 20
Double that number. — 40
Add 15. — 55
Double again. — 110
Subtract 30. — 80
Divide by 2. — 40
Divide by 2 again. — 20

3
Write any 2-digit number. — 11
Double that number. — 22
Add 43. — 65
Subtract 18. — 47
Add 11. — 58
Divide by 2. — 29
Subtract 18. — 11

4
Write the number of children in your neighborhood. — 15
Double that number. — 30
Add 15. — 45
Double it again. — 90
Subtract 30. — 60
Divide by 4. — 15

COMPLETE YEAR GRADE 4

160

Number Puzzles

Use the numbers in each box to make number sentences. Use each number only once.

Answers will vary. Examples follow.

$4 + 3 = 7$
$14 - 8 = 6$
$9 \times 4 = 36$

$5 + 3 = 8$
$12 - 3 = 9$
$4 \times 7 = 28$

$6 + 7 = 13$
$12 - 4 = 8$
$9 \times 3 = 27$

$5 + 5 = 10$
$13 - 4 = 9$
$6 \times 7 = 42$

$8 + 7 = 15$
$11 - 5 = 6$
$7 \times 3 = 21$

$9 + 3 = 12$
$16 - 9 = 7$
$5 \times 4 = 20$

COMPLETE YEAR GRADE 4

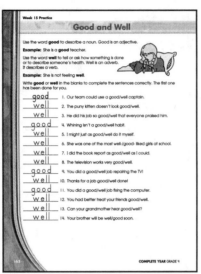

Week 15 Practice

Good and Well

Use the word **good** to describe a noun. Good is an adjective.

Example: She is a **good** teacher.

Use the word **well** to tell or ask how something is done or to describe someone's health. Well is an adverb. It describes a verb.

Example: She is not feeling **well**.

Write **good** or **well** in the blanks to complete the sentences correctly. The first one has been done for you.

<u>good</u> 1. Our team could use a good/well captain.
<u>well</u> 2. The puny kitten doesn't look good/well.
<u>well</u> 3. He did his job so good/well that everyone praised him.
<u>good</u> 4. Whining isn't a good/well habit.
<u>well</u> 5. I might just as good/well do it myself.
<u>well</u> 6. She was one of the most well-/good- liked girls at school.
<u>well</u> 7. I did the book report as good/well as I could.
<u>well</u> 8. The television works very good/well.
<u>good</u> 9. You did a good/well job repairing the TV!
<u>well</u> 10. Thanks for a job good/well done!
<u>good</u> 11. You did a good/well job fixing the computer.
<u>well</u> 12. You had better treat your friends good/well.
<u>well</u> 13. Can your grandmother hear good/well?
<u>well</u> 14. Your brother will be well/good soon.

COMPLETE YEAR GRADE 4

162

Week 15 Practice

Your and You're

The word **your** shows possession.

Examples: Is that **your** book?
I visited **your** class.

The word **you're** is a contraction for **you are**. A **contraction** is two words joined together as one. An apostrophe shows where letters have been left out.

Examples: **You're** doing well on that painting.
If **you're** going to pass the test, you should study.

Write **your** or **you're** in the blanks to complete the sentences correctly. The first one has been done for you.

<u>You're</u> 1. Your/You're the best friend I have!
<u>You're</u> 2. Your/You're going to drop that!
<u>Your</u> 3. Your/You're brother came to see me.
<u>your</u> 4. Is that your/you're cat?
<u>you're</u> 5. If your/you're going, you'd better hurry!
<u>your</u> 6. Why are your/you're fingers so red?
<u>your</u> 7. It's none of your/you're business!
<u>Your</u> 8. Your/You're bike's front tire is low.
<u>You're</u> 9. Your/You're kidding!
<u>your</u> 10. Have it your/you're way.
<u>your</u> 11. I thought your/you're report was great!
<u>you're</u> 12. He thinks your/you're wonderful!
<u>your</u> 13. What is your/you're first choice?
<u>your</u> 14. What's your/you're opinion?
<u>your</u> 15. If your/you're going, so am I!
<u>You're</u> 16. Your/You're welcome.

COMPLETE YEAR GRADE 4

163

Week 15 Practice

Good and Well; Your and You're

Choose the correct word for each sentence: **good, well, your,** or **you're**.

1. Are you sure you can see <u>well</u> enough to read with the lighting you have?

2. <u>You're</u> going to need a paint smock when you go to art class tomorrow afternoon.

3. I can see <u>you're</u> having some trouble. Can I help with that?

4. The music department needs to buy a speaker system that has <u>good</u> quality sound.

5. The principal asked, "Where is <u>your</u> hall pass?"

6. You must do the job <u>well</u> if you expect to keep it.

7. The traffic policeman said, "May I please see <u>your</u> driver's license?"

8. The story you wrote for English class was done quite <u>well</u>.

9. That radio station you listen to is a <u>good</u> one.

10. Let us know if <u>you're</u> unable to attend the meeting on Saturday.

COMPLETE YEAR GRADE 4

164

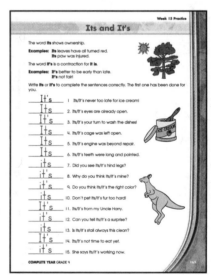

Week 15 Practice

Its and It's

The word **its** shows ownership.

Examples: **Its** leaves have all turned red.
Its paw was injured.

The word **it's** is a contraction for **it is**.

Examples: **It's** better to be early than late.
It's not fair!

Write **its** or **it's** to complete the sentences correctly. The first one has been done for you.

<u>It's</u> 1. Its/It's never too late for ice cream!
<u>Its</u> 2. Its/It's eyes are already open.
<u>It's</u> 3. Its/It's your turn to wash the dishes!
<u>Its</u> 4. Its/It's cage was left open.
<u>Its</u> 5. Its/It's engine was beyond repair.
<u>Its</u> 6. Its/It's teeth were long and pointed.
<u>its</u> 7. Did you see its/it's hind legs?
<u>it's</u> 8. Why do you think its/it's mine?
<u>it's</u> 9. Do you think its/it's the right color?
<u>its</u> 10. Don't pet its/it's fur too hard!
<u>It's</u> 11. Its/It's from my Uncle Harry.
<u>it's</u> 12. Can you tell its/it's a surprise?
<u>its</u> 13. Is its/it's stall always this clean?
<u>It's</u> 14. Its/It's not time to eat yet.
<u>it's</u> 15. She says its/it's working now.

COMPLETE YEAR GRADE 4

165

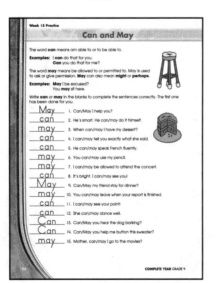

Week 15 Practice

Can and May

The word **can** means am able to or to be able to.

Examples: I **can** do that for you.
Can you do that for me?

The word **may** means be allowed to or permitted to. May is used to ask or give permission. **May** can also mean **might** or **perhaps**.

Examples: **May** I be excused?
You **may** sit here.

Write **can** or **may** in the blanks to complete the sentences correctly. The first one has been done for you.

<u>May</u> 1. Can/May I help you?
<u>can</u> 2. He's smart. He can/may do it himself.
<u>may</u> 3. When can/may I have my dessert?
<u>can</u> 4. I can/may tell you exactly what she said.
<u>can</u> 5. He can/may speak French fluently.
<u>may</u> 6. You can/may use my pencil.
<u>may</u> 7. I can/may be allowed to attend the concert.
<u>can</u> 8. It's bright. I can/may see you!
<u>May</u> 9. Can/May my friend stay for dinner?
<u>may</u> 10. You can/may leave when your report is finished.
<u>can</u> 11. I can/may see your point!
<u>can</u> 12. She can/may dance well.
<u>Can</u> 13. Can/May you hear the dog barking?
<u>Can</u> 14. Can/May you help me button this sweater?
<u>may</u> 15. Mother, can/may I go to the movies?

COMPLETE YEAR GRADE 4

166

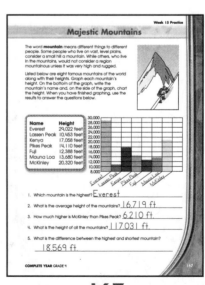

Week 15 Practice

Majestic Mountains

The word **mountain** means different things to different people. Some people who live on vast, level plains, consider a small hill a mountain. While others, who live in the mountains, would not consider a region mountainous unless it was very high and rugged.

Listed below are eight famous mountains of the world along with their heights. Graph each mountain's height. On the bottom of the graph, write the mountain's name and, on the side of the graph, chart the height. When you have finished graphing, use the results to answer the questions below.

Name	Height
Everest	29,022 feet
Lassen Peak	10,453 feet
Kenya	17,058 feet
Pikes Peak	14,110 feet
Fuji	12,388 feet
Mauna Loa	13,680 feet
McKinley	20,320 feet

1. Which mountain is the highest? <u>Everest</u>

2. What is the average height of the mountains? <u>16,719 ft.</u>

3. How much higher is McKinley than Pikes Peak? <u>6,210 ft.</u>

4. What is the height of all the mountains? <u>117,031 ft.</u>

5. What is the difference between the highest and shortest mountain?
<u>18,569 ft.</u>

COMPLETE YEAR GRADE 4

167

Answer Key

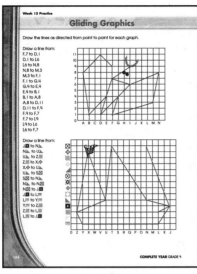

168

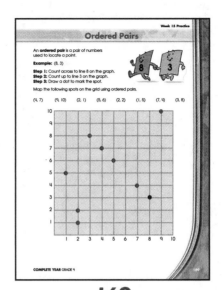

169

Graphing: Finding Ordered Pairs

Graphs or grids are sometimes used to find the location of objects.

Example: The ice cream cone is located at point (5, 6) on the graph. To find the ice cream's location, follow the line to the bottom of the grid to get the first number — 5. Then go back to the ice cream and follow the grid line to the left for the second number — 6.

Write the ordered pair for the following objects. The first one is done for you.

book (4, 8) bike (8, 6) suitcase (1, 4) house (8, 3)
globe (4, 4) cup (9, 9) triangle (7, 2) airplane (7, 8)

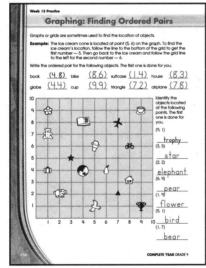

Identify the objects located at the following points. The first one is done for you.

(9, 1) ___trophy___
(3, 5) ___star___
(2, 2) ___elephant___
(6, 4) ___pear___
(1, 9) ___flower___
(5, 1) ___bird___
(1, 7) ___bear___

170

Its and It's; Can and May

Choose the correct word for each sentence: **its**, **it's**, **can**, or **may**.

1. "It looks as though your arms are full, Diane. ___May___ I help you with your full of those things?" asked Michele.

2. The squirrel ___can___ climb up the tree quickly with his mouth full of acorns.

3. She has had her school jacket so long that it is beginning to lose ___its___ color.

4. How many laps around the track ___can___ you do?

5. Sometimes you can tell what a story is going to be about by looking at ___its___ title.

6. Our house ___may___ need to be painted again in two or three years.

7. Mother asked, "Jon, ___can___ you open the door for your father?"

8. ___It's___ going to be a while until your birthday, but do you know what you want?

9. I can feel it in the air; ___it's___ going to snow soon.

10. If I'm careful with it, ___may___ I borrow your CD player?

172

Sit and Set

The word **sit** means to rest.

Examples: Please sit here!
Will you sit by me?

The word **set** means to put or place something.

Examples: Set your purse there.
Set the dishes on the table.

Write **sit** or **set** to complete the sentences correctly. The first one has been done for you.

___sit___ 1. Would you please sit/set down here?
___set___ 2. You can sit/set the groceries there.
___set___ 3. She sit/set her suitcase in the closet.
___set___ 4. He sit/set his watch for half past three.
___sit___ 5. She's a person who can't sit/set still.
___Set___ 6. Sit/set the baby on the couch beside me.
___set___ 7. Where did you sit/set your new shoes?
___sit___ 8. They decided to sit/set together during the movie.
___set___ 9. Let me sit/set you straight on that!
___sit___ 10. Instead of swimming, he decided to sit/set in the water.
___set___ 11. He sit/set the greasy pan in the sink.
___set___ 12. She sit/set the file folder on her desk.
___sit___ 13. Don't ever sit/set on the refrigerator!
___set___ 14. She sit/set the candles on the cake.

173

They're, Their, There

The word **they're** is a contraction for **they are**.

Examples: They're our very best friends!
Ask them if they're coming over tomorrow.

The word **their** shows ownership.

Examples: Their dog is friendly.
It's their bicycle.

The word **there** shows place or direction.

Examples: Look over there.
There it is.

Write **they're**, **their**, or **there** to complete the sentences correctly. The first one has been done for you.

___There___ 1. They're/Their/There is the sweater I want!
___their___ 2. Do you believe they're/their/there stories?
___there___ 3. Be they're/their/there by one o'clock.
___there___ 4. Were you they're/their/there last night?
___they're___ 5. I know they're/their/there going to attend.
___their___ 6. Have you met they're/their/there mother?
___there___ 7. I can go they're/their/there with you.
___their___ 8. Do you like they're/their/there new car?
___They're___ 9. They're/Their/There friendly to everyone.
___they're___ 10. Did she say they're/their/there ready to go?
___their___ 11. She said she'd walk by they're/their/there house.
___there___ 12. Is anyone they're/their/there?
___there___ 13. I put it right over they're/their/there!

174

175

Week 16 Practice

Sit and Set; They're, Their, There

Choose the correct word for each sentence: **sit, set, they're, there,** or **their**.

1. _Set_ your pencil on your desk when you finish working.

2. When we choose our seats on the bus will you _sit_ with me?

3. _There_ is my library book! I wondered where I had left it!

4. My little brother and his friend said _they're_ not going to the ball game with us.

5. Before the test, the teacher wants the students to sharpen _their_ pencils.

6. She blew the whistle and shouted, "Everyone _sit_ down on the floor!"

7. All the books for the fourth graders belong over _there_ on the top shelf.

8. The little kittens are beginning to open _their_ eyes.

9. I'm going to _set_ the dishes on the table.

10. _They're_ going to be fine by themselves for a few minutes.

COMPLETE YEAR GRADE 4

176

Week 16 Practice

This and These

The word **this** is an adjective that refers to things that are near. **This** always describes a singular noun. Singular means one.

Example: I'll buy **this** coat.
(Coat is singular.)

The word **these** is also an adjective that refers to things that are near. **These** always describes a plural noun. A plural refers to more than one thing.

Example: I will buy **these** flowers.
(Flowers is a plural noun.)

Write **this** or **these** to complete the sentences correctly. The first one has been done for you.

these 1. I will take this/these cookies with me.
these 2. Do you want this/these seeds?
these 3. Did you try this/these nuts?
this 4. Do it this/these way!
this 5. What do you know about this/these situation?
these 6. Did you open this/these doors?
this 7. Did you open this/these window?
these 8. What is the meaning of this/these letters?
these 9. Will you carry this/these books for me?
These 10. This/These pans are hot!
this 11. Do you think this/these light is too bright?
these 12. Are this/these boots yours?
this 13. Do you like this/these rainy weather?

COMPLETE YEAR GRADE 4

177

Week 16 Practice

Review

Complete the sentences by writing the correct words in the blanks.

good 1. You have a good/well attitude.
well 2. The teacher was not feeling good/well.
well 3. She sang extremely good/well.
good 4. Everyone said Josh was a good/well boy.
You're 5. Your/You're going to be sorry for that!
you're 6. Tell her your/you're serious.
Your 7. Your/You're report was wonderful!
You're 8. Your/You're the best person for the job.
_it's_ 9. Do you think its/it's going to have babies?
Its 10. Its/It's back paw had a thorn in it.
_It's_ 11. Its/It's fun to make new friends.
its 12. Is its/it's mother always nearby?
may 13. How can/may I help you?
may 14. You can/may come in now.
Can 15. Can/May you lift this for me?
can 16. She can/may sing soprano.
sit 17. I'll wait for you to sit/set down first.
set 18. We sit/set our dirty boots outside.
their 19. It's they're/their/there turn to choose.
There 20. They're/Their/There is your answer!
they're 21. They say they're/their/there coming.
this 22. I must have this/these one!
these 23. I saw this/these gloves at the store.
these 24. He said this/these were his.

COMPLETE YEAR GRADE 4

178

Week 16 Practice

Averaging

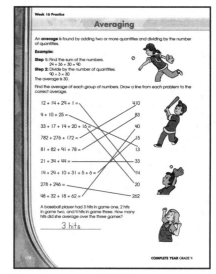

An **average** is found by adding two or more quantities and dividing by the number of quantities.

Example:
Step 1: Find the sum of the numbers.
24 + 36 + 30 = 90
Step 2: Divide by the number of quantities.
90 ÷ 3 = 30
The average is 30.

Find the average of each group of numbers. Draw a line from each problem to the correct average.

12 + 14 + 29 + 1 =   410
4 + 10 + 25 =   83
33 + 17 + 14 + 20 + 16 =   40
782 + 276 + 172 =   15
81 + 82 + 91 + 78 =   13
21 + 34 + 44 =   33
14 + 24 + 10 + 31 + 5 + 6 =   20
278 + 246 =   262
48 + 32 + 18 + 62 =

A baseball player had 3 hits in game one, 2 hits in game two, and 4 hits in game three. How many hits did he average over the three games?

3 hits

COMPLETE YEAR GRADE 4

179

Week 16 Practice

Averaging

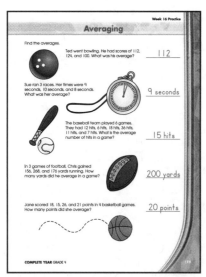

Find the averages.

Ted went bowling. He had scores of 112, 124, and 100. What was his average?   _112_

Sue ran 3 races. Her times were 9 seconds, 10 seconds, and 8 seconds. What was her average?   _9 seconds_

The baseball team played 6 games. They had 12 hits, 6 hits, 18 hits, 36 hits, 11 hits, and 7 hits. What is the average number of hits in a game?   _15 hits_

In 3 games of football, Chris gained 156, 268, and 176 yards running. How many yards did he average in a game?   _200 yards_

Jane scored 18, 15, 26, and 21 points in 4 basketball games. How many points did she average?   _20 points_

COMPLETE YEAR GRADE 4

180

Week 16 Practice

Work It Out

The **average** is the result of dividing the **sum** of addends by the **number** of addends. Match the problem with its answer.

```
  62
  79      76
+ 87  → 3) 228
 228
```

1. 80 + 100 + 90 + 95 + 10 = 375 ÷ 5 = _D_   A. 53
2. 52 + 56 + 51   _A_   B. 190
3. 85 + 80 + 95 + 95 + 100   _E_   C. 410
4. 782 + 276 + 172   _C_   D. 75
5. 125 + 248 + 214 + 173   _B_   E. 91
6. 81 + 82 + 91 + 78   _G_   F. 55
7. 40 + 60 + 75 + 45   _F_   G. 83
8. 278 + 246   _J_   H. 33
9. 75 + 100 + 100 + 70 + 100   _K_   I. 3
10. 0 + 0 + 0 + 0 + 15   _I_   J. 262
11. 21 + 34 + 44   _H_   K. 89
12. 437 + 509 + 864 + 274   _O_   L. 94
13. 80 + 80 + 100 + 95 + 95   _N_   M. 8
14. 4 + 6 + 7 + 12 + 11   _M_   N. 90
15. 75 + 100 + 100 + 100 + 95   _L_   O. 521

COMPLETE YEAR GRADE 4

Answer Key

Page 182

Review

Write the correct answers in the blanks using the words in the box.

good	well	your	you're	its
it's	can	may	sit	set
they're	there	their	this	these

1. ___This___ is an adjective that refers to a particular thing.
2. Use ___well___ to tell or ask how something is done or to describe someone's health.
3. ___It's___ is a contraction for **it is**.
4. ___These___ describes a plural noun and refers to particular things.
5. ___Sit___ means to rest.
6. ___Can___ means am able to or to be able to.
7. ___They're___ is a contraction for **they are**.
8. ___Your___, ___its___, and ___their___ show ownership or possession.
9. Use ___may___ to ask politely to be permitted to do something.
10. ___You're___ is a contraction for **you are**.
11. ___Set___ means to place or put.
12. ___Good___ describes a noun.
13. Use ___there___ to show direction or placement.

COMPLETE YEAR GRADE 4

182

Page 183

Misused Words

Sometimes people have difficulty using **good**, **well**, **sure**, **surely**, **real**, and **really** correctly. This chart may help you.

Adjectives	Adverbs
Good is an adjective when it describes a noun. That was a **good** dinner.	**Good** is never used as an adverb.
Well is an adjective when it means in good health or having a good appearance. She looks **well**.	**Well** is an adverb when it is used to tell that something is done capably or effectively. She writes **well**.
Sure is an adjective when it modifies a noun. A robin is a **sure** sign of spring.	**Surely** is an adverb. He **surely** wants a job.
Real is an adjective that means genuine or true. That was a **real** diamond.	**Really** is an adverb. Mary **really** played a good game.

Use the chart to help you choose the correct word from those in parentheses. Write it in the blank.

1. You did a very ___good___ job of writing your book report. (good, well)
2. The detective in the story used his skills ___well___. (good, well)
3. He ___surely___ solved the case before anyone else did. (sure, surely)
4. I ___really___ want to read that book now. (real, really)
5. Did it take you long to decide who the ___real___ criminal was? (real, really)
6. The doctor said the child was ___well___ and healthy. (well, good)
7. Detective Rains read the clues ___well___ as he worked on the case. (good, well)
8. You will ___surely___ get a good grade on that report. (surely, sure)
9. You had to ___really___ work hard to get those good grades. (real, really)

COMPLETE YEAR GRADE 4

183

Page 184

Shortening Words

| aren't |
| couldn't |
| doesn't |
| hasn't |
| he'd |
| I'd |
| she's |
| should've |
| they'll |
| wasn't |
| what's |
| who'd |
| won't |
| you've |

Write each contraction and the two words that form it.

1. ___aren't___ ___are___ ___not___
2. ___couldn't___ ___could___ ___not___
3. ___doesn't___ ___does___ ___not___
4. ___hasn't___ ___has___ ___not___
5. ___he'd___ ___he___ ___would___
6. ___I'd___ ___I___ ___would___
7. ___she's___ ___she___ ___is___
8. ___should've___ ___should___ ___have___
9. ___they'll___ ___they___ ___will___
10. ___wasn't___ ___was___ ___not___
11. ___weren't___ ___were___ ___not___
12. ___what's___ ___what___ ___is___
13. ___who'd___ ___who___ ___would___
14. ___won't___ ___will___ ___not___
15. ___you've___ ___you___ ___have___

Sometimes a contraction can represent different words. Circle the correct answer in each of the following.

1. In the sentence, "He'd had a cold," the **'d** stands for . . .
   a. would   **b. had**   c. did
2. In the sentence, "He'd like to go," the **'d** stands for . . .
   a. would   b. had   c. did
3. In the question "Who'd volunteer?" the **'d** stands for . . .
   a. would   b. had   c. did
4. In the question "Who'd you say it was?" the **'d** stands for . . .
   a. would   b. had   **c. did**

COMPLETE YEAR GRADE 4

184

Page 185

Analogies

An **analogy** indicates how different items go together or are similar in some way.

Examples: Petal is to **flower** as **leaf** is to **tree**.
Book is to **library** as **food** is to **grocery**.

If you study the examples, you will see how the second set of objects is related to the first set. A petal is a part of a flower, and a leaf is part of a tree. A book can be found in a library, and food can be found in a grocery store.

Fill in the blanks to complete the analogies. The first one has been done for you.

1. Cup is to saucer as glass is to ___coaster___.
2. Paris is to France as London is to ___England___.
3. Clothes are to hangers as ___shoes___ are to boxes.
4. California is to ___Pacific Ocean___ as Ohio is to Lake Erie.
5. ___Tablecloth___ is to table as blanket is to bed.
6. Pencil is to paper as ___paintbrush___ is to canvas.
7. Cow is to ___barn___ as child is to house.
8. State is to country as ___county___ is to state.
9. Governor is to state as ___president___ is to country.
10. ___Water___ is to ocean as sand is to desert.
11. Engine is to car as hard drive is to ___computer___.
12. Beginning is to ___start___ as stop is to end.

Write three analogies of your own.

___Answers will vary.___

COMPLETE YEAR GRADE 4

185

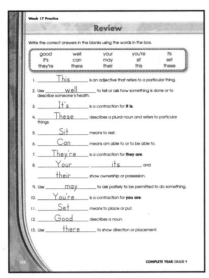

Page 186

Prize Words

Fill in the blanks. Each word is used only once.

1. **One** is to **once** as **two** is to ___twice___
2. **Reverse** is to **forward** as **sit** is to ___arise___
3. **Book** is to **library** as **typewriter** is to ___office___
4. **Shiny** is to **dull** as **foolish** is to ___wise___
5. **Teacher** is to **education** as **judge** is to ___justice___
6. **Illness** is to **doctor** as **crime** is to ___police officer___
7. **Tag** is to **label** as **cost** is to ___price___
8. **1, 2, 3** is to **count** as **A, B, C** is to ___alphabetize___
9. **Imagine** is to **think** as **guess** is to ___surmise___
10. **Wordy** is to **long-winded** as **brief** is to ___concise___

alphabetize	memorize	service
arise	office	surmise
concise	police	surprise
enterprise	price	twice
justice	prize	wise

Use the remaining words from the list to answer each question.

1. What do you usually get when you win a contest? ___prize___
2. What do actors do with their lines? ___memorize___
3. What is a risky or important project? ___enterprise___
4. What is a synonym for "helpfulness"? ___service___
5. What is a synonym for "astonish"? ___surprise___

COMPLETE YEAR GRADE 4

186

Page 187

Spinner Fun

Using what you know about probability, try to predict how many times your spinner would land on the following numbers if you were to spin the spinner 20 times.

Predictions

	Number of Times
Spinning a 1	
Spinning a 2	
Spinning a 3	
Spinning a 4	

Now, actually spin the ... with what you act... ...spins.

___Answers will vary.___

Actual Spins

	Number of Times
Spinning a 1	
Spinning a 2	
Spinning a 3	
Spinning a 4	

1. Were your predictions close to the actual? ___yes___
2. What did you notice about your predictions and the actual spinning? ___Some were less and some were more.___
3. Why do you think this is? ___Probability is not certain.___

COMPLETE YEAR GRADE 4

187

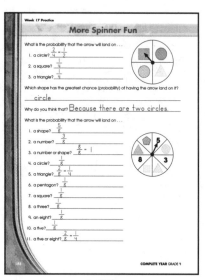

188

Week 17 Practice

More Spinner Fun

What is the probability that the arrow will land on . . .

1. a circle? $\frac{2}{4} = \frac{1}{2}$
2. a square? $\frac{1}{4}$
3. a triangle? $\frac{1}{4}$

Which shape has the greatest chance (probability) of having the arrow land on it?

circle

Why do you think that? Because there are two circles.

What is the probability that the arrow will land on . . .

1. a shape? $\frac{5}{8}$
2. a number? $\frac{3}{8}$
3. a number or shape? $\frac{8}{8} = 1$
4. a circle? $\frac{1}{8}$
5. a triangle? $\frac{2}{8} = \frac{1}{4}$
6. a pentagon? $\frac{1}{8}$
7. a square? $\frac{1}{8}$
8. a three? $\frac{1}{8}$
9. an eight? $\frac{1}{8}$
10. a five? $\frac{1}{8}$
11. a five or eight? $\frac{2}{8} = \frac{1}{4}$

COMPLETE YEAR GRADE 4

189

Week 17 Practice

Probability

One thinking skill to get your brain in gear is figuring probability. **Probability** is the likelihood or chance that something will happen. Probability is expressed and written as a ratio.

The probability of tossing heads or tails on a coin is one in two (1:2).

The probability of rolling any number on a die is one in six (1:6).

The probability of getting a red on this spinner is two in four (2:4).

The probability of drawing an ace from a deck of cards is four in fifty-two (4:52).

Write the probability ratios to answer these questions.

1. There are 26 letters in the alphabet. What is the probability of drawing any letter from a set of alphabet cards? — 1:26

2. Five of the 26 alphabet letters are vowels. What is the probability of drawing a vowel from the alphabet cards? — 5:26

3. Matt takes 10 shots at the basketball hoop. Six of his shots are baskets. What is the probability of Matt's next shot being a basket? — 6:10

4. A box contains 10 marbles: 2 white, 3 green, 1 red, 2 orange, and 2 blue. What is the probability of pulling a green marble from the box? — 3:10
   A red marble? — 1:10

5. What is the probability of pulling a marble that is not blue? — 8:10

COMPLETE YEAR GRADE 4

190

Week 17 Practice

Probability

Write the probability ratios to answer these questions.

1. Using the spinner shown, what is the probability of spinning a 4? — 1:8

2. Using the spinner show, what is the chance of not spinning a 2? — 7:8

3. Using the spinner shown, what is the probability of spinning a 6, 7, or 3? — 3:8

4. What is the probability of getting heads or tails when you toss a coin? — 1:2

Toss a coin 20 times and record the outcome of each toss. Then answer the questions. _____ Heads _____ Tails

5. What was the ratio of heads to tails in the 20 tosses? _____

6. Was the outcome of getting heads or tails in the 20 tosses the same as the probability ratio? _____

7. Why or why not? _____

The probability ratio of getting any number _____

Toss a die 36 times _____ *Answers will vary.*
on each number.

_____ _____ three _____ four _____ five _____ six

8. What _____ ratio for each number on the die?
   _____ one _____ two _____ three _____ four _____ five _____ six

9. Did any of the numbers have a ratio close to the actual probability ratio?

10. What do the outcomes of flipping a coin and tossing a die tell you about the probability of an event happening?
   _____

COMPLETE YEAR GRADE 4

192

Week 18 Practice

Watch for Grandpa's Watch

Each "watch" in the title of this activity sheet has a different meaning. One means "to look for," and the other means "a timepiece." Write two meanings for the words below.

	Meaning 1	Meaning 2
1. spring		
2. run		
3. ruler		
4. duck		
5. suit		
6. cold		
7. fall		
8. tire		
9. rose	*Definitions will vary.*	
10. face		
11. train		
12. play		
13. foot		
14. pen		
15. box		
16. fly		
17. seal		
18. bowl		
19. ride		
20. line		

COMPLETE YEAR GRADE 4

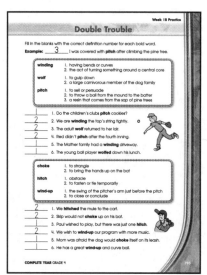

193

Week 18 Practice

Double Trouble

Fill in the blanks with the correct definition number for each bold word.

Example: __3__ I was covered with **pitch** after climbing the pine tree.

winding	1. having bends or curves 2. the act of turning something around a central core
wolf	1. to gulp down 2. a large carnivorous member of the dog family
pitch	1. to sell or persuade 2. to throw a ball from the mound to the batter 3. a resin that comes from the sap of pine trees

__ 1. Do the children's club **pitch** cookies?
__2__ 2. We are **winding** the top's string tightly.
__2__ 3. The adult **wolf** returned to her lair.
__2__ 4. Red didn't **pitch** after the fourth inning.
__ 5. The Mather family had a **winding** driveway.
__1__ 6. The young ball player **wolfed** down his lunch.

choke	1. to strangle 2. to bring the hands up on the bat
hitch	1. obstacle 2. to fasten or tie temporarily
wind-up	1. the swing of the pitcher's arm just before the pitch 2. to close or conclude

__2__ 1. We **hitched** the mule to the cart.
__2__ 2. Skip would not **choke** up on his bat.
__ 3. Paul wished to play, but there was just one **hitch**.
__2__ 4. We wish to **wind-up** our program with more music.
__ 5. Mom was afraid the dog would **choke** itself on its leash.
__ 6. He has a great **wind-up** and curve ball.

COMPLETE YEAR GRADE 4

194

Week 18 Practice

Book Words

Use a spelling word to replace the bold words in the story. Write the replacement word on the corresponding numbered line below the story.

No Spelling Today

(1) **Throughout the time of** the afternoon Joan sat on a (2) **pad** near the babbling (3) **creek** that meandered through the pasture. She knew she (4) **ought** to have been studying the words for her spelling test, but instead she was doodling on the (5) **stock of paper** on her lap. Across the stream several sheep were grazing. Their soft (6) **fleece** was growing back after the spring shearing. Joan (7) **was able to** hear a chirping wren in the (8) **thicket** nearby. Suddenly, the peaceful scene was disturbed by a (9) **female** calling her name. "Joan, Joan," the voice called out. "Come eat some (10) **custard** I just cooked," continued the loud voice. Joan (11) **realized** she'd dozed off and her mom was calling her to the house. Tucking her list of spelling words under her arm, she walked back home in the late afternoon sun.

brook	notebook	wolf
bush	pudding	woman
could	should	wool
cushion	sugar	would
during	understood	yours

1. During
2. cushion
3. brook
4. should
5. notebook
6. wool
7. could
8. bush
9. woman
10. pudding
11. understood

Write two sentences using two of the four words not used above.

1. _____
2. *Answers may vary.*

COMPLETE YEAR GRADE 4

Answer Key

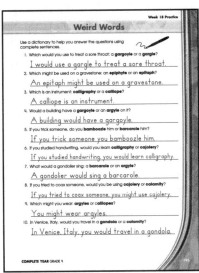

195

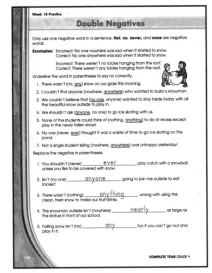

196

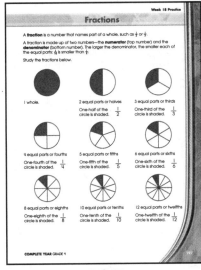

197

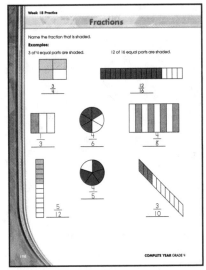

198

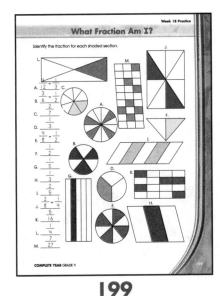

199

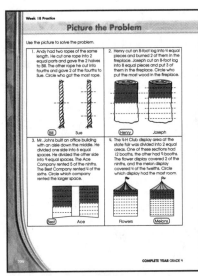

200

Answer Key

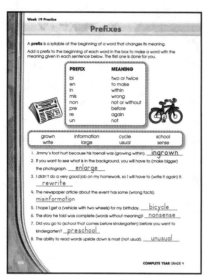

206

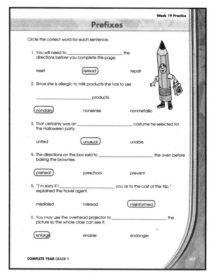

207

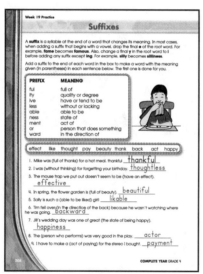

208

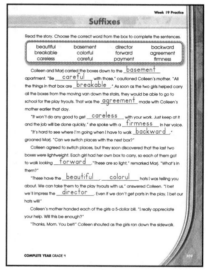

209

210

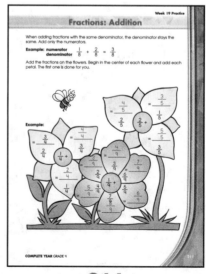

211

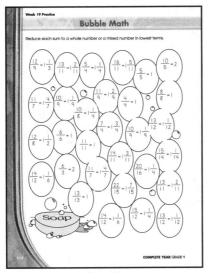

212

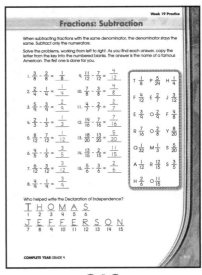

213

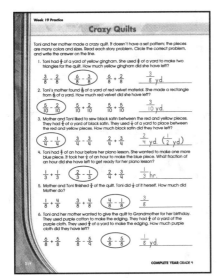

214

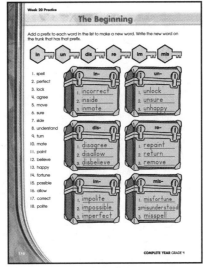

216

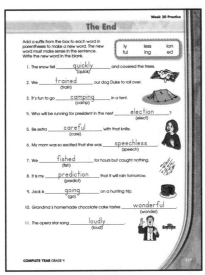

217

218

Answer Key

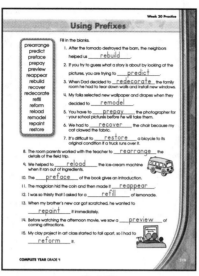

219

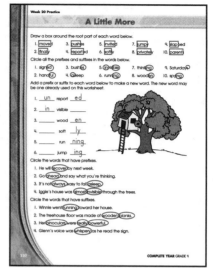

220

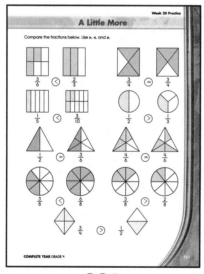

221

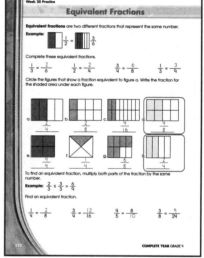

222

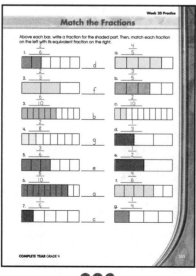

223

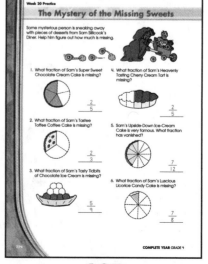

224

Answer Key

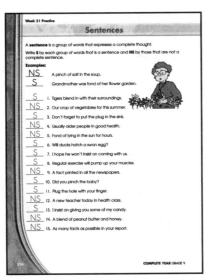

226

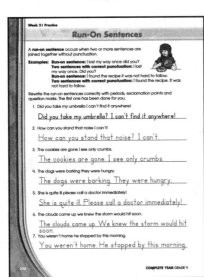

228

227

229

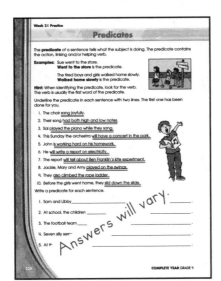

230

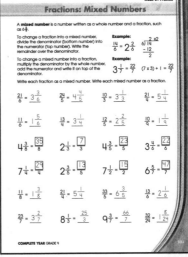

231

Answer Key

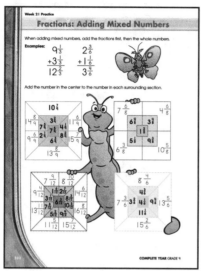

232

233

234

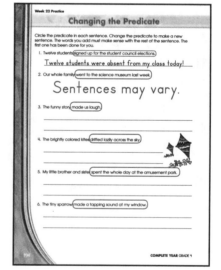

236

237

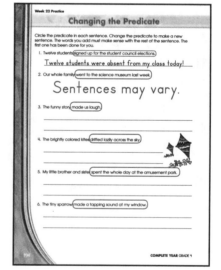

238

Answer Key

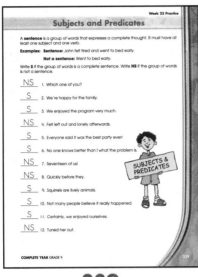

239

Subjects and Predicates

A **sentence** is a group of words that expresses a complete thought. It must have at least one subject and one verb.

Examples: Sentence: John felt tired and went to bed early.

Not a sentence: Went to bed early.

Write **S** if the group of words is a complete sentence. Write **NS** if the group of words is not a sentence.

NS 1. Which one of you?
S 2. We're happy for the family.
S 3. We enjoyed the program very much.
NS 4. Felt left out and lonely afterwards.
S 5. Everyone said it was the best party ever!
S 6. No one knows better than I what the problem is.
NS 7. Seventeen of us!
NS 8. Quickly before they.
S 9. Squirrels are lively animals.
S 10. Not many people believe it really happened.
S 11. Certainly, we enjoyed ourselves.
NS 12. Tuned her out.

COMPLETE YEAR GRADE 4

240

Subjects and Predicates

On the previous page, some of the groups of words are not sentences. Rewrite them to make complete sentences.

1.
2.
Answers will vary.
3.
4.
5.

COMPLETE YEAR GRADE 4

241

Fractions to Decimals

When a figure is divided into 10 equal parts, the parts are called tenths. Tenths can be written two ways—as a fraction or a decimal. A **decimal** is a number with one or more places to the right of a decimal point, such as 6.5 or 2.25. A **decimal point** is the dot between the ones place and the tenths place.

Write the decimal and fraction for the shaded parts of the following figures. The first one is done for you.

$\frac{6}{10}$ 0.6
$\frac{3}{10}$ 0.3 $\frac{9}{10}$ 0.9 $1\frac{5}{10}$ 1.5
$1\frac{8}{10}$ 1.8 $\frac{4}{10}$ 0.4 $\frac{8}{10}$ 0.8

COMPLETE YEAR GRADE 4

242

Fractions to Decimals

Compare the fraction to the decimal in each box. Circle the larger number.

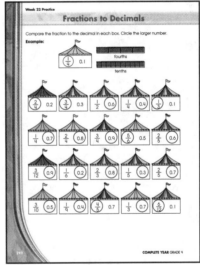

COMPLETE YEAR GRADE 4

243

Decimals: Hundredths

The next smallest decimal unit after a tenth is called a hundredth. One hundredth is one unit of a figure divided into 100 units. Written as a decimal, it is one digit to the right of the tenths place.

Write the decimal for the shaded parts of the following figures.

0.24   0.50   0.53   0.05
1.48   1.10

COMPLETE YEAR GRADE 4

244

Decimals

Add or subtract. Remember to include the decimal point in your answers.

Example: $1\frac{3}{10} = 1.3$ $1\frac{6}{10} = 1.6$

1.3 + 1.6 = 2.9

| 8.1 +1.7 = 9.8 | 4.1 +6.2 = 10.3 | 0.5 +1.6 = 2.1 | 7.6 −6.5 = 1.1 | 7.2 −2.6 = 4.6 | 1.2 +5.0 = 6.2 | 8.7 −3.9 = 4.8 | 6.8 −3.7 = 3.1 |

| 7.8 −6.8 = 1.0 | 16.5 −7.3 = 9.2 | 6.4 +5.3 = 11.7 | 10.0 +3.5 = 13.5 |

| 0.42 +0.35 = 0.77 | 0.98 −0.87 = 0.11 | 0.78 −0.13 = 0.65 | 0.83 +0.12 = 0.95 |

| 0.95 −0.14 = 0.81 | 3.23 +2.48 = 5.71 | 4.68 −2.65 = 2.03 | 5.86 −2.73 = 3.13 |

| 6.98 +1.40 = 8.38 | 3.27 +1.82 = 5.09 | 4.65 −1.32 = 3.33 | 5.97 +2.77 = 8.74 |

Mr. Martin went on a car trip with his family. Mr. Martin purchased gas 3 times. He bought 6.7 gallons, 7.3 gallons, then 5.8 gallons of gas. How much gas did he purchase in all?

19.8 gallons

COMPLETE YEAR GRADE 4

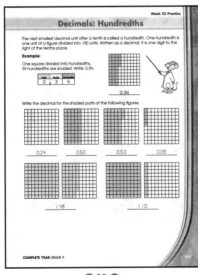

Answer Key

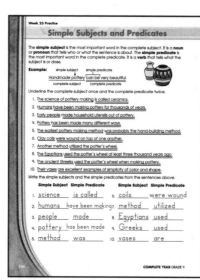

Page 246

Week 23 Practice

Simple Subjects and Predicates

The **simple subject** is the most important word in the complete subject. It is a **noun** or **pronoun** that tells who or what the sentence is about. The **simple predicate** is the most important word in the complete predicate. It is a **verb** that tells what the subject is or does.

Example: simple subject   simple predicate
Handmade pottery can be very beautiful.
complete subject   complete predicate

Underline the complete subject once and the complete predicate twice.

1. The science of pottery making is called ceramics.
2. Humans have been making pottery for thousands of years.
3. Early people made household utensils out of pottery.
4. Pottery has been made many different ways.
5. The earliest pottery making method was probably the hand-building method.
6. Clay coils were wound on top of one another.
7. Another method utilized the potter's wheel.
8. The Egyptians used the potter's wheel at least three thousand years ago.
9. The ancient Greeks used the potter's wheel when making pottery.
10. Their vases are excellent examples of simplicity of color and shape.

Write the simple subjects and the simple predicates from the sentences above.

	Simple Subject	Simple Predicate		Simple Subject	Simple Predicate
1.	science	is called	6.	coils	were wound
2.	humans	have been making	7.	method	utilized
3.	people	made	8.	Egyptians	used
4.	pottery	has been made	9.	Greeks	used
5.	method	was	10.	vases	are

COMPLETE YEAR GRADE 4

246

Page 247

Week 23 Practice

Compound Subjects

A **compound subject** is a subject with two parts joined by the word **and** or another conjunction. Compound subjects share the same predicate.

Example: Her shoes were covered with mud. Her ankles were covered with mud, too.

Compound subject: Her shoes and ankles were covered with mud.
The predicate in both sentences is **were covered with mud.**

Combine each pair of sentences into one sentence with a compound subject.

1. Bill sneezed. Kassie sneezed.

   Bill and Kassie sneezed.

2. Kristin made cookies. Joey made cookies.

   Kristin and Joey made cookies.

3. Fruit flies are insects. Ladybugs are insects.

   Fruit flies and ladybugs are insects.

4. The girls are planning a dance. The boys are planning a dance.

   The girls and boys are planning a dance.

5. Our dog ran after the ducks. Our cat ran after the ducks.

   Our dog and cat ran after the ducks.

6. Joshua got lost in the parking lot. Daniel got lost in the parking lot.

   Joshua and Daniel got lost in the parking lot.

COMPLETE YEAR GRADE 4

247

Page 248

Week 23 Practice

Compound Subjects

If sentences do not share the same predicate, they cannot be combined to write a sentence with a compound subject.

Example: Mary laughed at the story.
Tanya laughed at the television show.

Combine the pairs of sentences that share the same predicate. Write new sentences with compound subjects.

1. Pete loves swimming. Jake loves swimming.

   Pete and Jake love swimming.

2. A bee stung Elizabeth. A hornet stung Elizabeth.

   A bee and a hornet stung Elizabeth.

3. Sharon is smiling. Susan is frowning.

4. The boys have great suntans. The girls have great suntans.

   The boys and girls have great suntans.

5. Six squirrels chased the kitten. Ten dogs chased the kitten.

   Six squirrels and ten dogs chased the kitten.

6. The trees were covered with insects. The roads were covered with ice.

COMPLETE YEAR GRADE 4

248

Page 249

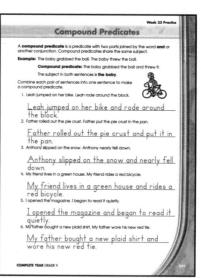

Week 23 Practice

Compound Predicates

A **compound predicate** is a predicate with two parts joined by the word **and** or another conjunction. Compound predicates share the same subject.

Example: The baby grabbed the ball. The baby threw the ball.

Compound predicate: The baby grabbed the ball and threw it.
The subject in both sentences is **the baby.**

Combine each pair of sentences into one sentence to make a compound predicate.

1. Leah jumped on her bike. Leah rode around the block.

   Leah jumped on her bike and rode around the block.

2. Father rolled out the pie crust. Father put the pie crust in the pan.

   Father rolled out the pie crust and put it in the pan.

3. Anthony slipped on the snow. Anthony nearly fell down.

   Anthony slipped on the snow and nearly fell down.

4. My friend lives in a green house. My friend rides a red bicycle.

   My friend lives in a green house and rides a red bicycle.

5. I opened the magazine. I began to read it quietly.

   I opened the magazine and began to read it quietly.

6. My father bought a new plaid shirt. My father wore his new red tie.

   My father bought a new plaid shirt and wore his new red tie.

COMPLETE YEAR GRADE 4

249

Page 250

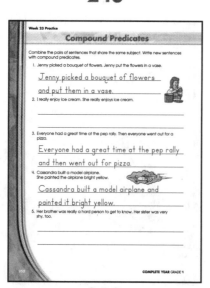

Week 23 Practice

Compound Predicates

Combine the pairs of sentences that share the same subject. Write new sentences with compound predicates.

1. Jenny picked a bouquet of flowers. Jenny put the flowers in a vase.

   Jenny picked a bouquet of flowers and put them in a vase.

2. I really enjoy ice cream. She really enjoys ice cream.

3. Everyone had a great time at the pep rally. Then everyone went out for a pizza.

   Everyone had a great time at the pep rally and then went out for pizza.

4. Cassandra built a model airplane. She painted the airplane bright yellow.

   Cassandra built a model airplane and painted it bright yellow.

5. Her brother was really a hard person to get to know. Her sister was very shy, too.

COMPLETE YEAR GRADE 4

250

Page 251

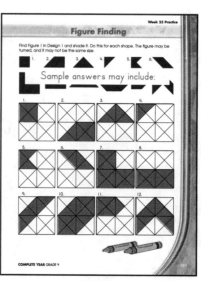

Week 23 Practice

Figure Finding

Find Figure 1 in Design 1 and shade it. Do this for each shape. The figure may be turned, and it may not be the same size.

Sample answers may include:

COMPLETE YEAR GRADE 4

251

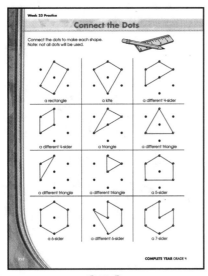

252

253

Statements and Questions

A **statement** tells some kind of information. It is followed by a period (.).

Examples: It is a rainy day. We are going to the beach next summer.

A **question** asks for a specific piece of information. It is followed by a question mark (?).

Examples: What is the weather like today? When are you going to the beach?

Write whether each sentence is a statement or question. The first one has been done for you.

1. Jamie went for a walk at the zoo. — statement
2. The leaves turn bright colors in the fall. — statement
3. When does the Easter Bunny arrive? — question
4. Madeleine went to the new art school. — statement
5. Is school over at 3:30? — question
6. Grandma and Grandpa are moving. — statement
7. Anthony went home. — statement
8. Did Mary go to Amy's house? — question
9. Who went to work late? — question
10. Ms. McDaniel is a good teacher. — statement

Write two statements and two questions below.

Statements:

Questions: *Answers will vary.*

256

Commands and Exclamations

A **command** tells someone to do something. It is followed by a period (.).

Examples: Get your math book. Do your homework.

An **exclamation** shows strong feeling or excitement. It is followed by an exclamation mark (!).

Examples: Watch out for that car! Oh, no! There's a snake!

Write whether each sentence is a command or exclamation. The first one has been done for you.

1. Please clean your room. — command
2. Wow! Those fireworks are beautiful! — exclamation
3. Come to dinner now. — command
4. Color the sky and water blue. — command
5. Trim the paper carefully. — command
6. Hurry, here comes the bus! — exclamation
7. Isn't that a lovely picture! — exclamation
8. Time to stop playing and clean up. — command
9. Brush your teeth before bedtime. — command
10. Wash your hands before you eat! — exclamation

Write two commands and two exclamations below.

Commands:

Exclamations: *Answers will vary.*

257

Four Kinds of Sentences

Write **S** for statement, **Q** for question, **C** for command or **E** for exclamation. End each sentence with a period, question mark, or exclamation mark.

Example:

E You better watch out!

S 1. My little brother insists on coming with us.
C 2. Tell him movies are bad for his health.
S 3. He says he's fond of movies.
Q 4. Does he know there are monsters in this movie?
S 5. He says he needs facts for his science report.
S 6. He's writing about something that hatched from an old egg.
Q 7. Couldn't he just go to the library?
Q 8. Could we dress him like us so he'll blend in?
E or Q 9. Are you kidding! or ?
Q 10. Would he sit by himself at the movie?
S or E 11. That would be too dangerous. or ?
S 12. Mom said she'd give us money for candy if we took him with us.
Q 13. Why didn't you say that earlier?
C or E 14. Get your brother and let's go. or !

258

Four Kinds of Sentences

For each pair of words, write two kinds of sentences (any combination of question, command, statement, or exclamation). Use one or both words in each sentence. Name each kind of sentence you wrote.

Example: pump   crop

Question: What kind of crops did you plant?
Command: Pump the water as fast as you can.

1. pinch   health

2. fond   fact   *Answers will vary.*

3. insist   hatch

exclamation   command   statement   question

259

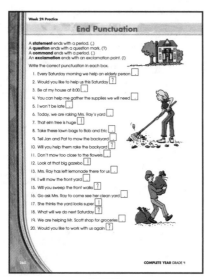

260

261

263

264

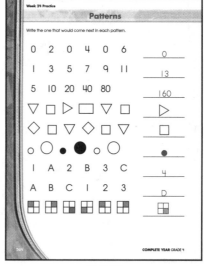

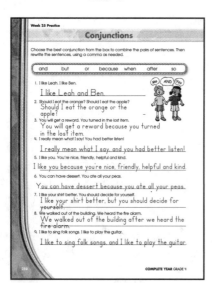

266

267

Answer Key

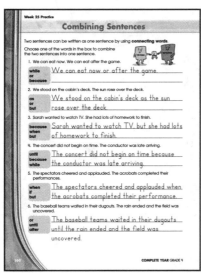

Page 268

Combining Sentences

Two sentences can be written as one sentence by using **connecting words**.

Choose one of the words in the box to combine the two sentences into one sentence.

1. We can eat now. We can eat after the game.
   (while / or / because) We can eat now or after the game.

2. We stood on the cabin's deck. The sun rose over the deck.
   (as / or / but) We stood on the cabin's deck as the sun rose over the deck.

3. Sarah wanted to watch TV. She had lots of homework to finish.
   (because / when / but) Sarah wanted to watch TV, but she had lots of homework to finish.

4. The concert did not begin on time. The conductor was late arriving.
   (until / because / while) The concert did not begin on time because the conductor was late arriving.

5. The spectators cheered and applauded. The acrobats completed their performances.
   (when / if / but) The spectators cheered and applauded when the acrobats completed their performance.

6. The baseball teams waited in their dugouts. The rain ended and the field was uncovered.
   (or / until / after) The baseball teams waited in their dugouts until the rain ended and the field was uncovered.

Page 269

Commas With Compound Sentences

A **compound sentence** contains two simple sentences joined by a comma and a connecting word such as "and." The simple sentences must be about the same topic.

Example: Jane helps prepare dinner, and Pat sets the table.

Write **compound** on the line if it is a compound sentence and add the needed comma. Write **no** on the line if it is not a compound sentence.

1. The porpoise looks very much like a fish. — no
2. It is a mammal, and it bears its young alive. — compound
3. The porpoise resembles and is closely related to the dolphin. — no
4. The top of a porpoise is mostly black, and its underside is white. — compound
5. It searches out and eats small fish and shellfish. — no
6. A mother porpoise has just one baby, and that baby is large. — compound
7. The mother nurses the baby while swimming through the water. — no
8. Porpoises seem to like humans, and they have saved people who were drowning. — compound
9. Porpoises are social animals and swim in large groups. — no
10. Porpoises often travel with tuna, and they are sometimes caught in the tuna nets. — compound

Use a comma and the word and to combine each pair of sentences.

1. Most species of dolphins live only in salt water. They can be found in almost all the oceans. Most species of dolphins live only in salt water, and they can be found in almost all the oceans.

2. The word "dolphin" also refers to a big game fish. This fish is good to eat. The word "dolphin" also refers to a big game fish, and this fish is good to eat.

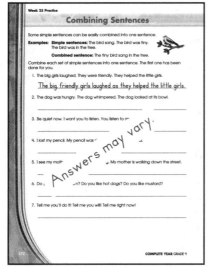

Page 270

Combining Sentences

Some simple sentences can be easily combined into one sentence.

Examples: Simple sentences: The bird sang. The bird was tiny. The bird was in the tree.

Combined sentence: The tiny bird sang in the tree.

Combine each set of simple sentences into one sentence. The first one has been done for you.

1. The big girls laughed. They were friendly. They helped the little girls.
   The big, friendly girls laughed as they helped the little girls.

2. The dog was hungry. The dog whimpered. The dog looked at its bowl.

3. Be quiet now. I want you to listen. You listen to me.

4. I lost my pencil. My pencil was ...

5. I see my mother ... My mother is walking down the street.

6. Do you ... ? Do you like hot dogs? Do you like mustard?

7. Tell me you'll do it! Tell me you will! Tell me right now!

Answers may vary.

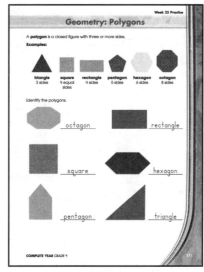

Page 271

Geometry: Polygons

A **polygon** is a closed figure with three or more sides.

Examples:

triangle 3 sides, square 4 equal sides, rectangle 4 sides, pentagon 5 sides, hexagon 6 sides, octagon 8 sides

Identify the polygons.

octagon — rectangle

square — hexagon

pentagon — triangle

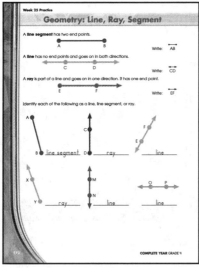

Page 272

Geometry: Line, Ray, Segment

A **line segment** has two end points.
A — B   Write: AB

A **line** has no end points and goes on in both directions.
C — D   Write: CD

A **ray** is part of a line and goes on in one direction. It has one end point.
E — F   Write: EF

Identify each of the following as a line, line segment, or ray.

line segment   ray   line

ray   line   line

Page 273

Geometry: Angles

The point at which two line segments meet is called an **angle**. There are three types of angles — right, acute, and obtuse.

A **right angle** is formed when the two lines meet at 90°.
An **acute angle** is formed when the two lines meet at less than 90°.
An **obtuse angle** is formed when the two lines meet at greater than 90°.

Angles can be measured with a protractor or index card. With a protractor, align the bottom edge of the angle with the bottom of the protractor. Line the apex point of the angle at the circle of the protractor. Note the direction of the other ray and the number of degrees of the angle.

right   acute   obtuse

Place the corner of an index card in the corner of the angle. If the edges line up with the card, it is a right angle. If not, the angle is acute or obtuse.

right   acute   obtuse

Use a protractor or index card to identify the following angles as right, obtuse, or acute.

acute   right   acute

obtuse   right   acute

Answer Key

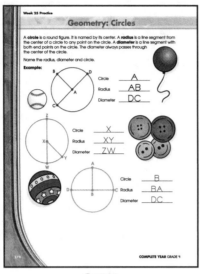

274

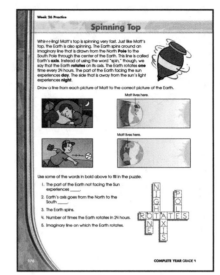

276

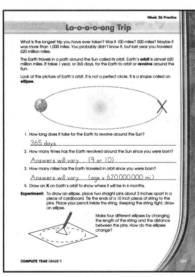

277

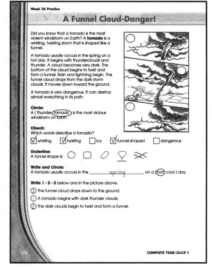

278

279

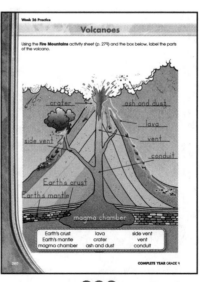

280

Answer Key

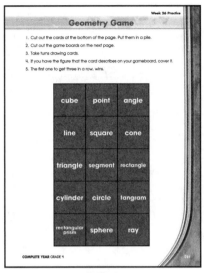

281

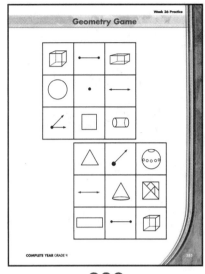

283

286

287

288

289

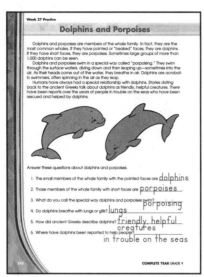

290

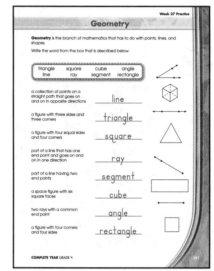

291

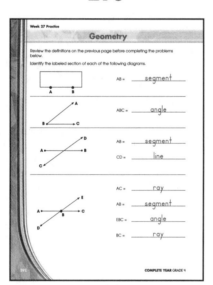

292

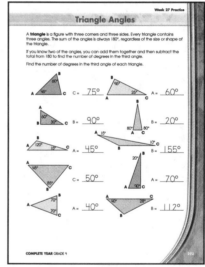

293

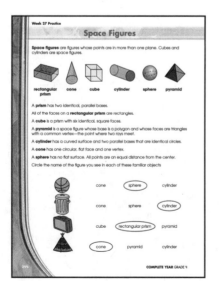

294

300

Answer Key

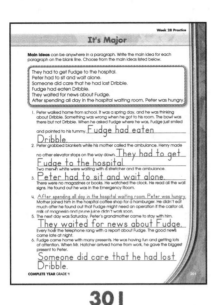

301

It's Major

Main ideas can be anywhere in a paragraph. Write the main idea for each paragraph on the blank line. Choose from the main ideas listed below.

> They had to get Fudge to the hospital.
> Peter had to sit and wait alone.
> Someone did care that he had lost Dribble.
> Fudge had eaten Dribble.
> They waited for news about Fudge.
> After spending all day in the hospital waiting room, Peter was hungry.

1. Peter walked home from school. It was a spring day, and he was thinking about Dribble. Something was wrong when he got to his room. The bowl was there but not Dribble. When he asked Fudge where he was, Fudge just smiled and pointed to his tummy. **Fudge had eaten Dribble.**

2. Peter grabbed blankets while his mother called the ambulance. Henry made no other elevator stops on the way down. **They had to get Fudge to the hospital.** Two men in white were waiting with a stretcher and the ambulance.

3. There were no magazines or books. He watched the clock. He read all the wall signs. He found out he was in the Emergency Room. **Peter had to sit and wait alone.**

4. **After spending all day in the hospital waiting room, Peter was hungry.** Mother joined him in the hospital coffee shop for a hamburger. He didn't eat much after he found out that Fudge might need an operation if the castor oil, milk of magnesia and prune juice didn't work soon.

5. The next day was Saturday. Peter's grandmother came to stay with him. **They waited for news about Fudge.** Every hour the telephone rang with a report about Fudge. The good news came late at night.

6. Fudge came home with many presents. He was having fun and getting lots of attention. When Mr. Hatcher arrived home from work, he gave the biggest present to Peter. **Someone did care that he had lost Dribble.**

COMPLETE YEAR GRADE 4

302

A Black Hole

Have you ever heard of a mysterious black hole? Some scientists believe that a black hole is an invisible object somewhere in space. Scientists believe that it has such a strong pull toward it, called gravity, that nothing can escape from it!

These scientists believe that a black hole is a star that has collapsed. The collapse made its pull even stronger. It seems invisible because even its own starlight cannot escape! It is believed that anything in space that comes near the black hole will be pulled into it forever. Some scientists believe there are many black holes in our galaxy.

Check:
Some scientists believe that:
- ☑ a black hole is an invisible object in space.
- ☑ a black hole is a collapsed star.
- ☑ a black hole will not let its own light escape.

Write:
A – gravity
B – collapse

B — To fall or cave in
A — A strong pull toward an object in space

Draw what you think the inside of a black hole would be like.

COMPLETE YEAR GRADE 4

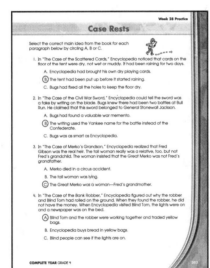

303

Case Rests

Select the correct main idea from the book for each paragraph below by circling A, B or C.

1. In "The Case of the Scattered Cards," Encyclopedia noticed that cards on the floor of the tent were dry, not wet or muddy. It had been raining for two days.
   A. Encyclopedia had brought his own dry playing cards.
   (B) The tent had been put up before it started raining.
   C. Bugs had fixed all the holes to keep the floor dry.

2. In "The Case of the Civil War Sword," Encyclopedia could tell the sword was a fake by writing on the blade. Bugs knew there had been two battles at Bull Run. He claimed that this sword belonged to General Stonewall Jackson.
   A. Bugs had found a valuable war memento.
   (B) The writing used the Yankee name for the battle instead of the Confederate.
   C. Bugs was as smart as Encyclopedia.

3. In "The Case of Merko's Grandson," Encyclopedia realized that Fred Gibson was the real heir. The tall woman really was a relative, too, but not Fred's grandchild. The woman insisted that the Great Merko was not Fred's grandfather.
   A. Merko died in a circus accident.
   B. The tall woman was lying.
   (C) The Great Merko was a woman—Fred's grandmother.

4. In "The Case of the Bank Robber," Encyclopedia figured out why the robber and Blind Tom had rolled on the ground. When they found the robber, he did not have the money. When Encyclopedia visited Blind Tom, the lights were on and a newspaper was on the bed.
   (A) Blind Tom and the robber were working together and traded yellow bags.
   B. Encyclopedia buys bread in yellow bags.
   C. Blind people can see if the lights are on.

304

Lucky Beth or Lucky Kim?

Kim thinks Beth is so lucky. Almost every day, Beth comes to school with something new. One day, she might be wearing a new outfit her mom bought her at the department store where her mom works. The next day, Beth may have something really unique from her father, like a watch that has the days of the week in a foreign language. He brings her gifts when he comes home from traveling on business.

Beth, however, does not think she is so lucky. Beth's mom works until 7 p.m. every night and also has to work every Saturday. Her father travels so much with his job, that Beth is lucky if she gets to see him one week a month. Beth loves her parents, but she wishes they were both home every night and every weekend like Kim's parents so they could do special things together. She also wishes she had a little brother like Kim does so she wouldn't be so lonely.

Check:
Kim thinks Beth is lucky because Beth . . .
- ☑ gets lots of neat gifts.
- ☐ doesn't have a brother or sister.
- ☐ has a father who travels a lot.

Circle:
Beth thinks Kim is lucky because . . .
(Kim has a little brother.)
Kim doesn't get a lot of new clothes.
(Kim's parents are home at night and on the weekends.)

Underline:
When something is unique, it is . . .
ugly   special   small   <u>unusual</u>   different

Write:
Who do you think is luckier, Kim or Beth? Why? **Answers will vary.**

COMPLETE YEAR GRADE 4

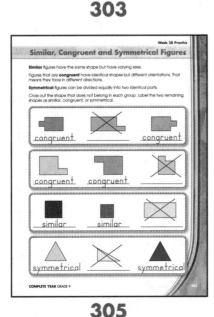

305

Similar, Congruent and Symmetrical Figures

Similar figures have the same shape but have varying sizes.

Figures that are **congruent** have identical shapes but different orientations. That means they face in different directions.

Symmetrical figures can be divided equally into two identical parts.

Cross out the shape that does not belong in each group. Label the two remaining shapes as similar, congruent, or symmetrical.

congruent ____ congruent
congruent   congruent ____
similar   similar ____
symmetrical ____ symmetrical

COMPLETE YEAR GRADE 4

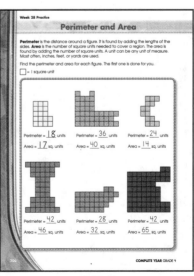

306

Perimeter and Area

Perimeter is the distance around a figure. It is found by adding the lengths of the sides. **Area** is the number of square units needed to cover a region. The area is found by adding the number of square units. A unit can be any unit of measure. Most often, inches, feet, or yards are used.

Find the perimeter and area for each figure. The first one is done for you.

☐ = 1 square unit

Perimeter = 18 units   Perimeter = 36 units   Perimeter = 24 units
Area = 17 sq. units   Area = 40 sq. units   Area = 14 sq. units

Perimeter = 42 units   Perimeter = 28 units   Perimeter = 42 units
Area = 46 sq. units   Area = 32 sq. units   Area = 65 sq. units

COMPLETE YEAR GRADE 4

Answer Key

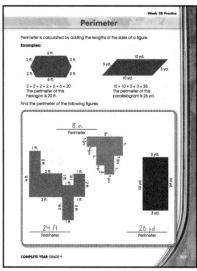

307

308

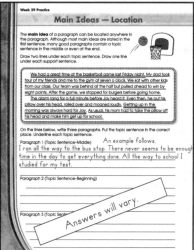

310

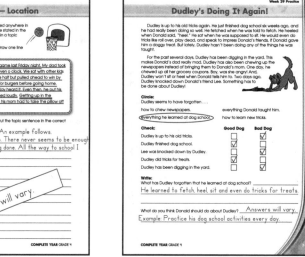

311

312

313

Answer Key

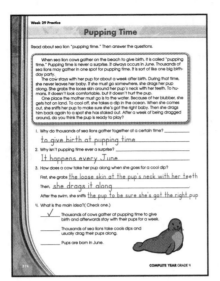

314

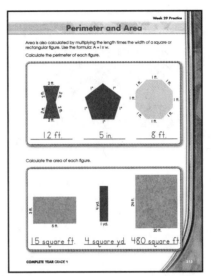

315

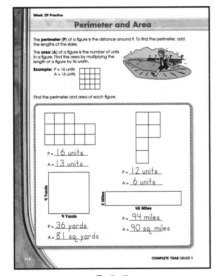

316

Perimeter and Area

Use the formulas for finding perimeter and area to solve these problems.

Julie's family moved to a new house. Her parents said she could have the largest bedroom. Julie knew she would need to find the area of each room to find which one was largest.

One rectangular bedroom is 7 feet wide and 12 feet long. Another is 11 feet long and 9 feet wide. The third bedroom is a square. It is 14 feet wide and 9 feet long. Which one should she select to have the largest room?   **the 11 x 9 room**

The new home also has a swimming pool in the backyard. It is 32 feet long and 18 feet wide. What is the perimeter of the pool?   **100 ft.**

Julie's mother wants to plant flowers on each side of the new house. She will need three plants for every foot of space. The house is 75 feet across the front and back and 37.5 feet along each side. Find the perimeter of the house.   **225 ft.**

How many plants should she buy?   **675 plants**

The family decided to buy new carpeting for several rooms. Complete the necessary information to determine how much carpeting to buy.

Den: 12 ft. x 14 ft. = **168** sq. ft.

Master Bedroom: 20 ft. x **18 ft.** = 360 sq. ft.

Family Room: **15 ft.** x 25 ft. = 375 sq. ft.

Total square feet of carpeting: **903 sq. ft.**

317

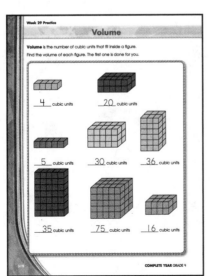

318

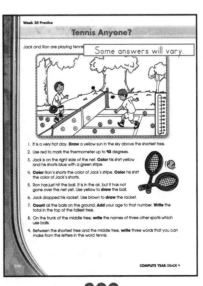

320

437

Answer Key

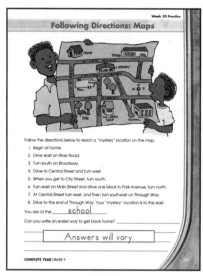

Week 30 Practice

Following Directions: Maps

Follow the directions below to reach a "mystery" location on the map.

1. Begin at home.
2. Drive east on River Road.
3. Turn south on Broadway.
4. Drive to Central Street and turn west.
5. When you get to City Street, turn south.
6. Turn east on Main Street and drive one block to Park Avenue; turn north.
7. At Central Street turn east, and then turn southeast on Through Way.
8. Drive to the end of Through Way. Your "mystery" location is to the east.

You are at the ___school___

Can you write an easier way to get back home?

___Answers will vary.___

COMPLETE YEAR GRADE 4

321

Week 30 Practice

Following Directions: Recipes

Sequencing is putting items or events in logical order.
Read the recipe. Then number the steps in order for making brownies.

> Preheat the oven to 350 degrees. Grease an 8-inch square baking dish.
> In a mixing bowl, place two squares (2 ounces) of unsweetened chocolate and ½ cup butter. Place the bowl in a pan of hot water and heat it to melt the chocolate and the butter.
> When the chocolate is melted, remove the pan from the heat. Add 1 cup sugar and two eggs to the melted chocolate and beat it. Next, stir in ¾ cup sifted flour, ½ teaspoon baking powder, and ¼ teaspoon salt. Finally, mix in ½ cup chopped nuts.
> Spread the mixture in the greased baking dish. Bake for 30 to 35 minutes. The brownies are done when a toothpick stuck in the center comes out clean. Let the brownies cool. Cut them into squares.

8 — Stick a toothpick in the center of the brownies to make sure they are done.
5 — Mix in chopped nuts.
2 — Melt chocolate and butter in a mixing bowl over a pan of hot water.
9 — Cool brownies and cut into squares.
3 — Beat in sugar and eggs.
6 — Spread mixture in a baking dish.
4 — Stir in flour, baking powder, and salt.
7 — Bake for 30 to 35 minutes.
1 — Turn oven to 350 degrees and grease pan.

COMPLETE YEAR GRADE 4

322

Week 30 Practice

Following Directions: Salt Into Pepper

Read how to do a magic trick that will amaze your friends. Then number the steps in order to do the trick.

> Imagine doing this trick for your friends. Pick up a salt shaker that everyone can see is full of salt. Pour some into your hand. Tell your audience that you will change the salt into pepper. Say a few magic words, such as "Fibbidy, dibbiddy, milkshake and malt. What will be pepper once was salt!" Then open your hand and pour out pepper.
> How is it done? First you need a clear salt shaker with a screw-on top. You also need a paper napkin and a small amount of pepper.
> Take off the top of the salt shaker. Lay the napkin over the opening and push it down a little to make a small pocket. Fill the pocket with pepper. Put the top back on the salt shaker and tear off the extra napkin. Now you are ready for the trick.
> Hold up the salt shaker so your audience can see that it is full of salt. Shake some "salt" into your hand. Close your fist so no one can see that it is really pepper. Say the magic words and open your hand.

9 — Say some magic words.
1 — Find a clear salt shaker with a screw-on top.
10 — Open your hand and pour out the pepper.
3 — Take off the top of the salt shaker.
7 — Show the audience the shaker full of salt.
4 — Place the napkin over the opening of the salt shaker.
2 — Get a paper napkin and some pepper.
5 — Put the pepper in the napkin pocket.
8 — Shake some "salt" into your hand and close your fist.
6 — Put the top back on the salt shaker and tear off the extra napkin.

COMPLETE YEAR GRADE 4

323

Week 30 Practice

Following Directions: Recipes

Follow these steps for making a peanut butter and jelly sandwich.

1. Get a jar of peanut butter, a jar of jelly, two slices of bread and a knife.
2. Open the jar lids.
3. Using the knife, spread peanut butter on one slice of bread.
4. Spread jelly on the other slice of bread.
5. Put the two slices of bread together to make a sandwich.

Write the steps for a recipe of your own. Be very specific. When you are done, give the recipe to a friend to make. You will know right away if any steps are missing!

Recipe for: _____

1. _____
2. _____
3. _____   *Answers will vary.*
4. _____
5. _____
6. _____

COMPLETE YEAR GRADE 4

324

Week 30 Practice

Volume

The volume of a figure can also be calculated by multiplying the length times the width times the height. Use the formula: V= l x w x h.

Example: 3 x 5 x 2 = 30 cubic feet

Find the volume of the following figures. Label your answers in cubic feet, inches or yards. The first one is done for you.

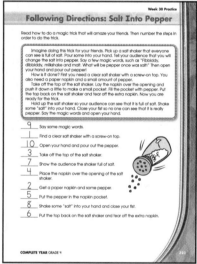

6 cubic inches

20 cubic feet   _60 cubic yards_

35 cubic yards   _36 cubic feet_

COMPLETE YEAR GRADE 4

325

Week 30 Practice

Volume

The formula for finding the volume of a box is length times width times height **(L x W x H)**. The answer is given in cubic units.

Solve the problems.

Example: Height 8 ft.
Length 8 ft.
Width 8 ft.

L	x	W	x	H	=	volume
8'	x	8'	x	8'	=	512 cubic ft. or 512 ft³

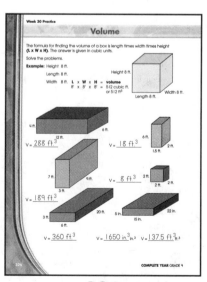

V = _288 ft³_   V = _18 ft³_

V = _189 ft³_   V = _8 ft³_

V = _360 ft³_   V = _1650 in³_   V = _137.5 ft³_

COMPLETE YEAR GRADE 4

326

438

Answer Key

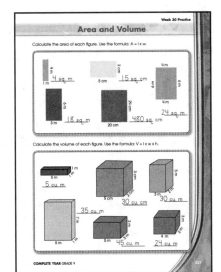

327

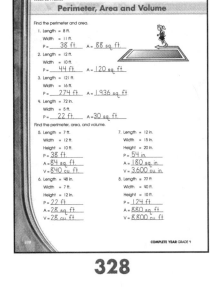

328

330

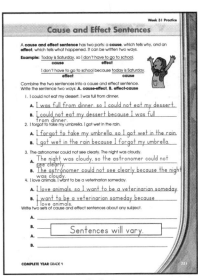

331

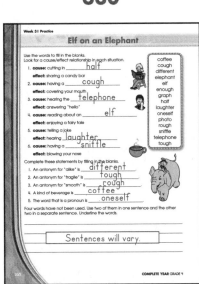

332

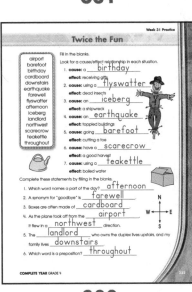

333

439

Answer Key

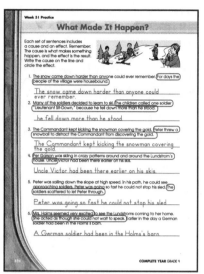

334

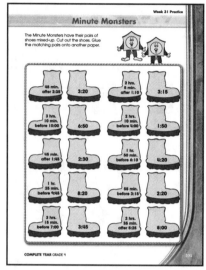

335

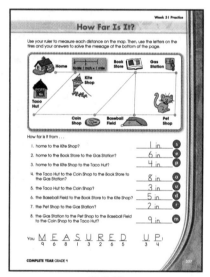

337

338

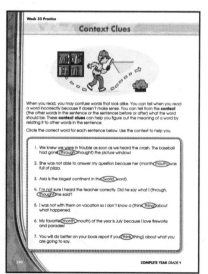

340

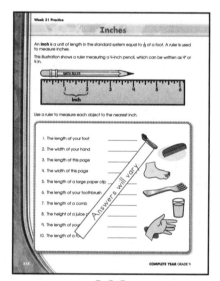

341

Answer Key

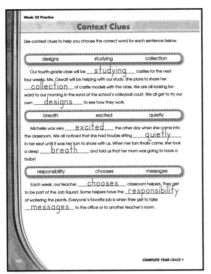

342

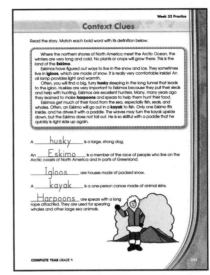

343

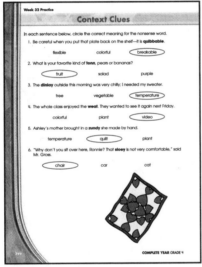

344

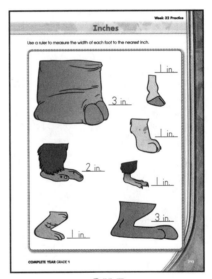

345

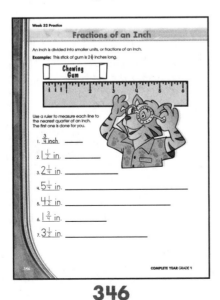

346

347

Answer Key

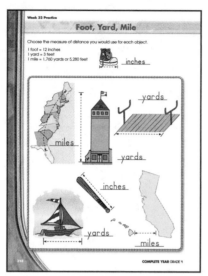

348

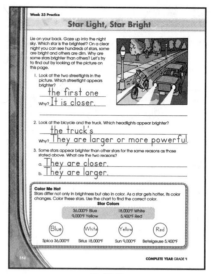

350

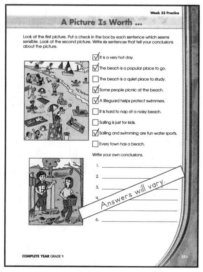

351

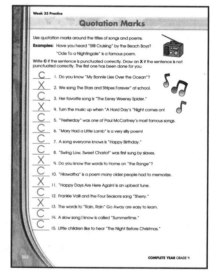

352

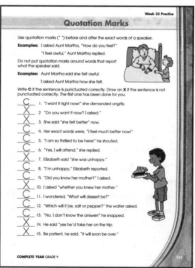

353

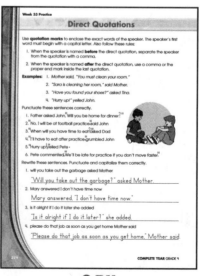

354

Answer Key

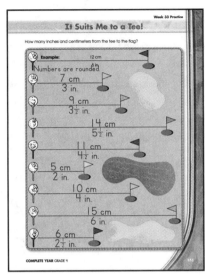

355

356

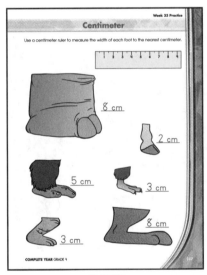

357

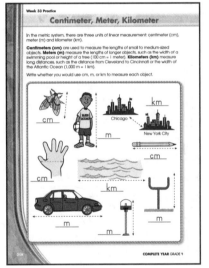

358

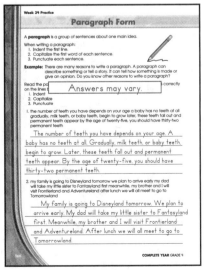

360

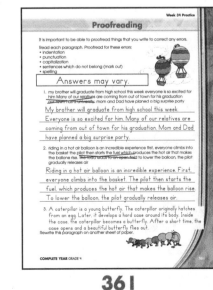

361

Answer Key

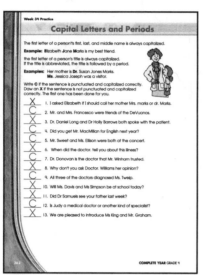

362

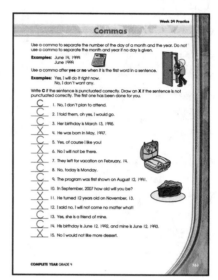

363

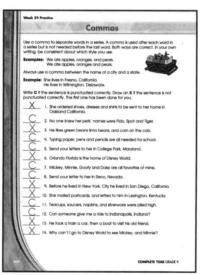

364

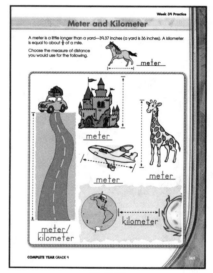

365

366

367

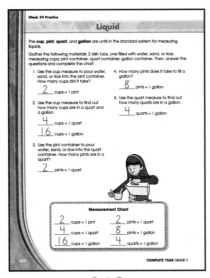

368

Week 34 Practice
Liquid

The **cup**, **pint**, **quart**, and **gallon** are units in the standard system for measuring liquids.

Gather the following materials: 2 dish tubs, one filled with water, sand, or rice; measuring cups; pint container; quart container; gallon container. Then, answer the questions and complete the chart.

1. Use the cup measure to pour water, sand, or rice into the pint container. How many cups did it take?
2 cups = 1 pint

2. Use the cup measure to find out how many cups are in a quart and a gallon.
4 cups = 1 quart
16 cups = 1 gallon

3. Use the pint container to pour water, sand, or rice into the quart container. How many pints are in a quart?
2 pints = 1 quart

4. How many pints does it take to fill a gallon?
8 pints = 1 gallon

5. Use the quart measure to find out how many quarts are in a gallon.
4 quarts = 1 gallon

Measurement Chart
2 cups = 1 pint
4 cups = 1 quart
16 cups = 1 gallon
2 pints = 1 quart
8 pints = 1 gallon
4 quarts = 1 gallon

COMPLETE YEAR GRADE 4

370

Week 35 Practice
Topic Sentences — Paragraphs

Read each topic listed below. Write a topic sentence for each topic.

Example: Topic: Seasons
Topic Sentence Examples:
There are four seasons in every year.
Of all the seasons, my favorite is summer.

1. Topic: Winter — Topic Sentence:
2. Topic: Skateboards — Topic Sentence:
3. Topic: America — Topic Sentence:
4. Topic: Horses — Topic Sentence:
5. Topic: Books — Topic Sentence:

Choose two of your best topic sentences from above.

Answers may vary.

COMPLETE YEAR GRADE 4

371

Week 35 Practice
Topic Sentences

A **paragraph** is a group of sentences that tells about one main idea. A topic sentence tells the main idea of a paragraph.

Many topic sentences come first in the paragraph. The topic sentence in the paragraph below is underlined. Do you see how it tells the reader what the whole paragraph is about?

Friendships can make you happy or make you sad. You feel happy to do things and go places with your friends. You get to know each other so well that you can almost read each others' minds. But friendships can be sad when your friend moves away—or decides to be best friends with someone else.

Underline the topic sentence in the paragraph below.

We have two rules about using the phone at our house. Our whole family agreed on them. The first rule is not to talk longer than 10 minutes. The second rule is to take good messages if you answer the phone for someone else.

After you read the paragraph below, write a topic sentence for it.

There are many ways you can earn money.

For one thing, you could ask your neighbors if they need any help. They might be willing to pay you for walking their dog or mowing their grass or weeding their garden. Maybe your older brothers or sisters would pay you to do some of their chores. You also could ask your parents if there's an extra job you could do around the house to make money.

Write a topic sentence for a paragraph on each of these subjects.

Homework:
Television:

Sentences will vary.

COMPLETE YEAR GRADE 4

372

Week 35 Practice
Support Sentences

The **topic sentence** gives the main idea of a paragraph. The support sentences give the details about the main idea. Each sentence must relate to the main idea.

Read the paragraph below. Underline the topic sentence. Cross out the sentence that is not a support sentence. On the line, write a support sentence to go in its place.

Giving a surprise birthday party can be exciting but tricky. The honored person must not hear a word about the party! On the day of the party, everyone should arrive early. A snack may ruin your appetite.

Example: When the birthday person comes in, everyone will yell "Surprise!"

Write three support sentences to go with each topic sentence.

Giving a dog a bath can be a real challenge!
Example:
1. First, you must make sure that you have supplies.
2. Then, you must convince your dog to stand still.
3. Finally, you must make sure that your dog is dried completely.

I can still remember how embarrassed I was that day!
1.
2.
3.

Sometimes I like to imagine what our prehistoric world...
1.
2.
3.

A daily newspaper ... kinds of news.
1.
2.
3.

Answers will vary.

COMPLETE YEAR GRADE 4

373

Week 35 Practice
Supporting Sentences

Supporting sentences provide details about the topic sentence of a paragraph.

In the paragraph below, underline the topic sentence. Then cross out the supporting sentence that does not belong in the paragraph.

One spring it started to rain and didn't stop for 2 weeks. All the rivers flooded. Some people living near the rivers had to leave their homes. Farmers couldn't plant their crops because the fields were so wet. Plants need water to grow. The sky was dark and gloomy all the time.

Write three supporting sentences to go with each topic sentence below. Make sure each supporting sentence stays on the same subject as the topic sentence.

Not everyone should have a pet.

I like to go on field trips with my class.

I've been ... about what I want to be when I get older.

Sentences will vary.

COMPLETE YEAR GRADE 4

374

Week 35 Practice
Topic Sentences and Supporting Details

For each topic below, write a topic sentence and four supporting details.

Example: Playing with friends:
(topic sentence) Playing with my friends can be lots of fun.
(details)
1. We like to ride our bikes together.
2. We play fun games like "dress up" and "animal hospital."
3. Sometimes, we swing on the swings or slide down the slides on our swingsets.
4. We like to pretend we are having tea with our stuffed animals.

Recess at school:

Summer vacation:

Brothers:

Answers will vary.

COMPLETE YEAR GRADE 4

Answer Key

Cup, Pint, Quart, Gallon

Circle the number of objects to the right that equal the objects on the left. The first one is done for you.

2 cups = 1 pint
2 pints = 1 quart
4 quarts = 1 gallon

= 1 cup   = 1 pint   = 1 quart   = 1 gallon

375

Week 35 Practice

Milliliter and Liter

Liters and milliliters are measurements of liquid in the metric system. A milliliter (mL) equals 0.001 liter or 0.03 fluid ounces. A drop of water equals about 1 milliliter. Liters (L) measure large amounts of liquid. There are 1,000 milliliters in a liter. One liter measures 1.06 quarts. Soft drinks are often sold in 2-liter bottles.

Choose milliliters or liters to measure these liquids.

Example: milliliters   milliliters
liters   milliliters
milliliters   liters
liters   liters

376

Week 35 Practice

Weight and Liquid

Choose grams (g) or kilograms (kg) to weigh the following objects. The first one is done for you.

rhinoceros	kg	person	kg
dime	g	airplane	kg
bucket of wet sand	kg	spider	g
eyeglasses	g	pair of scissors	g
toy train engine	g	horse	kg

Choose milliliters (mL) or liters (L) to measure the liquids in the following containers. The first one is done for you.

swimming pool	L	baby bottle	mL
small juice glass	mL	teapot	mL
gasoline tank	L	outdoor fountain	L
test tube	mL	ink pen	mL
washing machine	L	Lake Erie	L

COMPLETE YEAR GRADE 4

377

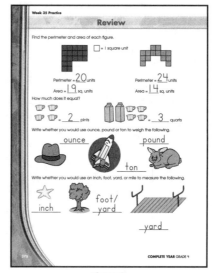

Week 35 Practice

Review

Find the perimeter and area of each figure.

☐ = 1 square unit

Perimeter = 20 units   Perimeter = 24 units
Area = 19 sq. units   Area = 14 sq. units

How much does it equal?

= 2 pints   = 3 quarts

Write whether you would use ounce, pound or ton to weigh the following.

ounce   pound   ton

Write whether you would use an inch, foot, yard, or mile to measure the following.

inch   foot/yard   yard

378

Week 36 Practice

What's the Point?

Write the correct purpose of each sentence on the line provided.

Persuade   Entertain   Inform

Answers may vary.

1. Inform
2. Persuade
3. Entertain
4. Persuade
5. Inform
6. Persuade
7. Inform
8. Entertain
9. Persuade
10. Persuade
11. Inform
12. Inform
13. Inform
14. Inform
15. Persuade

380

Week 36 Practice

From Whose Point of View?

Read each sentence below. Decide if it is the first or third person's point of view. If it is a first person's point of view, rewrite the sentence to make it a third person's point of view.

Answers may include:

1. I wanted to tell Anh and Thant the secret of our leaving, but I had given my word.
   Cindy wanted to tell Anh and Thant the secret of their leaving, but she had given her word.
2. The grandmother did not want to go aboard the boat.
   I did not want to go aboard the boat.
3. The people on shore were pushing to get on the deck of the boat.
   We were pushing to get on the deck of the boat.
4. Though I had worked many days in the rice paddies watching planes fly over, I never thought I'd be on one.
   Though Loi had worked many days in the rice paddies watching planes fly over, he never thought he'd be on one.
5. Loi made a net from pieces of string and caught a turtle with his new device.
   I made a net from pieces of string and caught a turtle with it.
6. I know of a place where we can wash our clothes.
   Anh knows of a place where everyone can wash their clothes.
7. The officer looked at them with great interest.
   The officer looked at us with great interest.
8. When I looked into the harbor, I could see the shape of the sampan boats.
   When she looked into the harbor she could see the shape of the sampan boats.
9. This is my duck and I choose to share it with everyone for the celebration of Tet.
   This is her duck and she chooses to share it with everyone for the celebration of Tet.

COMPLETE YEAR GRADE 4

381

Answer Key

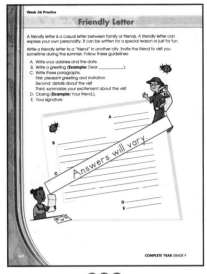

382

383

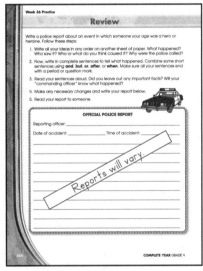

384

385

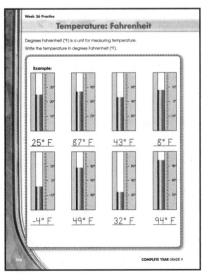

386

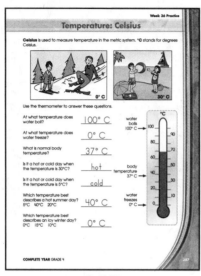

387

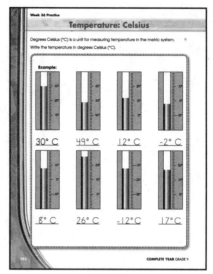

388